ARKANA

The Magus of Strovolos

Kyriacos C. Markides, a native of Cyprus, is Professor of Sociology at the University of Maine. He is married to Emily J. Markides from Famagusta, Cyprus. They have two children, Constantine and Vasia. He has also written *Homage to the Sun*, the sequel to *The Magus of Strovolos*, and *Fire in the Heart*, both published by Arkana.

The Magus of
Strovolos

The Extraordinary World
of a Spiritual Healer

KYRIACOS C. MARKIDES

ARKANA

PENGUIN BOOKS

Published by the Penguin Group
Penguin Books Ltd, 27 Wrights Lane, London W8 5TZ, England
Penguin Books USA Inc., 375 Hudson Street, New York, New York 10014, USA
Penguin Books Australia Ltd, Ringwood, Victoria, Australia
Penguin Books Canada Ltd, 10 Alcorn Avenue, Toronto, Ontario, Canada M4V 3B2
Penguin Books (NZ) Ltd, 182–190 Wairau Road, Auckland 10, New Zealand

Penguin Books Ltd, Registered Offices: Harmondsworth, Middlesex, England

First published by Routledge & Kegan Paul Ltd., 1985
Published in Arkana 1990
5 7 9 10 8 6 4

Printed in England by Clays Ltd, St Ives plc
Filmset in 10/11pt Sabon

To the memory of my mother
To my father
To Emily, Constantine and Vasia

Contents

Contents

Author's Note

I appreciate and I am well aware of feminist concerns about language. To avoid, however, stylistically cacophonous phrases such as his/hers or he/she I decided, reluctantly, to follow the traditional style. Therefore, whenever I write about 'Mankind' I mean both men and women. When I refer to God as 'He' I do so only because of customary usage without presuming that Divinity is masculine.

For the same reasons I decided to use the Greek style in addressing names. For example I speak of Daskal*os* in the third person. But when I address him I say Daskal*e*. Similarly with Kost*as* and Iacov*os*. When I call on them I say Kost*a* and Iacov*o*. Feminine names do not pose this problem. All names in the text are fictitious except historical names and those of my family. Other than names, nothing else in this study is fictitious.

The present research should be considered primarily as a phenomenological study of a spiritual healer and his close associates. It is not a study in parapsychology. My focus is not to test or ascertain the empirical validity of paranormal phenomena. Instead I try to present as accurately as possible the world as experienced by the subjects themselves. This does not imply that my role has been that of a passive observer. As the reader will discover, I have become an active participant within this group of healers in my effort to understand their world from within their system.

The material was gathered in four separate periods, during the summer of 1978, the period between December 1978 and September 1979, and the summer months of 1981 and 1983.

I wish to express my appreciation to the University of Maine for offering me a summer grant and a sabbatical leave of absence during the 1978-9 academic year. Without such generous support this study would probably not have taken

ix

place. Similar appreciation goes to my colleagues at the Department of Sociology and Social Work. I would also like to thank the staff of the Cyprus Social Research Centre for offering the use of their copying machines and tape recorders whenever I needed them.

Many thanks to my friends Stephen and Joan Marks who first triggered my interest in issues related to the study of consciousness and spirituality. Thanks too to my other friends, colleagues and fellow scholars who read the original manuscript and generously offered their supportive and critical appraisal: Stephen Cohn, Richard Fenn, Herbert Maccoby, Leonard Doob, Joanne Green, Erling Skorpen, Jacob Needleman, Marcello Truzzi, Michael Harner, James Laue and Colin Wilson.

Thanks to Marlene Gabriel, my literary agent, for her friendship, confidence in the book and first-rate professional expertise. Thanks also to Eva Meyn for superbly typing the manuscript. My love to my sister Maroulla Christou for being the great sister that she is and for the help she has always given us during our stay in Cyprus. To my wife Emily are reserved the deepest affections for, among other things, her spirited support, intellectual stimulation and outstanding editing of the first draft.

I wish, finally, to express my profound admiration for Daskalos and his close associates. My work with them has been truly a labor of love. In a very real sense this is their book.

1
The Magus of Strovolos

I knew of Spyros Sathi from childhood. His reputation as the island's leading specialist of the netherworld stirred in me a mixture of fascination, curiosity and fright. As children, we were warned by the priest of our parish to shun the 'Magus of Strovolos,' the man with 'satanic powers.' We listened with wide eyes to tales of possession and exorcisms and myths of his house overcrowded with disembodied spirits. His name was synonymous with occultism itself and anyone with the courage and desire to contact his dead mother had but to knock at his door. That was the image I had in my mind of Spyros Sathi when I left Cyprus for America in 1960.

Almost two decades later I hardly remembered the man whom I fantasized about but never met in my early youth. It was not until the summer of 1978 on a visit to Cyprus that my interest in the 'Magus of Strovolos' was reawakened. I was casually conversing with an old friend, a philologist, when she told me in confidence that she and her husband, a judge, belonged to a semi-secret 'Circle for the Research of Truth.' The spiritual master of this mystical cult, I was surprised to learn, was none other than the 'Magus of Strovolos.' I immediately expressed an interest in meeting him.

It was late in August when I drove with my friend to Strovolos, a Nicosia suburb, to meet Spyros Sathi. How ironic, I thought, that I had to spend eighteen years in America before I could meet this mysterious man who lived only two miles from my house. I expected to encounter a person of stern disposition and ferocious looks, at par with his reputation. None of my preconceptions were valid. He was a tall and sympathetic-looking grandfather in his mid-sixties, a retired civil servant who lived frugally on his government pension. Instead of a half-mad menacing sorcerer I encountered an ebullient and deeply religious person with a high sense of humor whose hobbies included painting and classical music. He thought of himself as a healer and a 'psychotherapist,' a doctor of the soul, whose primary concern in life was to alleviate pain around him, as he put it, and assist those interested and ready to embark on a journey of self-discovery.

'We have met before!' he exclaimed when I first met him, and placed his right hand on his forehead.

'I do not think so,' I said smiling, and extended my hand as my friend introduced us.

'We have met before,' he nodded with confidence, and invited us to sit in his small living room. I assumed he confused me with someone else and I left the subject at that.

Daskalos, as my friend called him, offered us coffee and inquired about my family background, a customary practice in Cyprus where in a population of slightly over half a million 'everybody is related to everybody else.' I then began asking questions about his life and teachings. To my pleasant surprise Daskalos was a talkative man and answered my questions without reservations. He even invited me to attend the meetings he held every fortnight. In that first encounter I understood that his teachings were a blend of Christian mysticism and Indian religion. The concept of Karma, or the law of cause and effect as he called it, and the doctrine of reincarnation seemed to play a central role in what he disseminated to his disciples. My curiosity about Daskalos' world was intensified as I realized that he was hardly a primitive shaman but a highly articulate and intellectually cultivated man. Yet the world within which he lived was mysterious and exotic from my vantage point.

'I have heard of miraculous cures that you have performed,' I pointed out. 'Is there a chance that I could witness such miracles?' I confessed to Daskalos that I had a hard time accepting the notion of 'miracles.' I went on to say that the anthropological literature is full of accounts of extraordinary feats of healing by shamans and healers. 'But I need to witness such phenomena myself before I can be convinced,' I said.

'First of all,' Daskalos replied, smiling, 'those cures you have heard about were not performed by me but by the Holy Spirit. I am nothing more than a channel of that super-intelligence. Whether you witness or not a so-called miracle is not up to me. If it is part of the Divine Plan for you to witness a miracle, then you will. But we just cannot order a miracle to happen.'

Before I left that day Daskalos invited me to attend a meeting that he was to have with some of his students the following afternoon in the Stoa. It was a small room in the back of his yard, detached from the rest of the house, where he trained his disciples. The Stoa was divided into two, the main part where the instructions took place, and the Sanctum where Daskalos carried out his meditations and prayers. The Sanctum was filled with religious artifacts, icons of Christ, of the Holy Virgin and white candles. On the altar there was a silver cup and next to it was a small sword without a point, resting on a cross. This Unpointed Sword, I learned later, was of great symbolic significance to Daskalos' circles.

I took up his invitation to attend his meeting with my wife, Emily, who met Daskalos for the first time. When we arrived at his house half an hour before the formal meeting, Daskalos had just completed a therapy and looked exhausted, sitting in an armchair and wearing a leather apron similar to the type butchers wear in Cyprus. Next to him sat a rough-looking and happily smiling villager.

'There comes the Doubting Thomas!' Daskalos exclaimed humorously as he saw me coming into the room with Emily. 'Had you been here ten minutes earlier you would have witnessed a miracle.' Daskalos explained that the visitor had been suffering from his spine for the last twenty years as a result of beatings he endured at the hands of British soldiers during the anti-colonial underground war of the 1950s.

'Now he is well,' he declared confidently. 'If he is now examined the X-rays will show a completely cured spine.'

The peasant, with a look of incredulity on his face, continued to smile happily as I asked him questions about his illness. He told me how well he felt and how the pains he suffered all those years were gone. 'I wish I had time to study this,' I murmured, 'but I am leaving for America tomorrow.'

'Do I owe you anything?' the villager asked after a while.

'Of course you do!' Daskalos replied. 'Do exactly as I advised you to do. Eat and drink less and take vitamins.' In spite of the man's persistence Daskalos refused to take any compensation for his services.

By the time the meeting was to take place Daskalos looked

revitalized as if charged by some mysterious energy. After a short prayer he began the lesson. Man, he said, is an eternal entity, an emanation of a 'Holy Monad' and after his passage through the 'Idea of Man,' an archetype within the Absolute, he acquires shape and existence. The moment we pass through the Idea of Man we embark on our incarnational cycles. The ultimate aim is to return to the source, carrying along the accumulated experiences of earthly lives.

Daskalos then spoke of Mind as the supersubstance by which the 'universes' are constructed. It is the stuff from which we as human beings build 'elementals.' We give birth to such elementals with our thoughts and sentiments. Once 'projected' they have an existence of their own and can affect those around us that 'vibrate' on the same frequency.

It was not easy for us to follow his talk as it was the first time we were exposed to such a language. I realized that to understand Daskalos' vocabulary and world view would require continuous exposure and discussions with him.

Emily and our children remained in Cyprus while I returned to Maine to teach during the fall of 1978. We were to reunite in Cyprus at Christmas and begin my sabbatical leave for the spring of 1979. This would provide us with nine continuous months in Cyprus, a great opportunity to enmesh ourselves once again in our native culture and rekindle old friendships as well as make new ones. At the same time I planned to complete a manuscript on the problem of international terrorism, the material for which I had already gathered.

In the back of my mind, however, there lurked Spyros Sathi. The brief encounters with him intrigued me and led me into further reading on shamanism and non-medical healing. By mid-semester while reading Doug Boyd's *Rolling Thunder*, a study of an American Indian medicine man, I was literally jolted by the thought of spending my sabbatical leave to gather material on Spyros Sathi with the intention of eventually writing a book about him. The manuscript on terrorism, I thought, could wait.

I was not, however, confident that he would allow me to be anything other than a disciple. I was aware of his distaste for publicity. Yet I felt I already had established a good rapport with him and I was hopeful he would not object. To prepare the ground I mailed him a letter and a book I published on the social and political developments in Cyprus. In my letter I mentioned nothing of my intentions but simply wrote, 'I am sending you this book because I realize how interested you are in the problems of Cyprus. See you in December.'

The second day of my return to the island I visited my philologist friend and revealed to her my intentions.

'Don't raise your hopes,' she cautioned me. 'Daskalos will not allow anyone to write about him. He is not even willing to give interviews.'

Disappointing as her warnings were, I thought I should try my luck. I hadn't seen Daskalos for more than three months and I was eager to reestablish contact with him as soon as possible. When I reached his home he was busy with a healing session. The door of the living room was shut but I could distinctly hear his voice. I sat in the hallway waiting as Daskalos diagnosed that the patient's skin problems were psychological and cure implied change of attitude on his part.

'Where have you been all this time?' he exclaimed when he saw me as he escorted his visitors to the door. To my disappointment he did not seem to remember that I had been in America during the last four months.

'Haven't you received my letter?' I asked, somewhat puzzled.

'What letter?' he replied, and feigned ignorance of ever receiving a copy of my book.

'Is this the one?' a young man who seemed to be one of Daskalos' apprentices said as he opened a drawer and pulled out my book.

'Yes, that is the one,' I replied.

'You mean you wrote that?' Daskalos exclaimed and pointed at the book.

Obviously not only did he not bother to look at my book and explore its content, but he did not even notice who the author was. My ego was hurt. I had the feeling that the prospect of letting me write a book about him seemed to me at that moment remote. Yet I decided to persist in spite of the awkwardness of the situation.

'I will be in Cyprus for the next nine months,' I said, 'I have my sabbatical from the university and. . . .'

'What is a sabbatical?' he interrupted. When I explained he shook his head in disbelief.

'You mean to tell me,' he went on as he raised his eyebrows in a mocking grimace, 'that you will be paid for such a long time without working? How great it is to have leisure!' he remarked to his young apprentice.

Before I had a chance to protest that a sabbatical was not a vacation he baffled me with an embarrassing question.

'By the way,' he said in a low and teasing voice, 'can you tell us how much you are making, if I may ask?' I felt cornered but he seemed to ignore my discomfort. I knew that people simply did not ask such questions.

'Sure,' I replied as I swallowed my excess saliva and revealed my salary.

'All that money!' he marvelled, and shook his head in amazement. I clumsily rushed to explain that such a salary may appear high but could hardly be considered even average by American standards. He seemed unsympathetic. His reactions made me feel as if I were a member of a parasitic class. At that moment I realized the wisdom of my friend's admonitions. I assumed that the chances of writing a book about him were, for all practical purposes, nil. Daskalos did not take me seriously at all.

'I would like to use my sabbatical to write a book about you,' I said after I gathered my courage, knowing full well what the answer would be.

He looked pensive and serious for a few seconds without saying a word.

'What is so important that you want to write about me?' he asked with a lowered voice.

I responded that a lot of people in the English-speaking world, particularly in America, would be very interested to hear his message about life.

'But what I teach is not my message,' he replied as he spread his hands outward to give emphasis. 'I am simply the channel of Yohannan and other invisible masters.'

'Who is Yohannan?'

Daskalos went on to explain that Yohannan was none other than Jesus' disciple, John the evangelist, who spoke through Daskalos' body.

'Quite often the vibrations of his presence are so intense that my material brain has a hard time channeling his teachings. In such cases I just leave my body and let Yohannan take complete possession of it while I sit in the audience listening to the talk. Do you understand now why I should not get any credit for the teachings?'

Daskalos paused for a moment and gazed at me piercingly. 'Fame is a trap in our spiritual path,' he said, as if to warn himself and myself of the dangers lurking in publicity. 'I must remain anonymous.'

That is the end of my project I thought and began resigning myself to this realization. But before I completed my thought, Daskalos surprised me.

'You can write about the teachings if you so wish, assuming that I do not get the credit,' he said quietly. I was delighted and promised that I would guard his anonymity as much as I could. The name Daskalos is after all a common title in Greek, the manner with which people address schoolmasters.

'I am very happy that you are letting me write about your world,' I said shortly. 'But I am puzzled. Why me? I know that so far you have refused to give even a single interview.'

He smiled and looked at me with intensity. 'Before I give you an answer tell me, do you believe in reincarnation?' I was taken aback by his pointed question and for a moment I was at a loss, not knowing what to say. In my training as a sociologist I learned to be a skeptic and avoid metaphysical questions considered to be unanswerable. Such questions, we were led to believe, interfere with the objectivity and detachment necessary for valid observation.

'I have no basis to believe or disbelieve,' I said, 'but I am open to persuasion.' I mentioned further that I am always impressed with the eloquence of arguments presented in favor of reincarnation throughout the ages from Plato to the Theosophists and Madame Blavatsky.

Daskalos appreciated my answer and nodded with approval. He then proceeded to answer my question.

'This is not the first time we have met,' he said in all sincerity. 'We have known each other in four previous incarnations. Our meeting in this life,' he continued as I noticed an eerie look on his face, while I must have appeared perplexed and incredulous, 'is not accidental as it is not accidental that you have a keen interest in politics and mysticism. You lived in

India at a time when I was a yogi and we knew of one another. Your major concern in that incarnation was to play the role of the mediator between several warring tribes. But you were so inept,' Daskalos went on and burst into laughter, 'that in spite of your good intentions you caused a war to break out.

'During the time of Queen Isabella of Spain,' he said further, 'when the Spaniards pushed the Moors out of the Iberian Peninsula, you were again in the midst of political turmoil. Your mother was Moorish and your father a Spaniard. You tried to mediate between the two warring groups, again unsuccessfully. It was an adventure that almost cost your life.

'Your interest in mysticism developed in Tibet where you incarnated several times. Your obsession with finding the Truth led you to wander from one lamasary to another. In your present incarnation your lamasary is the university where you now teach.'

With that last remark I could not hide a smile. The notion of the University of Maine as my present lamasary was very amusing.

'You have come close to enlightenment several times in the past,' Daskalos went on as he concentrated on my face, 'but you habitually turn back at the last moment.'

'In what way?'

'Your attention gets distracted by other more earthly considerations. By the way,' Daskalos said suddenly, before giving me a chance to digest my incarnational history, 'have I introduced you to Iacovos?'

The young man who had been listening quietly smiled as we were introduced.

'Iacovos,' Daskalos announced matter-of-factly, as if to shock me even further, 'is four thousand years old.'

'Strange,' I said humorously, 'he seems to be no more than twenty.'

Daskalos argued that he and Iacovos were 'old friends,' their friendship dating thousands of years back.

'To whom can I tell such stories without being pronounced insane?' Daskalos said laughing as he tapped my knee. 'Even some of us,' he went on as he turned towards his young apprentice, 'in spite of our experiences wonder sometimes whether the powers we have are real or not. He is only nineteen now,' Daskalos said as he turned towards me, 'and he often questions the reality of his own experiences. I had doubts myself at that age.'

'Logic sometimes gets in our way,' Iacovos murmured, as if thinking aloud.

'Logic, logic . . . ,' Daskalos reacted and shook his head with impatience. 'If you stick to logic you cannot go very far. What is logic other than the conventional way of thinking at a particular time and place? Our concern is with Logos, Reason, Truth which are beyond time and space.'

He then mentioned that each night he and some of his students became 'invisible helpers.' They carried out 'exomatosis,' that is, they left their bodies and traveled to faraway places 'to be of service.' Those capable of exomatosis were his most advanced disciples who had put on the 'white robe,' a symbolic uniform implying initiation into the exclusive inner circle.

'With my invisible helpers,' Daskalos said, 'we go all over the Middle East, including Iran and Turkey. In our work there is no nationality, no religion, no race.'

When I asked how exomatosis is possible, Daskalos replied that every human being has three bodies, not only one, as people commonly assume. We have, he said, in addition to our 'gross material body,' a 'psychic body,' the body of sentiments, and a 'noetic body,' the body which expresses our mental state. Each of the three bodies lives within a different dimension of existence, the gross material dimension, the psychic dimension and the noetic dimension. The three bodies express our 'present personality,' which is a manifestation of our inner self, the 'permanent personality.' When our gross material body dies we continue to live within the psychic worlds with our 'psycho-noetic body.' An experienced mystic, according to him, can leave his material body at will, travel with his psychonoetic body as complete self-consciousness and then return to his material body fully conscious of the experiences he had while in exomatosis.

Each of the three bodies, Daskalos went on, has its corresponding 'etheric-double,' the energy field that keeps the three bodies alive and linked to one another. Etheric vitality, which makes healing possible, is the cosmic energy which scientists have yet to discover. This energy is absorbed by our bodies through certain psychonoetic centers, the 'chakras' or 'sacred discs.'

Daskalos said that these are truths that someday I would experience when I embark on the path for the research of truth.

'It is better,' he continued slowly, 'not to talk about such matters publicly because people get scandalized.'

I mentioned that in America there is a growing interest in mysticism and people are not so easily scandalized.

'Perhaps it is so in America but not here in Cyprus.'

'I see what you mean,' I nodded, realizing that Daskalos referred to the various attempts on the part of the local church to excommunicate him.

'Tell me,' Daskalos said abruptly, 'why are you interested in writing this book?'

His question took me by surprise since I assumed I had already explained myself.

'I have no way of knowing,' I replied with determination, 'whether the world you live in is real or not. But I must confess I am fascinated with what you have told me so far about it. I would be a hypocrite if I do not admit that my ambition is to write a good book which will portray as accurately as possible the world as you experience it. I also want to learn how to proceed to have similar experiences like yourself. I am ready to follow your instructions on meditation exercises and try to understand your teachings on the nature of reality.'

'What else?' Daskalos said softly and looked at me in earnest. I realized he found my answer inadequate.

'Well,' I said somewhat perplexed, suspecting what Daskalos had in mind, 'in the event that I evolve and acquire psychonoetic powers I would like to become a healer myself and be of service to my fellow man.'

'Good!' Daskalos exclaimed, and leaned back in his chair with a satisfied look on his face. 'This is our mission in life. To be of service to our fellow man. Remember, the harvest is bountiful but few are the harvesters. You,' he went on and pointed his finger at me, 'with your knowledge of society could be of special service. You could construct beautiful worlds in which men could live in peace and harmony.'

'I'll try my best,' I said naively, not having the foggiest

notion what Daskalos meant by his ultra-idealistic utterance.

He went on to say that the whole region of the Middle East is plagued with violence and suffering and that the urgency to act is more pressing than ever. Moral standards, he said, with sadness in his face, are collapsing everywhere and there is so much savagery and injustice.

When I went home that evening I pondered over my encounter with Daskalos which seemed to have defined for me the nature of my relationship with him for the months and years to come. My spontaneous responses to his questions clarified in my mind the appropriate methodological procedure I should follow in studying Daskalos' world.

Even before our last encounter I understood that a conventional sociological approach to the study of Daskalos' circles would be inappropriate. Such a study, I thought, would have forced me to raise questions at the exclusion of others which appeared to me much more significant and enticing. I preferred instead to become a participant observer in the fullest sense of the word. To understand Daskalos' reality I had to become a disciple myself and try to observe his world from within his experience. I decided to use his own language in conversing with him without any preconceived notions on the objective validity of his reality. Instead of imposing my own theories to explain Daskalos' world I thought it proper to follow a phenomenological approach and let him explain his own world in his own language and categories of understanding. My ambition as a researcher, therefore, was to use my training in field research and observation in order to bring to the surface of social consciousness the life, work and world view of an extraordinarily gifted spiritual master.

2
Exorcising the Nazi Spirits

I woke up early in the morning and began working on my field notes. I was not to see Daskalos until four o'clock that afternoon when a meeting was scheduled with his students. Daskalos told me the day before that he could not see me earlier because he had several errands.

At about eight o'clock the phone rang. It was Maro, a friend of my sister. She wanted to know whether I would be willing to arrange a meeting with Daskalos on behalf of some friends of hers. She said they were Jewish and had just arrived from Israel. Their daughter was having severe psychological problems. The medical doctors could do nothing and they had resorted to many psychiatrists but to no avail. The girl, I was told, was quite normal until one night when she dreamed of demons tormenting her. Since then she heard their voices and saw them in her dreams. She desperately needed help because her situation was deteriorating. This girl had come to Cyprus with her mother to visit an aunt. Maro asked whether it would be possible for me to arrange a meeting with Daskalos that very day.

After several phone calls I managed to locate Daskalos. We made an appointment for eleven thirty. By that time, he said, he would be through with his errands. Maro arrived at our house with her friends shortly before the meeting with Daskalos. She introduced me to the three Jewish women, mother, daughter and aunt. They spoke broken English and, given their apparent uneasiness, carrying on a conversation with them was not easy. The girl appeared 'normal' but I noticed deep anxiety and sadness in her face.

It took us only fifteen minutes to drive to Daskalos' house. Maro did not come with us because she said she was petrified of 'these matters.' She had never met Daskalos but knew of his reputation as a specialist in the occult. The mere thought of him filled her with dread.

Daskalos was with Loizos, one of his close students who was studying medicine at the University of Athens. I asked the three women to introduce themselves. Then I briefly explained to Daskalos the nature of our visit. He made himself comfortable in his armchair and looked at the girl intensely.

'You have a talisman on you,' he said, 'right at the heart. It is a six-pointed star.'

I saw the faces of all three of the women lighting up. The girl's mother, in her heavily accented English, noted that underneath her daughter's dress, at the spot where Daskalos mentioned, there was, in fact, a talisman in the shape of David's star made for her daughter by a Jewish rabbi. This demonstration of psychic power by Daskalos apparently established in their eyes his credibility as a healer. He then asked Hadas, the girl, to describe to him what happened. With the help of her mother and aunt she explained that whenever 'they' come she felt that they took her soul away and that her body was dead. Whenever this happened she experienced pains in her stomach and in the back of her head.

'I am abnormal,' she concluded, 'these demons will not let me rest for a single moment.'

'How can you say you are abnormal,' Daskalos interjected, 'when you explain to me what happens to you in such a lucid and comprehensible manner?'

'This is what her mother believes,' said the aunt with excitement. 'It is all in her imagination.'

I noticed that Daskalos was not impressed with this diagnosis of the girl's predicament and continued asking questions.

'Did you ever ask these spirits who they were and what they wanted from you?'

'No, I did not,' Hadas replied.

'How old are you?'

'Twenty-six.' Actually she did not look to me more than twenty.

'What is your religion?'

'Jewish.'

'Close your eyes, please.' She apparently did not understand what Daskalos said and her aunt interpreted his words in Hebrew. Hadas showed eagerness to cooperate and closed her eyes while Daskalos focused on her face. In a few seconds she opened her eyes and Daskalos began to talk again.

'If you want me to help you,' he said, 'you must tell me whether you genuinely believe in God or not.'

'I do, I do,' the girl replied in earnest.

'Good! I could not have helped you otherwise.' Daskalos then offered his diagnosis of the problem.

'Your daughter,' he said to the mother, 'is not suffering from demonic possession.' Then he looked at me and continued, 'Neither is she possessed by elementals.' Finally addressing himself to Hadas he said, 'Those you see and whose voices you hear tormenting you are not illusions. They are human beings. They are Nazis.' I saw horror expressed in the faces of the three Jewish women. 'They are,' Daskalos continued, 'two spirits, husband and wife, who died during the bombardment of Hamburg by the Allies. They took part in the Holocaust and physically tortured a great number of Jews. When they departed to the other world they carried with them their hatred for Jews. So they managed to get possession of you at a time when their vibrations and yours were on the same frequency. The husband took possession of your solar plexus and the woman the chakra of your genitals. But they have not been able to take over the chakra of your brain. They have managed to send to the asylum four other Jewish women. But you need not be afraid because today we will cut the connection and send them away. Since your religion is Jewish we will do the exorcism in accordance with the Jewish Cabbala.'

Daskalos then asked Loizos to go upstairs to the bedroom and fetch the White Eagle, a small statue Daskalos kept at his bedside. It was Daskalos' symbol of white magic, a very ancient mystical symbol, I found out later. Loizos was also instructed to bring along a silver six-pointed star, a gift to Daskalos from a Jewish mystic. In its center there were inscriptions in Hebrew of the Ten Commandments. Daskalos told Loizos that on his return to the living room he should have his hands crossed over his chest holding on one hand the White Eagle and on the other the six-pointed star. He also told Loizos not to utter a word while holding the two objects in that fashion. Loizos went upstairs and Daskalos began his preparations. He first lit a white candle and filled a glass of water which he placed on the table next to the candle. Then he got a piece of white paper and markers of various colors. He went into the Sanctum and brought back the Unpointed Sword, kissed it and placed it over the paper. When Loizos returned, looking somber and silent just as he had been told, Daskalos took the statue, placed it next to the candle, and held the six-pointed star with his other hand.

'Come forward,' he said to the girl. She stood up and came close to the table.

'Can you read Hebrew?' Daskalos asked.

'Yes,' said the girl softly. Then Daskalos extended his arm and held the six-pointed star firmly in front of her face. He asked her to read aloud the Ten Commandments. After she had finished, he gave her the six-pointed star and told her to sit down and hold it with her right hand tightly over her heart.

'Repeat after me,' Daskalos commanded, 'Shalom Alehem, Shalom Alehem.'

'Shalom Alehem, Shalom Alehem,' the girl repeated it in a broken voice. I noticed a look of awe in the eyes of the other two women upon hearing the Hebrew words.

Daskalos then sat in front of his desk, kissed the Unpointed Sword, and asked Hadas to do likewise. Then he asked her to begin a prayer she knew in Hebrew. While she recited her prayer, Daskalos continued to murmur 'Shalom Alehem, Shalom Alehem' and using the Unpointed Sword and a red marker he began to draw several lines that appeared to me like several six-pointed stars, one almost on top of the other. His movements were slow and determined. After a few minutes he stopped murmuring 'Shalom Alehem' and began talking slowly while still drawing the red lines. I could not make out what he was saying. I could only see his lips moving. Loizos was standing behind Daskalos and joined in murmuring monotonously 'Shalom Alehem' while his eyes were fixed on Daskalos' drawings. Hadas continued her prayer, held the six-pointed star firmly against her chest, and focused her gaze on the flame as Daskalos had instructed her to do. I noticed the other two women were sitting on the couch next to each other holding firmly each other's hand and watching with watery eyes what was going on. It was an emotional scene. At that moment Daskalos appeared more like a rabbi than a Greek

Cypriot medicine man. By following Jewish mystical procedures he apparently eased the tension of the Jewish women, making it easier for them to participate meaningfully in the healing session. I suppose had the girl been a Muslim he would have followed Sufi methods to accomplish the same task.

'No, you are not Christians. You are swine. No pity on you,' he said in English with a loud severe voice, while concentrating on the flame and moving his hands around it. The flame was behaving in a rather strange manner. I had noticed this procedure on several occasions. Daskalos would concentrate his eyes on the candle and from a distance, usually two to three feet away, he would move his palm rapidly left and right in a trembling fashion. As he was doing this, the flame would become thin and elongated, black smoke flying away from its tip. Then it would shrink and vacillate violently. The flame appeared to respond to Daskalos' hand movements. Subsequently he would bring his palm forward and pass it over the flame as if trying to grasp it. He would then open his fist right over his drawings as if throwing something onto the paper, murmuring words no one could hear.

Daskalos shook his head disapprovingly while focusing and working on the candle's flame. 'They are stubborn,' he said, as if to inform his audience of the difficulties he was facing. 'No, you are not Christians,' he repeated loudly and severely, 'I am Jewish now! Shalom Alehem.'

Daskalos spent about twenty minutes working with the flame, a rather long period in comparison with other times that I had witnessed similar procedures. When he stopped I saw an expression of relief and satisfaction on his face. I also observed that the moment he stopped working with the flame it became still.

Hadas continued to repeat her prayer and Daskalos folded the white paper in the shape of a triangle. He then placed the edge of the folded paper over the flame, setting it on fire. Loizos, who was still murmuring 'Shalom Alehem,' took the burning paper from Daskalos' hands and placed it outside in a special container until it burned completely. Daskalos then asked the girl to put out the flame herself and then drink of the 'magnetized' water.

'You have nothing to worry about from now on,' he

declared authoritatively. 'They can no longer harm you or anyone else. Both of them are now gone to a place where they can rest in peace until they come to their senses. You may still feel heavy in the head but do not worry. These are the aftereffects that will gradually go away. But they can never again take possession of your aura. They may try to affect you telepathically but they cannot take possession of you. If you feel them near you, just say the prayer you have been saying here and concentrate on the flame of the white candle. The moment you do that they will be scared and will go away.'

Then Daskalos returned to his armchair. He looked tired. Little Marios, his three-year-old grandson, who had in the meantime come into the room, climbed on Daskalos' lap and rested his head on his grandfather's chest. Daskalos began stroking the boy's head. After a few moments of silence he said to the three women who sat there looking overwhelmed, 'It is amazing, is it not? People carry their hatreds even beyond the grave.'

Hadas' aunt, who was sitting next to me, leaned close to my right ear and asked in a low voice how much they owed Daskalos for his services. Apparently this was what they were waiting to hear before departing. I somehow expected it and said to the women in a half serious, half joking tone, 'Why don't you ask him?' Then I explained to Daskalos what we were talking about. 'You don't owe me anything,' was the standard response. 'Do you remember the case in the Old Testament of the Syrian king,' Daskalos continued, 'who suffered from leprosy and was cured by the Hebrew prophet?' The Jewish lady was apologetic for her ignorance of the Old Testament. So Daskalos briefly explained.

'When the Syrian king asked how much he owed the prophet his reply was "Nothing. The grace of the Lord is not paid with money." But one of his students got greedy. So when the king left with his entourage, this disciple followed them and told the king that the prophet had changed his mind. The king then offered him gold. But the prophet saw in his own way what had happened and when the student came back he told him, "The leprosy of the king is on you." And the disciple did, in fact, get leprosy. We cannot accept money for something which is not ours.'

'Are you saying, Daskale,' I interjected, 'that the prophet cursed his student?'

'No, of course not,' Daskalos replied, 'the prophet was good and loved his student. But he saw what was coming. It was the disciple's greediness that caused him to get the leprosy, not the prophet.'

'I don't understand,' Daskalos remarked after a few moments' pause, 'how a psychotherapist could ask for money for something which is not his, the life-giving ether of the Holy Spirit. You have been freely given, you should freely give,' he concluded.

After this short lesson the three women stood up, thanked Daskalos, and we all left. As we were coming out of the house the aunt inquired once again whether indeed they owed nothing. For some reason it sounded unbelievable to her. I reminded her of the story in the Old Testament, and got into the car.

A week later I paid the Jewish ladies a visit. I wanted to know how Hadas felt after her encounter with Daskalos. I had already been informed by Maro that Hadas had stopped hearing the voices since the day of the meeting with Daskalos. I was also told that she had gone out with a young man to a disco and was no longer afraid to walk in the streets by herself. 'Everybody was very happy,' Maro said.

It was the day before she was to return to Israel with her mother that I saw Hadas again. Unlike the last time I had seen her, she was quite talkative and willing to describe her experiences to me in more detail. Her mother and aunt were present. All three of them seemed pleased.

'Hadas,' I asked, 'can you describe to me what exactly happened to you?' With occasional help from her mother and aunt, Hadas began to narrate her ordeal.

'My problem started four years ago when my mother was on a trip to Romania. One night I went out with my friends. Something happened between me and my boyfriend and I left him. I went home and took a shower. When I went to bed I felt something entering my head. I was very upset. I felt changed. I went to a doctor who told me that it was only my nerves. He gave me pills. When my mother returned from Romania she took me to many doctors. All of them repeated that I was suffering from my nerves. I couldn't sleep even though I took many pills. Then I went to a rabbi. He told me that I must pray because something like a demon had gotten into me. I started praying and every morning I would vomit everything I ate.'

'But you still did not hear any voices?' I inquired.

'No, at first I didn't. But I dreamt that I lived in two kinds of worlds, in this world and in another world underground. A rabbi told me that after forty days I would vomit something very big and yellow, mixed with other colors. He said that after this I would be myself again, and this is what happened. I was vomiting every day and the fortieth day I vomited a lot and felt well again. I went out with my friends and had a new boyfriend. But once more something happened between us and we broke it off. I was very upset. This time it was more difficult for me because all my friends were married and I was very lonely. I remember I was sleeping on the sofa when something entered inside my body. It began in the legs and then entered in my stomach. I felt it penetrating me but did not hear any voices. After that it began to torture me. I went to many rabbis and told them what happened. "You are only upset. Forget it," they said. I couldn't forget it. It was hurting too much. After that I tried to convince myself that my problem was only psychological and that I should forget it, and then I went to sleep. But now I began to hear voices right here in the lower part of my neck and then they moved inside my head. The voices told me in my dream "In the world you are in, you cannot have a life like others. We will keep you away from your world. We will torture you and make you go mad. We will keep you in our world and get you married here." '

'They got you married in the other world?' I asked.

'Yes they did. They married me to a tall man with a mustache. I had never met him before. If I see him again I will recognize him. I know him so well! And they told me, "Because we forced you to marry in our world you cannot marry in your world." Every morning when I would wake up I would go to my mother's bed and ask her, "Please help me. Something very strange happened to me. Can you help me?" She couldn't. Nobody could help me! I felt the voices were destroying my mind. I didn't know what to do. I went to another psychiatrist. "There is nothing wrong with you," he said. "It is only in your mind." '

Hadas' mother mentioned that her daughter was sent to a mental institution from which she ran away after a week.

'They gave me very strong pills,' Hadas continued. 'My back began to hurt, I had trouble moving about, and the voices tormented me continuously. My mother then took me to another psychiatrist who told me that I was normal like everyone else. I visited this psychiatrist regularly, but he couldn't help me.'

'Did you,' I asked, 'describe your situation to the doctor the way you are describing it to me now?'

'No. I only talk about it to people who are open to these matters. I went to the rabbi again. "If you don't stop thinking about it," he said. "you will go mad." I couldn't stop. Every night they would come to me. They wanted me to commit suicide. Now I no longer hear them. I feel that my body is free. But I am not yet completely well. My head seems empty.'

I reminded Hadas of what Daskalos had said, that she was bound to have some aftereffects which would gradually go away. Her mother added that she saw a big difference in her daughter. The others agreed. I thanked them for their time and wished them farewell. My next task was to see Daskalos and hear his version of the story.

The next morning I took the bus and went to Strovolos. When I arrived I noticed that Daskalos had some visitors so I waited in the Stoa until they left. Later I went to the living room where I found Daskalos waiting. When I mentioned to him that I had seen the Jewish girl and that she was quite well, he showed no surprise or particular interest. 'I know,' he said matter of factly. Daskalos was a healer sure of his craft and he was in no need of reassurance about the effects of his intervention. When he said to Hadas, 'You are cured,' he was not simply trying to impress her and create in her a favorable psychological state for her recovery. Daskalos himself was absolutely convinced that objectively speaking she was cured, that the spirits had been exorcised and therefore she had nothing to fear. I was quite certain that Daskalos was not play-acting.

I did not elaborate on the details of my interview with Hadas when speaking to Daskalos. I just mentioned that I had seen her and that she was well. Now I wanted Daskalos to explain to me the details of the exorcism.

'It is a case,' Daskalos began, 'which I have encountered on several occasions. So far six or seven Jews, men and women, have come from Israel so that I could free them from "possession." ' Then, leaning back in his chair, Daskalos continued. 'In this case we are dealing with humans who died and who, during their lives, had relentless hatred against certain people or situations and who failed to make a complete transition to the psychic world. Instead they found themselves oscillating between the etheric of the gross material world and the psychic world. They thus found themselves in a position that allowed them to come in touch with this world. The way they do it is by taking possession of a human being who lives here on Earth and has certain phobias or is in a certain psychological state that permits these spirits to enter the person.'

'But as I understand it,' I added, 'possession can also happen by a demon or an elemental.'

'Of course!' Daskalos exclaimed. 'But possession, be it by a demon, an elemental, or a departed human, can take place only if there are reasons, that is, when the individual vibrates analogously with whoever or whatever tries to enter him. In other words the person must himself have the predisposition to hurt.'

'Are you suggesting, Daskale, that the Jewish girl had such a predisposition?'

'That girl had certain phobias that, had they been left unchecked, could have grown and hurt certain people. Therefore, for possession to take place, the sperm of something similar must exist in the one to be possessed. These Nazis tried gradually and in stages to get possession of the body of this girl, and they succeeded. These spirits were pushing her to self-destruction. You see they were not elementals of her own making that left her and then came back to her. Nor were they elementals of black magic sent to her by someone who wanted to harm her. So, as you see, possession can be by demons, by humans that have departed, or by elementals. The most difficult type of possession to cope with is by departed humans. They have a peculiar persistence. It is not easy to send them away. And you cannot destroy or dissolve them. They are eternal beings and cannot be destroyed. That's where the difficulty lies. For example, I can and I have the right to destroy and dissolve an elemental, no matter how powerful and terrifying it may be. In this case did you notice the persistence of those spirits?'

Apparently Daskalos expected me to give an affirmative response, forgetting for a moment that I was not a clairvoyant like himself and could not notice what he was seeing. So I must have sounded idiotic to him when my reply was, 'Notice what, Daskale?'

'Did you not notice that they refused to leave her? I would get them out of her and then they would return. I had a hard time passing them through fire.'

'Is that why the flame behaved in such a strange manner?' I asked.

'Yes. I was trying to pass them through the element of fire so that I could isolate them and then thrust them into Erevos.'

'To where?' I asked in surprise. I had never heard of such a word before.

'To Erevos,' he said emphatically. 'It is a form of psychonoetic abyss which is not punishment but a necessary condition similar, I would say, to oblivion where their memories will be erased so that when they return to consciousness they will not remember anything. You will see that what separates the various worlds, the etheric of the gross material, the psychic and the noetic, is the veil of Erevos or abyss. When one enters there one ceases to remember, reflects no impressions, yet one knows that one exists. Quite often human beings enter there during deep sleep. The ancient Greeks called it "The Dregs of the Water." It is a necessary condition to force human spirits that vibrate satanically, so to speak, to forget.'

'But Karma,' I said, 'will not forget.'

'No, of course not. They will come down to get their experiences and pay their debts. Erevos is just an expression of Divine Mercy.'

'So,' Daskalos continued, 'I tried to confine them in Erevos. Now they are in a state of deep sleep. They don't have the desire and they don't have the power to harm anybody. Therefore, the Jewish girl has nothing more to fear. But, because they stayed within her for such a long time, they brought about a certain amount of turbulence in her subconscious. There are still memories in her of what they had done. Now, you may ask, could I not have brought her into such a state that she could forget everything? It would have been very dangerous. She must gradually replace those memories herself. And she *is* now in a position to defend herself and to realize that it was *they* who created these pseudo-elementals in her. Now, had I uprooted these memories one by one, I might have disturbed her personality.'

'So what you are saying, Daskale,' I remarked, 'is that this girl may hear voices again but in that case they will be elementals, left over from her possession. And the prayer you asked her to say is to dissolve such elementals herself the moment she feels them near her.'

'Exactly! That is why I gave her a method which she can apply to dissolve these pseudo-elementals.'

'It is a form of autosuggestion,' I noted.

'Precisely. This is what it is. But what is autosuggestion? Self-conscious construction of elementals for a particular purpose. Therefore, that girl has a way to cure herself completely and at her own pace. Jesus once said that when we notice weeds growing in a field where we had just planted good seed, we should not uproot the weeds right away. We must wait until the good seed matures.'

'Daskale,' I said, 'you were carrying on a conversation with those spirits. And you said certain things such as "You are not Christians, you are swine." Did you say anything else?'

'Yes, a lot of things, through thought. I said those words in English, not for the spirits, since I could communicate with them mentally, but so that the subject, the Jewish girl, would understand how I characterize them. Do you understand now? I was working on both sides.'

'What else did you talk about?' I then asked.

'One of them said, "You are a Christian. What do you care about the Jews? They are enemies of Christianity. We are Christians." I told them, "You are not Christians because you trampled underfoot all Christian values." "We are!" they insisted. I noticed that in a past incarnation they had been members of a fanatical Protestant sect.

'So,' Daskalos continued, 'I then brought those two into a

situation which would make them realize that, not only are they not Christians, but they are swine, like those spirits that Jesus sent into the herd of pigs in order to destroy them.'

'When you said, Daskale, that you thrust them into Erevos, did you mean you created angelic elementals that escorted them there?'

'Exactly.'

'And in order to do that,' I continued, 'did you have to pass them through the element of fire?'

'Yes, of course. And I had to pass through fire myself, as consciousness, that is, so that I could bring them into a hypnotic state and dress them with Erevos. Now the Erevos that they got into is triadic. First, it is the etheric Erevos which they cannot break through and thus descend down to the gross material plane. Second, it is the psychic Erevos which will create the analogous psychic conditions for their sobering up, that is, the awakening within them of what we call conscience. And, third, the noetic Erevos which will calm them down and put them under the influence of reason so that they become conscious of the evilness of their thoughts and actions. Had I thrown them into the Erevos of total forgetfulness, they would not have received any benefits. I put them into the Erevos of forgetting particular incidents and episodes, but kept them awake in terms of conditions, so that conscience may work on them. I replaced the vibrations of hatred, antipathy and so on with the vibrations of compassion, and, if not love, at least tolerance. Therefore those two will be working through the elementals that I sent inside them. You see it was not just a question of helping the Jewish girl, but also the two Nazis. So I planted within them an elemental like a punishing angel, which will not really punish them for the sake of punishment, but rather an elemental which will awaken in them their own situation. Do you understand now what is happening? I dressed them in their thoughts with an elemental which has three dimensions in terms of vibrations. And the first dimension, as I told you, is the etheric so that it will not permit them to possess another human organism, which is done usually through the liver and the spleen. That's where they enter. In the psychonoetic Erevos specific incidents will be forgotten but the conditions will not be forgotten.'

'What does that mean, Daskale?' I asked.

'In other words,' Daskalos answered quickly, 'the memory that "I am an evil person because I hated, I tried to kill another person, I tried to obliterate and destroy another person" will remain. And there were specific episodes with places, names, circumstances, and so on. Those we now set aside in the psychic and noetic Erevos and we turn the roles around. In their thought they now become the persecuted instead of the persecutors. They will be the ones who will want to protect themselves from others who are trying to harm them. You see I turn things around. This is, after all, what Karma does day and night. They don't remember details of who they are. They just live vicariously, like a child who goes to the cinema and then in his dreams he sees himself being the hero, doing this and that. He has certain experiences and then he wakes up without remembering persons that he thought were himself. You see a characteristic of human nature is that people identify with the role of those they sympathize with or fear. So in this case I removed the memory that they were Germans fighting Jews so that other intense thoughts and emotions of nationalism will not be there. Instead I placed within them an elemental which with time will transform the persecutor into the persecuted. The persecutor is not a real one but an elemental. That is why I call it a punishing angel. It will awaken in them their consciences so that they will be able to differentiate between good and evil, to be able to develop the meaning of the good. That is how Karma works.'

'It seems,' I added, 'that they are in a kind of purgatory.'

'That's it. I created the circumstances which will lead them to the purgatory which they, *themselves*, have created. The Divine Plan will place them there. I am not myself creating Karma on them. I simply take them by the hand and accelerate their entrance into the situation they must live in which they themselves have created. Now, if they perceive it as relative hell or purgatory, it is their business. They constructed it and they are solely responsible for it. However, had I allowed them to stay inside that girl, not only would they have destroyed her, but they would have lost precious time themselves by creating worse Karma. Most likely they would have made more persons unhappy. But let me tell you something. These persons that become possessed are not the saintly types that are considered to be tormented by those that are bad. I don't believe that anyone can be hurt by an evil person if he does not have inside himself something analogous. Do you understand now what is happening? However, we shall never be the judges of either individuals or conditions. Instead we shall intervene to modify evil and in its place we shall prepare the circumstances so that the meaning of goodness, helpfulness and creativeness will dawn in the hearts of men, replacing the destructiveness that preceded it. Therefore, whoever is working with these matters must first rid himself of his own conceptions and sentiments about politics, religion and social questions. He must stand high above such questions and with impartiality and objectivity evaluate each case in accordance with its nature. Had I, for example, had a bias in favor of the Germans, and, had I had antipathy for Jews, I would not have been able to help that girl. Because if one has sentiments for or against one side or the other, one is bound to invent rationalizations to condemn or to excuse. You see, our work as Researchers of the Truth is polymorphous. We fight black magic, we do exorcisms, we heal, we fight injustice, we fight evil elementals and dissolve them and replace them with benign ones. All these are part of the duties of the invisible helper.'

'Daskale,' I asked, 'what were you doing when you were drawing the six-pointed star with the red marker?'

'I drew the six-pointed star because the procedure I used was taken from the Jewish Cabbala. I used a method which was appropriate for the girl as a Jewish person and which could have the greatest influence on her. Of course the six-pointed star is also our symbol.'

'But what, exactly, was happening when you were drawing the lines?' I probed further.

'Did you not notice? I was talking either with my mind or with words. First, I sought to entrap those spirits and place them where I wished them to be. Then I placed them in a symbolic space-prison so that they could not react. As you know, space is for the gross material body. But what about the psychonoetic body? There space exists as meaning, as conception. So I created a symbolic prison and placed them there. And then, after I forced them out of the girl and put them where I wanted them to be, I burned the six-pointed star in order to redeem them and thrust them into Erevos. And again I had to pass it through the element of fire so that this symbol-prison which I created might not remain in the gross material plane. Of course the Cabbala is very complicated. For example, with the Egyptian Cabbala you have to follow a different procedure. The same with the Christian Cabbala.'

'Daskale,' I said, 'it seems to me that very few people are capable of doing what you did with that girl the other day. Suppose she had never met you. Would that mean that she could never be cured?'

'No. There are certain rabbis in Israel who could have helped her.'

'So you had actually become a Jewish rabbi that day,' I commented.

'Precisely. You cannot help someone unless you become like that person. As you noticed, I asked her to pray with me in Hebrew. The fact that I am Christian is of no importance. Had I used Christian symbols and prayers she would not have accepted them. She would not have been able to understand. And her vibrations that were attuned to the pan-Hebraic way of thinking would not have permitted the elementals that I was sending to get inside her. That is why we had to start with the "Shalom Alehem," which means "Peace be with you." You may have noticed that all three of them were surprised when they heard me speak the Hebrew words.

'So,' Daskalos continued, 'with "Shalom Alehem" I was bringing peace between the three Jewish women on one side, and the German spirits on the other. For whatever reasons, Karma brought Germans and Jews together. I wanted to harmonize the relations of the two sides. I wanted to get these hostile spirits out of the Jewish girl and isolate them first, but I had to make very sure that the Jewish women would not become the aggressors themselves. Do you understand now what is happening?

'Had the girl been a Christian I would have used the circle and the cross. Also, I could have used the six-pointed star and placed crosses at the three top triangles. For this particular case I did not use these crosses so that the Jews would not react. Now you may ask why do we place these crosses? In the six-pointed star the topmost triangle symbolizes the Absolute. The other two are the Holy Spirit and the Christ Logos. Then we have the three lower triangles that symbolize the descent of the lower self into matter.'

Daskalos then proceeded to elaborate on the differences between the various Cabbalas. After that our conversation revolved around the question of talismans. I mentioned to him that everybody, including myself, was surprised that he 'saw' the talisman on the Jewish girl. He said he 'saw' it the moment he laid eyes on her. 'But,' he continued, 'that was not a very powerful talisman. It was like a shield that offered only partial protection around the chest. What about the rest of the body? The kind of talismans that we make are general and protect not only the whole physical body but also the psychic and the noetic. It is like a diving suit that protects the whole body. That is what I call a real talisman. That is what the ancient Egyptians used to make.'

Our conversation ended after Loizos arrived. Daskalos informed me that he had to go with him to the hospital and visit some patients. He promised to continue our discussion on the subject of possession, which he said was inexhaustible, some other time.

'Kyriaco,' Daskalos said, laughing, 'you can spend the rest of your life writing book after book about these matters.'

3
Elementals

Iacovos called me early in the morning and said he would be glad to talk to me about how he became a member of Daskalos' inner circle. He was one of his closest disciples and was being groomed by the master to succeed him. I had repeatedly expressed a desire to meet him and talk about his life but somehow he was hard to locate. Three weeks had passed since I had last seen him. I was very pleased to hear from him. In spite of his young age he seemed to be exceptionally knowledgeable about Daskalos' teachings. Most importantly he was one of Daskalos' beloved disciples and I assumed that through the young adept I could have an even easier access to the master. With time both of my assumptions proved to be valid.

Daskalos had mentioned to me that in 1974 during the Turkish invasion of the island Iacovos was taken prisoner to Turkey and remained there for five months. During that time he exemplified great courage and even though he was only fourteen he was an inspiration to the other inmates. He allegedly used to stand in front of the guards trying to block their way every time they came into the cell to abuse some of his fellow prisoners. Iacovos was badly beaten as a result of his actions. He purportedly said to one of the guards as he was hitting him, 'You are hitting at yourself but you don't know it.' One of the invisible helpers, said Daskalos, that was assisting Iacovos during his ordeal was 'brother Ismael,' a Sufi master who, in his last corporeal existence, lived as a Turk.

At a local café Iacovos told me of his relationship with Daskalos which began when the latter cured his father of a cancerous tumor on the neck. From that day on Iacovos became one of Daskalos' closest disciples. His psychonoetic powers began developing before he was sent to Turkey. There he kept contact with Daskalos through clairvoyance and exomatosis and informed his fellow-prisoners of events in Cyprus, which, according to Iacovos, he was later able to verify.

'You know,' Iacovos said, 'the first time I began consciously to leave my body I became quite confused. I reached a point when I was not sure which world was more real, the one we are in now or the various psychonoetic planes where I found myself while in exomatosis. Later on I learned that both this world and all the psychonoetic planes are illusions in the final analysis and that Reality is beyond all the worlds.'

Iacovos' puzzlement reminded me of the classical Chinese tale when Lao Tzu woke up one morning very confused. He dreamt of being a butterfly but he was not sure whether it was he who dreamt of the butterfly or whether he was in reality a butterfly dreaming of being Lao Tzu. Did Iacovos and Lao Tzu, I wondered, have a comparable experience?

Iacovos went on to tell me that when he was being sent to Turkey, and while on the boat, memories of similar experiences from past lives entered his mind. 'While the other prisoners were crying and screaming I suddenly experienced the Logos coming to me in the form of white light and felt peaceful.'

'Have you ever encountered the Logos again?' I asked.

'Yes, just before the day I was about to become initiated into Daskalos' inner circle.'

'Was it a dream?'

'No. I was fully awake when Christ appeared in front of me in a vision. He made me understand certain things about my life.'

'And what did he reveal to you?' I asked and noticed that Iacovos hesitated.

'He stood in front of me,' he said in a low and sad voice, 'and showed me the scars on His hands from the Crucifixion.'

'What was the message?' I persisted.

'That I too will have to bear a cross in my life,' Iacovos replied softly. Realizing that he wished to discuss the subject no further I shifted the conversation to other topics. We agreed to meet at Strovolos the following day when Daskalos was scheduled to give a lesson.

I arrived at Daskalos' much earlier than the scheduled meeting. Before every formal encounter with his students,

Daskalos usually met with some of his closest associates and chatted casually on a potpourri of topics, from local politics to the various techniques for journeying out of one's body. When I reached his home Daskalos was having lunch with Iacovos and Kostas, another one of his closest associates, a forty-year-old engineer. I found them in the midst of a discussion about the Greeks of old. I politely declined their earnest invitation to join their feast but merrily plunged into their debate. Daskalos brooded on the over-zealousness of the ancient mystics in guarding 'the secrets.'

'They should have tried to educate the people, particularly the philosophers,' he said forcefully, 'rather than keeping the knowledge egotistically to themselves.'

'But Daskale, what about Plato?' I pointed out. 'As far as I know he was involved with the Eleusinian mysteries. Much of what you teach about the higher noetic world reminds me of Plato's world of ideas.'

'There are some similarities but our teachings are not quite the same. Incidentally, Plato was not involved with the Eleusinian mysteries.'

'That is what some authorities say,' I noted.

'They are wrong. Plato went to Egypt and became initiated into the Egyptian mysteries. That is why he was called Plato.'

'I don't get that,' I said. I had learned in school that he was called by that name because he had a broad chest. The name Blaton (Plato) allegedly was a derivative of a Greek word meaning the 'broad one' or the 'wide-shouldered one.'

'That is historical nonsense,' Daskalos scoffed. 'His name comes from Baal, meaning God, and Aton which in ancient Egyptian meant "the Invisible God." Baalaton was cut into Blaton and in the English translation became Plato.' Daskalos then went on to make a similar case for another ancient sage, Pythagoras. It was he, according to Daskalos, who introduced the idea of reincarnation to the Greeks.

'Pythagoras traveled to India and was introduced to Oriental mysticism. He adopted his name from a Sanskrit word meaning "he who has been initiated into the temple." '

I commented that his interpretation of the names of these ancient philosophers would probably raise the eyebrows of many a scholar. Daskalos was not the least concerned. His information, he said, was based on the 'Akashic Records' and not on historical interpretations. He explained that the Akashic Records is another word for Universal Memory. Whatever exists, existed and will exist is imprinted in this pan-universal supercomputer. Furthermore, a single atom contains within it all the knowledge of the cosmos. It is, therefore, possible, by concentrating on a single atom, to acquire information of something or some event that took place in the distant past. It is done by entering into the Akashic Records just like a scholar enters into a library to investigate a particular issue. But like the scholar, the mystic must have prior knowledge of the subject he is investigating. Otherwise he will not be able to acquire any information. For example, if one is to use the Akashic Records to obtain information on nineteenth-century physics, one must be familiar with physics to begin with.

'I am glad,' I said jokingly, 'that in the order of things there is room for conventional knowledge. Otherwise it would be pointless to attend universities and read books.'

While I was finishing my sentence a white Mercedes parked outside Daskalos' door. A tall grey-haired and gentle-looking man stepped from the car and with slow movements walked into the house. Daskalos' eyes lit up. 'Theophani, what brings you to Nicosia?' All three of them were very happy to meet the man, who seemed to be close to Daskalos' age, around sixty.

'Kyriaco,' Daskalos said, 'let me introduce you to Theophanis, the "Magus of Paphos."' We shook hands and I expressed my pleasure to have met him, mentioning that I had heard a lot about him from Daskalos and Iacovos.

Theophanis was probably Daskalos' oldest close disciple and friend, their association going back for over forty years. He was from Paphos, the southwestern port of the island, one hundred miles from Nicosia. It was the place where Saint Paul was arrested and whipped for preaching Christianity to the pagans. The Paphians were known as devout worshipers of Aphrodite.

Theophanis had the reputation of being a healer himself and had his own disciples but at the same time he was also a member of Daskalos' 'inner circle.' Given their long association, there emerged a strong bond of friendship between the two old men. Theophanis, I was told, was particularly devoted to Daskalos. Unlike him, however, who was of an ebullient disposition, Theophanis was a quiet man who spoke only when spoken to. I later learned that he had never married. When he was twenty-five years old he was engaged to a girl with whom he was madly in love who died from tuberculosis before their wedding day. Theophanis never fully recovered from that loss and preferred instead to live with her memory. He devoted himself to healing and his profession. He held a high administrative position in the co-operative movement, an institution so developed and well entrenched in Cypriot life that it often served as a model for other developing societies.

As we were talking Theophanis inquired whether Daskalos was planning a trip to Greece during the summer months. Daskalos spent several weeks every summer in Athens giving 'crash courses' to his disciples there. During the rest of the year he sent them tapes. The invention of the tape recorder, said Daskalos, made his work much easier. He could now reach a greater number of people.

'I'll take a ten-day vacation myself and I'll join you,' said Theophanis.

'Great. But we'll have to go by boat.' Daskalos turned to me and mentioned that Theophanis was terrified of the sea. His stomach had a hard time adjusting to the waves.

'But,' Daskalos added, 'he should not worry about sea sickness. We'll make sure the sea calms down so that his Excellency may have a pleasant trip.'

I assumed Daskalos was either joking or was speaking metaphorically. I was wrong. He was dead serious, even though there was a strong dose of humorous irony in his remarks.

'I hope you will be able to pacify the sea as you did the year when we went to Tinos,' responded Theophanis, noticing my incredulous look. One summer, he went on to explain himself, he, along with Daskalos, sailed on a pilgrimage to the Greek island of Tinos, famous for the miraculous nature of an icon of the Virgin Mary. The sea around Tinos is renowned for being always turbulent. Daskalos, according to Theophanis, used his special powers and calmed the waters. When they disembarked the local fishermen and sailors were puzzled by the sudden tranquility of the sea.

'How did you do that?' I asked.

'I just wanted the sea to calm down for the sake of my

friend, Theophanis, and the sea listened,' Daskalos replied in all seriousness.

'But how did you do it?' I insisted.

'There you go again. You keep asking me this question all the time. How do you do this, how do you do that. . . . Suppose you had in front of you Paganini with his violin and asked him, "Mr Paganini, how do you play this violin?" what do you think he would tell you? Do you think he could explain to you how he plays his instrument? It is the same in my case. I just do it but don't ask me how. I can't explain it to you.'

Such phenomena, Daskalos said, should not scandalize us. These are powers latent in every human being. After all Jesus Himself calmed the waves. Since every human being has inside him the Christ Logos, it means that every human being can potentially master such powers.

It was already four o'clock in the afternoon and Daskalos' disciples were gathered in the Stoa waiting for their master to give the scheduled lecture. We terminated our conversation after a brief foray into the current confusion of local politics. It seemed that nobody in Cyprus could avoid discussing politics. It was the central topic of conversation among young and old alike. Faced with an occupying force in the north, politics acquired an intensity of existential proportions.

The subject of Daskalos' talk was elementals. At first he summarized many of the ideas he had discussed during previous meetings. It was his pedagogic method to repeat old material on a routine basis until his students had fully digested it.

Elementals, he said, have a life of their own just like any other living form and can have an existence independent of the one who projected them. Any thought and any feeling that an individual projects is an elemental. He then proceeded to explain that there are two kinds of elementals: those that are produced subconsciously, which he called elementals of 'desires-thoughts,' and those consciously constructed and called elementals of 'thoughts-desires.'

An individual, he went on, can vibrate through thoughts and sentiments. The way a person vibrates determines the type and quality of the elementals he creates. When he vibrates primarily through sentiments, he is under the impact of emotions and desires, thought playing a subservient role. These are the elementals of desires-thoughts. When an individual is under the influence of thought, he builds elementals made of noetic substance and becomes a master of the power of visual imagery. A Researcher of Truth should train himself to build powerful but benign elementals made up of strong thoughts within which desire and sentiment play a supportive role. Such elementals of thoughts-desires last longer, are more powerful and tend to accomplish the task for which they were constructed much faster.

Elementals of desires-thoughts are characteristic of ordinary people who lack an understanding of the nature of thought and desire. Consequently they often fall prey to the very elementals they themselves create. It is the law of Nature that once elementals are projected outwards they eventually return to the subconscious of the person who created them. Then they surface from the pool of his memory to the conscious level in order to acquire new energy and withdraw again. The same cycle is repeated until such elementals succeed in staying within the subconscious of the person on a more permanent basis. They then absorb energy from the etheric-double of the individual and in this manner they extend their life. This is how habits and obsessions such as smoking, gambling and drinking are being formed.

The tendency of elementals to return to their source is what makes the law of Karma possible. An individual sooner or later will be confronted with the elementals that he consciously or subconsciously creates. In a conversation I once had with Daskalos he maintained that elementals of strong desires may return to the person that gave them birth at a time when he least desires them. Daskalos then claimed that in a previous incarnation as an Italian during the Renaissance, he was obsessed with the idea of inventing a printing machine. The end result of that obsession was to spend his present life working as a linotypist in the government printing office.

Our present personalities, Daskalos went on, and the circumstances within which we live, are the sum total of the elementals we have constructed ever since our descent into the three-dimensional world and the beginning of our cycles of incarnation. Elementals are built with the very substance with which personality and the universes in general are built, that is, with etheric matter of the noetic, psychic, and gross material worlds.

'Let us examine,' Daskalos continued as the audience of about thirty persons listened attentively, 'the process by which an elemental is being formed. You will notice that it is not possible for a human being to desire something before he becomes aware of its existence. For example, when I see an object it means that etheric vibrations of light hit its surface and transfer images and forms to my eyes. They cause an irritation on the optic nerve and then on the brain which is imprinted as "seeing." Suppose now that I see an object which men consider precious, say a diamond necklace. I become aware of the existence of this object through my sight. Suppose that I am a person who has a strong desire for diamond necklaces. What happens then? Psychic matter is gathered around the image of the necklace. Desire is formed. It is precisely psychic matter that makes possible the birth of a desire which is followed by thoughts on how to satisfy it, in this case how to acquire the necklace. Around that object a series of elementals is being formed having as their ultimate goal the acquisition of that object by the person who projected them. An awareness of its existence and desire to know or possess it are not, alone, sufficient. Thoughts about it must follow in order for such an elemental to be created. The individual subconsciously begins the process of visual imagery.

'Suppose we take this person to a place away from the desired necklace and ask him to bring it to his mind. Most likely he will recreate it in the greatest detail. Someone else who saw the same object but who was not impressed by it will not be able to reconstruct it in his mind so accurately. Therefore, concentration and desire lead us to the construction of images made of noetic matter. This is what thought is all about, the condensation of noetic matter. We begin to see that object through noetic light. Now pay attention. What are real possessions? Are they those objects which ordinary people consider real? Or are they the elementals that we have constructed inside us? Suppose we take a precious object that we own and lock it up in a safe. The elemental of that object is inside us, is part of us. It exists in the pool of our memory and we can bring it to consciousness any time we wish. It is ours. It seems to you, however, that it is not real. And yet if you cannot bring it to your memory, how can you have knowledge of the material object in the safe? Think about it. Let me put it differently. Suppose that a very wealthy individual who knows that in a secret safe he has some very valuable objects suffers from amnesia. Everything within his memory collapses and is dissolved. What value do you think the objects outside his mind will have? None. Therefore, where is the real source of value of things? Pay attention to these points which you need to study. Otherwise you will not be able to penetrate and understand the nature of Life. What is Life in reality other than receiving impressions and interpreting them. Just think of the world around you. Can you perceive it outside of these elementals?

'You must realize by now that whether we perceive the world as good or as evil will depend on the kinds of elementals we construct inside us and project outward. Nothing, absolutely nothing, has any value in the world of the three dimensions if it does not also have value within us. It is what has value inside us which bestows value to whatever is outside of us. What, for example, does the phrase "lack of interest" mean? When an object outside of us does not have its counterpart inside us it has no value. So where has this condition come from? From the object or from within us? Everything is inside us.'

Daskalos stopped his talk for a few seconds and then proceeded to elaborate on the physical appearance of elementals, or more precisely on how elementals are perceived by a clairvoyant like himself.

'When an elemental is created, its image will appear at the base of the nose right on the chakra that lies between the two eyes. A clairvoyant will notice that it appears first in the shape of a needle's head. The moment it is thrust out of the etheric-double of the individual, it begins to acquire its natural size and shape. It will then move into the psychic worlds and will make a cyclical movement the size of which will depend on the strength of the desire. Then it will return to the person. At this moment it will enter into his psychic body but not in the same place from which it exited. It will make an entrance through a different center, that which is at the back of the skull.

'The shape of an elemental will depend on its type. It may be a desired house, a bicycle, or a car, and so on. These are examples of concrete images of desires-thoughts that remain within the subconscious for a relatively short time. They do so because such elementals, as I have said, seek a new lease on life in the same manner that an embryo seeks food. It will surface again at the disc between the two eyes and will seek an exit. The analogous vibrations in the psychic body of the person will begin again. He will remember it and the desire will become stronger. The elemental will detach itself once more and move on its cyclical trajectory. An ordinary individual does not realize what is happening. The elemental will tend to dominate him. It may become so powerful that he may not be able to control it. In such a case the individual is a slave to his desire which sometimes may be so intense that it could lead him to the asylum. It is possible that such an elemental may absorb so much etheric substance from the individual that it may even enable it to literally materialize itself. Let us not talk about this unfortunate development for the time being.

'What about morbid conditions that emerge directly as a result of our egotism such as anger, ostentation, hatred, feelings of being hurt, of showing off and the like? These elementals are constructed in the same way as all other elementals. Note that egotism is itself an elemental which is already formed within the self-conscious personality. It is the product of the repetition of many elementals. It is so sensitive that the slightest provocation sets it in motion. Egotism can create a variety of elementals. For example we have noticed from experience that when an individual has evil and malicious thoughts against someone, the elementals he creates have the shape of snakes with various dark colors, usually putrid green. They come out either from the heart or from the base of the nose. They move towards the person against whom we consciously or subconsciously direct them and they tend to stick to the aura of that person. Eventually they return to us. Sometimes such elementals acquire the size of an anaconda and when they return to us we feel our heart tighten.

'Have you ever considered how many such elementals people create daily? Had they been able to see the form of the elementals they project, they would have been filled with terror. This is what is commonly called the "evil eye." I once saw a painting of a man confessing his sins and there were snakes coming out of his mouth. Do not think that they were the fantasies of the artist. A clairvoyant can literally see these snakes. How often do you see such elementals come to you during sleep and frighten you? These elementals are either sent to you by others or they are your own creation. It is also possible that you might have picked them up in your sleep from the pool of elementals floating and wandering in the etheric world. Elementals of desires-thoughts have shape, power and a life of their own. They can become snakes and bears and other animals. Children often see them in their sleep and have nightmares.'

Daskalos then went on to explain that we can close the door of perception of such elementals by making appropriate autosuggestions such as a prayer before going to sleep. 'We can also calm down by sending thoughts of love even to those who dislike us. By doing so we disarm them. They can no longer send us elementals that haunt us in our sleep.'

'Daskale,' I interrupted, 'why do elementals of hate and jealousy look like snakes and not like something else? Is shape inherent in the very nature of the elemental?'

'Elementals of hate and jealousy look like snakes because in our culture we have this association. There is nothing inherently evil about snakes or any other animal for that matter. The way an elemental appears depends on the language of the person and the place from which he comes. Elementals are psychonoetic energy charges that can assume any shape depending on who creates them. A clairvoyant can see them in a shape consistent with his background.'

'So,' I continued, 'a clairvoyant from another culture may see the same elementals in the shape, say, of coyotes rather than snakes.'

'Exactly. But both will see the same causal connection between the projected elementals and their effects.'

'Daskale,' a middle-aged man asked, 'how can we dissolve and neutralize the power of elementals that we ourselves have subconsciously created?'

'You must keep in mind,' Daskalos replied, 'that the power and form of elementals will not be dissolved until they have accomplished the task for which they have been built. It is for this reason that we must be ready to face the consequences of our thoughts and actions. An elemental will keep us accountable not only in this life but also in succeeding incarnations. Therefore the builder of an elemental will have to sooner or later confront the elementals that he himself has constructed.

'You may wonder whether we can today avoid the influence of former conditions. Yes, assuming that we employ equal power with that of the elementals that we have constructed. But we need wisdom and a desire to redress past errors. We can resist the impact of old elementals or we may succumb to them by creating similar ones and by reinforcing the old elementals.'

'How can we fight,' someone asked, 'elementals such as smoking or drinking? Is it by avoiding situations where people smoke or drink?'

'First of all you must not fight such elementals. The enemy is invisible and is bound to defeat you. By waging an aggressive war against such an elemental you energize it. The way to neutralize its power is to ignore it. Let me give you an example. In our society today we see a lot of people quarreling fanatically over politics. Political fights are on a daily basis often leading even families to split up. These are terrible things that turn people into fools. I knew someone like that who tried repeatedly to avoid political fights but to no avail. He always managed somehow to get entangled into political quarrels and tremble with rage. "I can't stand hearing them talk like that," he told me. You see the elemental of narcissism was very powerful in him. He wanted to show off, to prove that he knew more than others and to impose his views. I explained to him that it was a personal weakness on his part which he could overcome with self-analysis. I advised him not to fight his urge but to consciously try to be indifferent. "Tomorrow," I suggested, "when you go to your office and they start the political arguments, you will most probably have the desire to join in. At that moment try to remind yourself that you must avoid losing your self-control. The elemental inside you will urge you to intervene in order to show your knowledge and wisdom. Listen carefully, judge and weigh their arguments, but say nothing." "But isn't it better to just leave?" he asked. "No," I replied, "you will not gain anything by running away."

'Naturally it was hard for him to practice this exercise. At first he could not resist the temptation. But at the end of the day he evaluated his actions. After three or four attempts he mastered his problem. One day he came to me and thanked me for helping him win back his friends.

'With indifference you extract the power of elementals and you neutralize them. Either they get dissolved or they float in the etheric sphere where they may be picked up by others. When we advance spiritually we become conscious of our responsibility for the fall of our fellow man as a result of elementals left over by us in the etheric world. Do you understand now why Christ said, "Do not judge lest you be judged"? Because you shall be judged by your own inner self. You created these elementals regardless of whether you have transcended the condition that led you to the creation of them.

'I urge you not to be concerned about how others judge or think of you. Fear only the judgment of your own inner self. Someone asked me once whether I was afraid of God. I said no, I love God and I try to be worthy of His love. What about, he said, the people around you? No, I said, I don't judge them and I don't care about their opinions of me. Aren't you afraid of anything? I am afraid of myself because I cannot deceive myself. When I sit down to meditate and practice my analysis, my inner self will ask, "What did you say? What did you do? What should you have done and you failed to do?" When we begin to listen to our inner self we are on the right path. We will no longer create evil elementals which will be floating in the etheric spheres and tormenting those around us. The Researcher of Truth must reach a point where he does not create elementals of desires-thoughts but, rather, elementals consciously constructed that are under his full control. When they leave him he will be able to govern and guide them regardless of how far away they may be. Such elementals of thoughts-desires are more concrete, more effective, and of a greater duration. For this reason we are more responsible for them. The person of benevolent thoughts must be certain that what he constructs receive the blessings of the higher spheres. No prayer has ever remained unanswered and no curse has remained unpunished.'

'What happens,' someone in the audience asked, 'when we

send a good thought to a person who is not receptive?'

'As I have pointed out to you before, it is the Law that whatever elemental we project will eventually return to us. In the case of evil elementals, whether subconsciously or consciously constructed, the punishment is inherent in them. When they return they acquire more strength and extension of life. The person against whom we project an evil elemental will be affected only to the extent that he, too, vibrates on the same frequency as ourselves. Otherwise it will hit his aura and bounce back to us seven times its original force. These are the types of elementals that a Researcher of Truth must learn how not to create. Jesus called them "spirits mute and deaf" that come out of the human being and, finding no rest, return to the individual, dragging along more of the same kind.

'In a similar manner, when we project a benign elemental and the person is not prepared to receive it as yet, it will hit his aura and come back to us. But in such a case the elemental will leave its mark on his aura. That power will be there to benefit that person at any moment when he will be ready to vibrate analogously. Therefore, you must always be aware that good is never lost. And if you love someone who you think does not deserve it, do not give up or despair. Continue sending him elementals of love and goodness. Sooner or later they will have an effect on him either in this or in succeeding incarnations. Remember what Christ said, "Love thine enemies." Bear in mind that those we consider as our enemies are in reality persons suffering from ignorance. For us the word "enemy" does not exist. We shall not call the mindless our enemies. Keep in mind that when we love those who love us it is understandable and very human. But when we love those who hate us, it is a divine condition. It uplifts us spiritually. When we hurt those who love us it is satanic. Unfortunately there is too much of that in our society today.'

'Does one generate elementals while asleep?' someone asked.

'Yes, of course. When we say a person is asleep, it is only his gross material body that is sleeping. But as a self-conscious personality he is using Mind in the form of sentiments and abstract thoughts. He mixes them up and subconsciously creates and projects elementals. Let me add that when a man is asleep he is more under the influence of his own elementals than when he is awake and preoccupied with the affairs of everyday life. You will notice that many things you desire and that you forget while awake will come to you either just before you fall asleep or during sleep. It is when the individual is in these receptive states that he is under the bombardment of his own self, of the elementals he has constructed earlier. It is for this reason that one of the promises of the Researcher of Truth is that every night before falling asleep one must spend a few minutes in self-analysis. It is exactly at that point when one begins to open up and become receptive to his own thoughts and desires. It won't be difficult to dredge them up from the pool of memory. It is at that moment when it is easier for him to study, know and master them. By learning how to use Mind properly we will discover who we really are and we will begin to distinguish our true selves from the conditions around us that keep us enslaved.

'I now want you to sit comfortably in your seats,' Daskalos said.

There was some commotion as everyone was trying to relax his limbs. Daskalos was going to give an exercise.

'Close your eyes. I want you to create with your minds a snake.' A few moments passed and then Daskalos continued slowly in a mesmerizing voice. 'Hold it with both your hands. It is not as terrible as you imagine. It is an elemental which can obey you. Imagine that you are holding it by its neck and tail. It moves. Here we go,' Daskalos said with disappointment. 'You are horrified! Had I asked you to hold an inanimate golden snake you would not have felt terrorized. But you are afraid to hold in your hands the breath of life. Very well then. Hold in your hands a golden snake. Now it is easier for you,' Daskalos said with humorous irony. 'I want some of you now to give it life. It can neither bite you nor hurt you. It is an innocent elemental. Let it down to the ground and with your thought say: "No snake will ever be able to hurt me." I am telling you, you will have nothing to fear from snakes from now on. This elemental will enter inside any snake which may be ready to hurt you and it will calm it down. This is a method you can use to tame animals around you. Don't forget that we, ourselves, are responsible for making animals our enemies.'

Daskalos on several occasions had talked of how men have

made the creatures of the Earth their adversaries and that there was a time when animals and men lived in peace and harmony. If you genuinely love an animal, he said, no matter what it is, you have nothing to fear from it. It is our hostility towards animals that causes them to attack us. Daskalos claimed he could carry on conversations with animals, including snakes. He once described to me how a snake sat at the top of a canvas he was painting and how he got some sugar, put it in his mouth and, after mixing it with his saliva, invited the snake to help itself right from his mouth. The snake took up the invitation and with its tongue licked up the sugar. There was an eye-witness to this episode who allegedly almost fainted.

On another occasion Daskalos, at the age of ten, sneaked into the cage of a circus lion and played with it. He said it was the lion which invited him in. As a grown man, a grandfather, on a visit to the British zoo, he accomplished a similar feat. According to his brother-in-law who was with him, Daskalos, like a mischievous youngster, managed to enter into the lions' den and played with the beasts. At one point he put his head inside the mouth of one of the lions. He did this in front of the horrified eyes of spectators and the zoo keeper was so impressed that he made Daskalos a job offer.

Once we train ourselves, Daskalos said, to construct live and powerful elementals, we will be able to accomplish as much. This is how Daniel managed to calm the lions. Daniel created, with his mind, elementals of tamed lions and projected them inside the hungry beasts in the den.

'Now,' Daskalos continued while everybody had his eyes closed, 'imagine that you are holding with your left hand a beautiful orange. Make it as perfect as you can. Scratch it with your right hand and smell it. You can smell it. Keep it tightly in your hands and visualize it as real as possible. You have now created the etheric model through which the orange may take material existence. Until the next lesson I want you to create with your mind an object once or twice a day, a few minutes at a time. Concentrate on it. Make it as perfect as you can. At first construct an object such as a fruit or a flower. Then construct a living creature such as a sparrow or a pigeon. But I must warn you. Do not make the mistake of a student of mine who created an elemental of a dog and could not control it. This most naive fellow learned the way to build powerful elementals and assumed, the fool, that it would be a good idea to create a dog with noetic matter so that it could guard his home without having to feed it. For forty days through intense concentration he infused this elemental with ether. He reached a point when he could no longer control it. It became so powerful that the neighbors could even hear it howl at night.

'You must know that when such an elemental is built it acquires the characteristics of the person who created it. If that person has an antipathy towards someone, the elemental will attack. Similarly, when someone has negative thoughts or feelings against the creator of the elemental, again the elemental will attack. This is exactly what happened in this case. One night he was desperate and came to me. "Save me," he implored. He could not control the dog anymore and it even began attacking him. With great effort I managed to dissolve that elemental. I had no choice but with great sorrow to expel him from our circles. I took away his white robe, so to speak. I just took away the cloth. The white robe will always be around him to guide him through the aeons.

'You must understand that when you create elementals of thoughts-desires you are handling divine substance. You are not dealing with clay. The acquisition of such powers is a great responsibility. We should experiment but we must be wise enough to create elementals of thoughts-desires which will benefit our fellow man, not to satisfy egotistical desires. Our aim is to become psychotherapists, not black sorcerers. May the love of the Most Beloved One be with you and in your homes and with the whole world.'

After Daskalos ended the lesson I spent a few minutes in the Stoa talking to Iacovos while most of the others chatted outside under Daskalos' grapevine arbor. A middle-aged woman, who seemed to know Iacovos well, returned to the Stoa and asked for Iacovos' help. She was about to have an operation at the hospital and wondered whether it would be possible to avoid it through healing. Daskalos had advised her not to worry and to proceed with the operation. He then sent her to Iacovos for assistance. I assume it was part of Daskalos' method of training Iacovos in the art of healing, in the same way that a surgeon trains an intern.

She briefly explained to Iacovos her problem and her fears of lying under the surgeon's lancet. Iacovos tried to allay her anxiety with comforting words and then asked her to sit on a chair. He then placed his hands over her head, closed his eyes, and breathed deeply. He remained in that position for about five minutes.

'Think of me when you are about to have the operation and I will be there,' Iacovos said to the woman.

'Just what did you do to her?' I asked with curiosity after the woman thanked him and joined the others in the yard.

'I just built a therapeutic elemental,' Iacovos said confidently. 'The patient will think of me just before the operation. When she does that the elemental I created will become activated and will do exactly what I would do were I to be there in person. Her thought will create the contact between her and myself. The elemental will absorb energy from my etheric-double to work.'

'What will you be thinking at that moment?' I asked.

'I will perhaps feel some exhaustion or I will become absent-minded. It is hard to explain.'

'How did you build that elemental?' I probed further as I noticed that most of Daskalos' students had already gone.

'I have employed certain properties of etheric vitality to shape an elemental which will be appropriate for her situation.'

'You mean one therapeutic elemental differs from another?' I asked again.

'Certainly. It differs in terms of its shape and the intensity of desire it encloses.'

'What exactly did you do at that moment when the woman asked you for help?'

'I created a white-blue ball of light which I projected on her etheric-double. That ball of light will become energized the moment the patient thinks of me.'

'Sounds very simple,' I said wryly.

'It is not as simple as it seems. You must employ intense concentration to build such an elemental. Otherwise it will be dissolved.'

'Come,' I said, 'Daskalos is waiting for us.'

4

The Authenticity of Experience

When Zoe, Emily's good friend, learned of my 'secret project,' she expressed a strong desire to meet Daskalos. She was a bright woman in her early thirties, a local writer, who was once a student of Piaget in Switzerland. Zoe was a thorough secularist, steeped in contemporary French thinking and culture. Even though she accepted the possibility that humans may have latent powers, the concept of the soul, life after death, and reincarnation were to her complete absurdities. The visit to Daskalos was more out of curiosity, she admitted, than a desire to search for a master.

I went to Daskalos with Zoe during the early evening. Emily was to join us later, along with Stelios, a close friend of mine, and his wife. On the way Zoe appeared somewhat apprehensive and uneasy. As a child, she experienced terror every time the name of Daskalos was mentioned by her parents, she confided in me. She knew that her father was acquainted with Daskalos but was not certain in what capacity. Her childhood fear of Daskalos was the result of a tale that circulated among friends of the family. He allegedly caused a pair of scissors to move by themselves in order to tease some friends. This feat took place in the middle of the night while everyone was asleep. The scissors flew over the middle of the room and were nailed on the floor. These childhood memories aroused in Zoe feelings of discomfort. I reassured her that his reputation among certain circles as a frightful sorcerer was totally unfounded and that once she met him she would be quite at ease. She agreed that her fear was totally irrational.

Daskalos was exceptionally friendly to Zoe and after the preliminary courtesies he mentioned in passing that her father, a prominent architect and former minister in the government, was Daskalos' student for many years. The revelation came as a shock to her. In the meantime the others arrived and the five of us sat in anticipation of what we expected to be an enchanted evening.

'Daskale,' I began, 'the other day I had a discussion with Zoe on the nature of mysticism and the relationship between mind and body. She claims that she can easily accept the possibility of paranormal phenomena but dismisses that soul and body are two distinct realities. Perhaps we can start our discussion tonight with this issue.'

Daskalos seemed to be in a lively mood and appeared to have taken a liking for Zoe. He mentioned to me on a different occasion that he preferred to discuss spiritual questions with well-intentioned atheists than with the fanatically religious. With a critical atheist, he said, you can have a rational conversation. Not so with the superstitiously religious.

'Do you know what matter is?' Daskalos began in an assertive tone after looking Zoe intensely in the eyes. Without waiting for an answer he continued, 'Do you think that the chemists with their elaborate formulas know what matter is? For us there is no matter. There is only Mind.' Zoe asked several questions trying to understand Daskalos' language and challenging his diminution of matter.

'What is wrong with matter?' she protested.

'Matter as master is evil. Matter as servant is a blessing,' Daskalos replied and spent some time elaborating on what he meant by matter.

'What is the purpose of matter?' Zoe, who had quickly overcome her initial reservation about Daskalos, asked.

'Its purpose is to make possible for us, as eternal entities, to acquire experiences. It is a manifestation of the Absolute that makes possible for us the development of our self-consciousness.' Daskalos then summarized his philosophy on the nature of Being, the nature of thought, elementals, the difference between permanent and present personality and so on. He explained that matter is not what it appears to be. We imagine something as solid simply because we vibrate at the same frequency with that object.

'Is it possible,' Daskalos continued, 'to build a city without an architect? Is it possible to build a house without a blueprint?' After raising the questions he went on to argue that there are immutable laws, causes that exist in the higher noetic plane, the world of ideas. These archetypal ideas are the real causes of phenomena.

'I find it very hard,' commented Zoe, 'to accept that my thoughts and feelings can be heard by anyone other than myself.'

'Many of my students often ask me this question. "Does the Absolute feel, see, hear as we do? Is Christ listening to us right now as we are talking to one another? Is He aware of the lesson that we are having at this very moment?" My answer is a categorical yes. He hears and feels this lesson both from His own perspective as the Pan-Universal Logos and from the perspective of each one of us, as we ourselves understand and feel it. Why? Because He is the Light that enlightens every man descending upon the Earth. It is this Light that makes possible for us our own self-conscious intelligence. Never has any conversation been carried on by humans that He has not heard. Never has any thought or idea been conceived by human intelligence that He does not know. Believe me, there is no secret which will not one day be revealed through Karma because we as phenomena of life do not exist within dead matter. The Universe is not a lifeless machine. Dead matter cannot create life. Sooner or later each one of us will realize that as human intelligences on a certain stage of our evolution we live simultaneously within a Superintelligence. It would be foolhardy to assume that the builder of eyes and ears can neither see nor hear. And it would be equally irrational to conclude that what gave us the ability of self-awareness is not aware of itself.'

We listened attentively as Daskalos continued his dialogue with Zoe. No longer feeling apprehensive, she continued to question Daskalos like a good investigator. It appeared as if the lesson was given primarily for her.

'What evidence do you have,' she asked, 'that you have a soul and that the world you have described to us is real and not an illusion or a hallucination?'

Apparently Zoe's question was the type that Daskalos expected and which elicited a prolonged response. I was certain it was not the first time that Daskalos had confronted such a question.

'Perhaps,' Daskalos said, after leaning back in his chair with a smile on his face, 'the best way to answer your question is to describe a few personal experiences.

'I was once traveling by boat to Greece. There was heavy rain and I went to my cabin to lie down. I came out of my body. I spread myself all over the boat. I saw everything that was going on in that ship. I saw what was happening in the captain's cabin, in the kitchen, in the dining room, on the deck. I then soared higher and spread myself over a wider area. I saw sea gulls following the boat. I penetrated the deep and observed life there. I experienced the saltiness of the sea. I was one with the boat. I spread further and higher and saw an island ahead. I was able to see the smallest detail on that island, creeks flowing, rabbits running up the hills, trees. The boat, from up there, appeared like a match box. Suppose it sank and everybody drowned, what would have happened to me? Nothing. I would not feel a thing. This is really what Christ meant when he said that those who follow Him will not taste death. Christ used to take his students into the olive groves and give them exercises and experiences in exomatosis.

'When I came back to my body,' Daskalos went on, 'I stepped out of my cabin and walked on the deck. The rain had already stopped and the sun had come out. The captain, an Athenian, was standing there gazing at the horizon. I asked him whether there was a little island ahead of us. "Yes, Daskale," he replied, "there is one a few miles away. Did you see it?" "How did you know my name?" I wondered. He said his brother was a student of mine and coincidentally he had in his cabin a couple of mimeographed volumes of my talks. Later on we passed by the island that I had seen in exomatosis. It was exactly the way I experienced it.' Daskalos stopped his narrative and addressed himself exclusively to Zoe. 'Now is this hallucination or a real experience which validates the reality of my world?'

'In this case,' Stelios commented from his corner, 'you were able to confirm your experience because what you saw was on the material plane. How can you confirm experiences that are not of this world when people with an ordinary consciousness have no access to them?'

'You can also check what you experience on the psychonoetic level.'

'Can two people on the psychic dimension have identical experiences that can be confirmed by each other? Can they see the same things?' Stelios asked again.

'They may see the same things differently. Suppose I take ten people to gaze at a landscape and then bring them back and ask them to describe what they saw. Do you think they will describe that landscape in the same way? Or will they observe and notice whatever attracts their interest? They will see the landscape. But they will not describe it the same way unless they have identical interests. When two Researchers of Truth with the same concerns find themselves within a psychic subplane they see and observe with the greatest detail the same landscape. In this way we confirm the authenticity of our psychic experiences that cannot be validated through the five senses.' Daskalos then turned towards Zoe and began to narrate another psychic experience he had had.

'Four miles away from Strovolos there is a farm owned by a friend of mine. He once invited me to spend the weekend with his family and volunteered to give me a lift with his car. I preferred to walk to his house. The following day just before I was about to wake up I spread myself and surveyed the territory between my house and my friend's farm. I noticed that on the road just before his farm there were two snakes fighting one another. I saw the big snake chasing the small one. It grabbed its tail, bit it and slowly swallowed it. Then it tried to cross the street but at that moment a car coming from the direction of Tseri ran over it and crushed its neck. I saw the snake squirming convulsively and with spasmodic movements it crawled into the ditch.

'In the meantime I woke up, put on my clothes and started walking towards the farm. It took me about an hour until I reached the spot where I had seen the fight between the two snakes. As I was approaching, a car stopped and four persons stepped out. I laughed. I said to myself they must have seen the dead snake. "Are you looking at the black snake?" I asked them as I came closer. One of them turned towards me with amazement. "How do you know there is a black snake?" he asked. "In fact," I said, laughing, "there is a yellow snake inside the black one." "What did you say?" the fellow responded with suspicion. "There is another snake inside this one?" You see,' Daskalos continued, 'I was naive at that time and talked openly about my experiences. I admit it was a mistake.

'I described to them in detail what happened and how a car passed over the snake, crushing its neck, how it crawled into the ditch and so on. That man suddenly took out a pocket knife, stepped over the head of the snake with his foot, and sliced its belly in two. He found there the yellow snake. He looked at me in horror. "Are you Spyros Sathi?" he muttered. "Yes," I nodded. "Get away from here. You are the Devil," and he pointed his finger at me. "Why, mister, do you think I am the Devil?" I protested. "How did you know there was a yellow snake inside the black snake?" he asked with a trembling voice.

'Could I explain to him how I knew?' Daskalos said with an air of despair in his voice. 'Do you think he could have understood? I just said, "It seemed to me that way." "It didn't seem to you," he said, "you are the Devil," and he started crossing himself. I discovered later that he went to the priests and announced to them that he had encountered Satan and narrated the episode with the snakes.

'One has to be very careful about these matters. At the same time these are the very experiences that offer me unshakable convictions on the reality of my world. Now do you understand? I have continuous experiences like these which prove to me that the world I live in is neither a hallucination nor an illusion.

'Some time ago,' he went on, 'a stupid fool borrowed my binoculars and lost them on a trip up on the Troodos mountains. He hung them on a pine tree, forgot which tree he had hung them on, and left them there. He got into his car, came down to Nicosia, and with the greatest audacity he announced, "You know, Daskale, those binoculars of yours are gone, they flew away." "What do you mean they flew away?" I said angrily. "I just don't know where I put them." "What do you mean, you don't know?" I responded with exasperation. "Those are powerful and expensive binoculars that I cannot find today." "But what can I do, Daskale? I just lost them." "You must go and find them," I ordered him. "How am I going to do that?" "Just wait a minute," I said to him. "Let me find out where they are and then you go and fetch them. Where did

you go?" I asked him. "We went to many places, Troodidissa, Platres, all around the mountains. We went...." "Just a moment," I said, "I can coordinate myself with my binoculars because they are embedded with my aura." I closed my eyes. "Did you pass by such and such a road?" I asked. "Yes." "Did you climb up the hill?" "Yes," he said reluctantly, "and I didn't even have paper . . . I went up there for this job and. . . ." '
Daskalos roared with laughter and continued his story.

' "I went," he said, "behind the hill so that they would not see me while I relieved myself. Don't tell me more," he said. "Don't tell me that I wiped myself with rocks." "I don't care," I said, "how you wiped your ass. What I care about is my binoculars that you left behind, hanging on that pine tree. You must go right away and bring them back." "Are you sure? Okay, I'll go," he promised. He got into his car, traveled a hundred miles all the way to the mountains and back, walked up that hill, found my binoculars hanging from the tree, and brought them back the same day. "Son of a gun," he said, "I forgot that I put them up there." '

Daskalos interrupted his narrative and whispered that these phenomena are no longer allowed. Before, he admitted, such incidents escaped him and often caused a great deal of trouble, with the church in particular.

'How can I not be convinced?' he went on. 'This is my life, my every-day reality. How can anyone who does not share similar experiences convince me that my world, my reality is illusory? Anybody has the potential to have such experiences.'

'In science, Daskale,' I said, after a few moments had passed, 'one scientist can check the results and observations of another scientist. . . .'

Daskalos understood what I was about to say and proceeded to answer my question before I completed the sentence.

'You can check these experiences also. Had it not been so, you could not believe. I speak of psychic planes and subplanes. I am not the only one who talks about these realms. Others see and experience the same things as myself. The work that I do others also do. They may not remember fully, but they remember a great deal. Do you follow me? Take Marios, my three-year-old grandson. When he was two years old he wanted to do exomatosis with me.'

'Did the child himself ask for it?' I inquired.

'Yes he did,' Daskalos replied and continued. 'I was conversing with Theophanis and the mayor of Paphos. Marios was there also. He was anxious. I asked the others to wait while I took him for a "walk." They understood what I meant. They knew about these matters. "Come, my love," I said to Marios. "Come out and I will join you." He closed his eyes and began to breathe deeply while I continued talking to the others. In the meantime he came back. "Grandpa," he said, "come on, I am waiting. When are you coming out yourself? Come, come," he said. "Okay, my love. Go back and I'll follow you right away." I saw him come out of his body and stand right in front of me waiting. I excused myself and lay on a couch. I came out of my body and joined Marios. Like lightning we went to the southwest coast near Limassol somewhere between the city and the British bases. There are some huge cliffs facing the sea. Marios liked it there. He enjoyed standing on the side of the sea facing the land and the rocks. As we were roaming around we saw a big snake coming toward the edge of the precipice. The snake saw us. Animals are clairvoyant, you see. My grandson went towards the snake and played with it. He stood in front of it trying to stop it from moving forward. The snake raised its head and started hissing.' Daskalos, like a good actor, imitated the snake and continued.

'I stood there watching and laughing. Marios passed his etheric hand through the body of the snake which continued to hiss. "Come on, my dear," I said to him, "we have to go back because we have guests." I woke up first, laughing, and told the others about my experience while Marios was still out of his body. In a few minutes he woke up. Theophanis immediately asked him, "Where did you go, my love?" "To the sea where the big rocks are," he replied. "And what did you see there, my love?" Theophanis asked again. "We saw mister snake. He stood up and said hissss. . . ."' Daskalos imitated how little Marios described the behaviour of the snake. Then he leaned back and looked at Zoe.

'Well,' he said, 'is this not proof for me? Is this not a validation of the reality of my experiences? You may ask, "Do all those who are capable of conscious exomatosis remember their experiences?" I would say some a great deal, some a little.

In order to remember your experiences fully you need a great deal of practice. Then you will reach a stage where you will be in full control.'

'How does one begin to develop these abilities?' Stelios inquired.

'Through certain meditation exercises.'

'Why are they necessary?' Stelios asked again.

'Tell me something,' Daskalos replied with a dose of irony in his voice, 'can one play the violin without practice? It is exactly the same with the development of one's psychonoetic powers.'

'Is it not possible to be born with such abilities?'

'Yes. But you must have developed these powers somehow, sometime in the past. If you are born with such abilities it means you have brought them with you from previous lives.'

'How should one start practicing?' Zoe asked.

'With concentration,' Daskalos said slowly and emphatically. 'Let me ask you a question. "How many things do you concentrate on with full awareness during your everyday life?" Very few. When you train yourself to concentrate you will become aware of much more in your life. At first you devote a quarter of an hour every day. During that time you may take a walk and will fully notice everything around you. Nothing should escape your attention, nothing. You may feel tired at first because you are not accustomed to paying attention to everything around you, the ant walking, the flowers, the sounds, the voices. You perceive everything, you feel everything. When you start this exercise you learn that during that quarter of an hour you live much more fully, much more intensely, than at any other period of the day. You will discover that what is considered ordinarily as the awakening state is in reality a form of semihypnosis. You will discover that your consciousness of the world will expand· tenfold during that quarter of an hour. Usually you do not retain in your memory more than a fraction of the day's impressions which you receive within the gross material world. Therefore, how much do you expect to bring back and remember from experiences you receive within the psychic world? Consequently one must begin exercising on the gross material plane and then continue exercising on the psychic plane. It is a matter of practice. Do you understand now? Today man does not know how to live, how to concentrate, how to express himself within the realms of Creation. Would you call the person who knows how to concentrate superior to others? No. I do not consider him any more skillful than a person who plays Paganini on the violin or Beethoven on the piano. It is a question of training and practice. The "I am I" of the person who lives in ignorance does not differ from that of the mystic. Do you understand what I am saying? It is not a question of discovering the "I" but of expressing it. This is the purpose of the Research for Truth, to find out who you are and to express yourself as you ought to. I tell you, you will discover that you grow neither bigger nor smaller. The field of vision of receiving impressions may get bigger but you are you as you have always been.'

When Daskalos completed his sentence the telephone rang. He walked up the steps and we heard him carry on a rather loud conversation. It seemed that the call was long-distance, probably Athens. When he returned, ten minutes later, he looked severe. He explained that a woman in Athens wanted to find out who stole forty thousand drachmas from her house. Daskalos said he could not tell her. It would not be proper to say anything, nor did he have the right to 'see.' 'But without my intentionally trying to see, I saw. How could I tell her that it was her seventeen-year-old son and her husband who stole the money? I just mentioned that it was not a stranger.'

After this brief interruption Zoe asked about Daskalos' reputed powers. Specifically she wanted to know what exactly happened in the case of the scissors that had caused her so much fear during her childhood. Daskalos burst out laughing and marveled that she remembered the episode. Without any hesitation and as if he had experienced this incident a short while ago, Daskalos narrated what happened.

'A young doctor from Famagusta came to me one day and told me that he had lost a pair of tailor's scissors. He searched for them for months but in vain. The scissors were very precious to him because it was his only inheritance from his late father who had been a tailor. He suspected his sister who insisted, however, that she was innocent. On several occasions he quarreled with his sister and exchanged bitter words. He said he hadn't talked to her for five months. His wife remained neutral in this dispute but she also suspected her of stealing the scissors while her brother was drunk.

'He asked me to help him find them. At first I refused and sent him away. I thought his problem was nonsensical and one should not misuse these powers. But after he left I had second thoughts. I realized that it was not a matter of a pair of scissors but a dispute between two people, brother and sister. When I went to bed this issue was still in my mind. I closed my eyes and I saw, on the top of a closet under a folded cotton blanket, the pair of scissors. He must have placed them there and forgot it. A few minutes later I received a phone call. He asked me whether I had changed my mind. All he wanted to know was whether his sister had stolen them or not. "Don't tell me she didn't," he said, "otherwise they should be in the house." "They are there," I told him but I did not specify the location. I advised him to go to bed and that soon he would know. I then left my body and traveled to his house forty miles away. I thought of materializing a hand to pull the scissors from under the blanket and push them onto the floor.'

'Why did you not tell him where the scissors were?' I asked.

'I wanted to experiment, to be playful. I made a mistake. The closet was in one room and their bed in another. An open door linked the two rooms. The distance between the chest and their bed was about sixteen feet. The floor was made of wood. I materialized a hand, pulled the scissors from under the blanket, and dropped them on the floor. I assumed they would fall in front of the closet. But I was inexperienced at the time and miscalculated the force I applied from one dimension to another. The scissors opened up, flew over to the other room, and like a knife, got imbedded on the floor near their bed. The noise woke them up. They were only three feet from his body. I could have killed him. He got very anxious, pulled the scissors from the floor, and called me up. It was eleven-thirty at night. "Daskale," he said, "you nearly killed me. Where did you find them and why did you dart them so close to my body?" I explained to him what had happened but he did not believe me. He got into his car and came to Nicosia with the scissors. He insisted that his sister was the thief and that I dematerialized the scissors from her house and rematerialized them in his bedroom. It took me some time to make him understand what had happened.'

Such phenomena are no longer allowed, Daskalos repeated. Power should be used only for healing. When one uses 'materialization' for moving objects, one has to be extremely careful. The intensity of the force applied may be ten times stronger than when one uses his material hands.

'Why is this so?' I asked.

'I don't know. You can see this with seances. Heavy objects are moved with the concentration of several individuals.'

Zoe listened attentively to Daskalos' story. There was a look of fascination in her face as she tried to assess the value of his experiences. Yet, as if to reassure herself, she murmured that for her reality still rested in matter.

'It is the only thing that I know exists. It is what I can feel, touch, see, smell.'

'There you go again,' Daskalos said laughing. 'You think that in order to exist one must eat, drink and go to the bathroom. There is nothing more misleading than the five senses.'

'I am not quite clear about the relationship between the soul, the permanent personality and the present personality,' Zoe commented after we calmed down from laughing.

'The soul,' Daskalos explained, 'is that part of ourselves which is pure and uncolored by earthly experience. The soul is beyond the Idea of Man, beyond all manifestation. It has never been born and it will never die. It is that part of ourselves which is qualitatively identical with the Absolute. If the Absolute is the ocean, we, as souls, are drops in the ocean. Qualitatively we are like the ocean. The soul is our divine essence, unchangeable and eternal. The permanent personality is that part of ourselves upon which the incarnational experiences are recorded and are transferred from one incarnation to the next. The present personality is made up of the noetic, psychic and gross material bodies. It is what ordinary people consider their personalities. The present personality is the lowest expression of ourselves which is constantly evolving and tends to become one with the permanent personality.

'Let us assume,' Daskalos said, 'that the permanent personality is a large circle. Imagine another circle outside without a periphery. We call that the soul which is within God, within infinity and boundlessness. It is always pure and unspoiled.

There is also a small circle inside the other two which I call the present self-conscious personality. All three circles have the same center. As the small circle spreads out, the distance between the periphery of the small circle and that of the larger circle merges until the two become one, the smaller circle being absorbed by the larger. The point at which the periphery of the smaller circle rests is the degree of one's perfection. The center of the present and permanent personality, as well as the self-conscious soul, is the same. "I am," says the present personality. "I am," says the permanent personality. If you ask them both which of the two says "I am," you will hear one voice, "I." But which "I"? It is the same voice with its echo. In reality it is the selfconsciousness in its totality that says "I am." And it is the experiences within gross matter that caused the separation of the two conditions within ourselves.

'The more the present self-conscious personality opens up as a circle, the more the permanent personality penetrates into the present personality. The higher you evolve on the spiritual path, the greater the influence and control of the inner self over the present personality. We habitually say, for example, that this man has conscience whereas another one does not. In reality there is no human being who does not have a center. The level of conscience of an individual depends upon the extent to which the present personality is spread out inside the permanent personality.'

It was already late in the evening. Daskalos' liveliness, however, was at its peak. Discussions like these seemed to energize him. I had repeatedly seen him come alive with the start of a conversation. He would look totally exhausted by the end of a hard day's work, but the moment a discussion began on metaphysical questions, he would become literally transformed.

We stood up, ready to leave, but my friend Stelios asked whether one can create, with one's mind, anything one wishes.

'Yes,' Daskalos replied, 'assuming that you are within the realm of possibilities and potentialities. A yogi may plant a seed of an orange tree and with prayers and meditations he may be able to have it grow much faster than usual. But he could not plant a seed of an orange tree and with his mind make that seed grow into a eucalyptus. You cannot work outside the world of ideas, laws, causes. You can, however, do something else. You may be able to first change the nuclear composition of a seed of an orange tree and make it into a seed of a eucalyptus and then plant it and get a eucalyptus tree. This is different. It is within the realm of possibilities and potentialities.'

'I have one last question,' my inquisitive friend said as the others headed towards the car. 'What is the purpose of meditation and exercise?'

'The immediate aim is to develop your psychonoetic powers so that you can be of service to your fellow human beings. The ability to carry out exomatosis is a means of psychotherapy, not an end in itself. The ultimate goal is to realize who you are, to become one with God, to become a god. This is what we call Theosis. We are gods,' Daskalos said, 'but we are not aware of it. We suffer from a self-inflicted amnesia. The aim,' he reiterated many times, 'is to reawaken that which we have always been and we shall always be. This is the purpose of the Research for Truth.'

'If that is so,' I volunteered to add, 'then one's self-realization as a god must be something other than a form of blissful unconsciousness. If I am not mistaken, this is how the Eastern concept of Nirvana is often interpreted.'

'This is nonsense,' Daskalos said forcefully. 'The idea of redemption or liberation is a word that is not desirable to many because it is assumed that it implies entering into a state of some unknowable bliss. As a good clergyman and friend once told me, this state hardly differs from a form of stupor and inertia. "Since I will not be able to understand anything," he said, "I will feel happy." That is how he envisioned paradise and liberation. It is far from the truth. Liberation means knowledge of and assimilation with the Truth through experience. It means the acquisition of abilities and psychonoetic powers. The worlds become open to ourselves whether we wish to have impressions and experiences or whether we wish to close the doors of external perceptions and recede into ourselves, within our divine self-sufficiency. Blissfulness and divine self-sufficiency are far from being a condition that resembles inertia and stupidity as many fantasize.'

'When you become theosized,' my friend went on, 'does it mean that you never incarnate into matter again?'

'You can incarnate if you choose to do so.'

'Will you then have to start all over again? Will you have to go through the cycles of incarnation?'

'Of course not. That would be pointless. If you choose to return, you come back as a captain of the boat and not like a common sailor,' Daskalos replied and laughed. 'Masters who attain Theosis may decide to incarnate into matter in order to help their fellow human beings evolve. They are not obligated by Karma to return. They have already attained their liberation. We shall talk these issues in greater detail in the future. I believe your wife is getting impatient waiting in the car.'

We thanked Daskalos for the evening and Zoe expressed the desire to continue the conversation sometime in the future. 'In the meantime, I am going to have a long talk with my father,' she murmured.

We all got into the car and decided to spend the rest of the evening at a local café.

5
Karma

'Daskale,' I asked, 'is it possible to avoid Karma?'

'Yes, definitely so,' Daskalos responded without hesitation. 'We can clearly see this in the case of Jonah. God tells the prophet that Nineveh has become so sinful, that it has created such evil elementals, that it is to be destroyed in three days. The prophet went to the Ninevites and announced to them the bad news. The people cried and repented. When the three days had passed Nineveh was not destroyed. The prophet was embittered. "God," he said, "you proved me a liar in the eyes of these people."

'According to the law of Karma Nineveh should have been destroyed. Jonah in a sense was right. Yet it was not destroyed. The people repented. They learned their lesson. Jonah later had that beautiful dialogue with God, after Jonah found his pumpkin plant on the ground one night, eaten up by a worm. "God," Jonah sighed, "my pumpkin plant is ruined and I am sad." And then God replied, "You are sad over the loss of a pumpkin plant. How should I feel losing a whole city? Should I let the law of Karma destroy my city?"

'The grandeur of Divine Mercy cannot be conceived by our brains. This does not mean that there is no law of cause and effect. When there is no repentance that would allow Divine Mercy to intervene, payment will have to come, in full, sooner or later. It may take centuries, but it will come. Christ put it quite correctly when he said that even a single glass of water that we offer to someone will eventually be returned to us.'

Daskalos appeared pensive and then, after a few moments' pause, he continued with a severe tone in his voice.

'We Christians, Catholics and Orthodox alike, get into the habit of making a mockery of ourselves and of God. We have the audacity, with three candles that we light in church, even to demand the Kingdom of Heaven. What are we offering, and what are we asking in return? I am telling you that I respect and prefer an atheist who cuts in two the only piece of bread he has and gives one piece to a hungry stranger without expecting any future rewards. I see this "atheist" much closer to God and the Christ Logos than someone who may give a lot but who is bargaining with God. To me most of the charities given today seem to be more an expression of egotism than of good. We see a lot of people who appear to be charitable but who in reality do so in order to humiliate their fellow human beings and prove to themselves and to others that they are superior. Whatever charity one gives, one should do it secretly. Send an anonymous envelope to someone in need, put thirty pounds in it and write nothing else except "with my Love." We must try to get rid of our egotism completely.'

There was silence for a few moments during which time everybody seemed pensive, pondering, I suppose, on what Daskalos had just said. Emily, who was sitting next to Daskalos, broke the silence.

'Daskale,' she asked, 'in what way will you answer the argument of someone that the effort to teach the law of cause and effect is not an attempt to impose a system of ethics so that humans will become better? How are you going to persuade such an individual that Karma is not yet another ethical system?'

'I have been asked this question before. My answer was this: study your actions, see what you pay, look around you to see what is happening, and arrive at your own conclusions. Things are so clear around us in our society that this sophistry is rather superficial. If you cannot see today, you will see tomorrow or the day after.'

'But you have not,' Emily insisted, 'answered this person's rational argument.'

'Just a minute,' Daskalos said in reply, 'the great truths cannot always be answered with words just as you cannot answer the question of the existence of God Himself. There are so many things that you cannot answer with words, with logic. You can answer these questions through your own experience by observing the results of your actions. There is no way you can avoid observing the results of your actions. Sooner or later you will. So you don't believe in Karma? When you get two or three lashes from Karma's whip you will know it because you will feel the pain.'

'This person,' Emily continued, 'will bring you the following argument, "I may not believe in your God and the ethical system which you call Karma, but I believe in humanity." '

'You can ask him this,' Daskalos responded quickly, 'why should you believe in humanity?'

'Because,' Emily replied, 'he also believes the world should get better.'

'Why?' Daskalos continued, with an almost mischievous look in his face, 'Why should it get better? Now I can guide him where I want him to be. Why should one believe so?'

'Because he believes in the good,' Emily said.

'You can persuade such an individual with his own logic and arguments,' Daskalos said. 'In an atheist who does not believe in an imaginary god like most people, I may see the Divine inside him.'

'Perhaps,' Emily continued, 'in such a person you may see a Researcher of Truth who is searching, however, through a different path.'

'Very true,' Daskalos said. 'There are many paths toward our ascent to God. It is not only those who have been initiated into the mysteries who are searching. I am telling you that there are persons who have never heard of the phrase Research for Truth and who may even be atheistic and yet at a higher step on the spiritual path than many of us. We should judge people not on the basis of their beliefs but on the basis of their actions. But I have this to add. I am not aware of anyone who sincerely struggles toward the Truth who has not eventually been enlightened. Remember Christ's words, "Ask and you shall be given, knock and you shall be answered." ' Then, with an abrupt change in the tone of his voice as if he remembered something, Daskalos said, 'Let me tell you of an encounter I had with a famous British philosopher who had the reputation of being an atheist. In a correspondence we had for some time I elaborated to him on the nature of elementals. One time he wrote to me: "In the gods of the priests, of whatever religion, I cannot believe. You explained to us that these gods as elementals have power. I accept that. Thought must be a form of power. But the gods that were produced by the thought of man I cannot accept as gods. I can accept them as supports that men create to cope with their difficulties. But you raise the question, who created Man who creates gods: You have explained to us a lot of things about what you call Absolute Beingness. But why not call it Absolute Being?" I answered him, "The term Absolute Being implies limits. But Absolute Beingness is more correct. I break the limits." What do you think he replied? "I believe in this Absolute Beingness of yours which is not God, but the Beingness in you and me. Its expression is kindness and all that we believe and understand as good. Now, you can show a god far from the witnesses of men. Because all the gods that men have created have human characteristics of weakness and evil. Now you show a god which you call Reality, you call Life. In this I believe. But why call it God? Yes, I like the words Absolute Beingness."

'Now, is this man an atheist? Answer me!' Daskalos said in a loud voice.

'But he has the reputation,' I said, 'that he is an atheist and wrote eloquent apologetics on the subject.'

'Because he rejected all those gods and christs that men created "Onward good Christian soldiers marching to the war,"' Daskalos said with a mocking tone in his voice, gesticulating with his hands. 'The man could not tolerate these. He was a pacifist. He believed in Love. How I succeeded with this philosopher was to help him accept "Absolute Beingness" which is Life, which is Love. In his last letter, written to me before he died, he said: "You are the only human being who has lighted the torch of Reality and Light, and Wisdom. For this Absolute Beingness' sake, hold it high and light the World."'

Just after Daskalos finished speaking a car stopped outside and we soon heard a knock on the door. I hardly remember a time when I would go to Daskalos' house without having visitors arrive seeking his services.

I opened the door and invited the strangers in. They were a middle-aged couple from Larnaca who asked Daskalos for a diagnosis of a relative who was incurably ill.

'Do you have a picture of him?' Daskalos inquired.

They must have known how Daskalos worked because they readily provided a photograph of the patient. Daskalos took the picutre, held it tightly in his right hand and closed his eyes. After about a minute of concentration he opened his eyes.

'The problem,' he said, 'is in his brain. There is something there that should be removed.'

'The doctor,' said the man as he put away the picture, 'did not mention anything about a brain tumor.'

'There is something there,' Daskalos insisted categorically. 'He should have an encephalograph.' The visitors thanked Daskalos for his time and left.

After Daskalos returned to his armchair and was getting ready to continue our discussion I asked him whether the affliction of that man was due to karmic debts.

'All illnesses are due to Karma,' Daskalos replied. 'It is either the result of your own debts or the debts of others you love.'

'I can understand paying for one's own Karma but what does it mean paying the Karma of someone you love?' I asked.

'What do you think Christ meant,' Daskalos said, 'when he urged us to bear one another's burdens?

'Karma,' Daskalos explained, 'has to be paid off in one way or another. This is the universal law of balance. So when we love someone, we may assist him in paying part of his debt. But this,' he said, 'is possible only after that person has received his "lesson" and therefore it would not be necessary to pay his debt in full. When most of the Karma has been paid off someone else can assume the remaining burden and relieve the subject from the pain. When we are willing to do that,' Daskalos continued, 'the Logos will assume nine-tenths of the remaining debt and we would actually assume only one-tenth. Thus the final debt that will have to be paid would be much less and the necessary pain would be considerably reduced. These are not arbitrary percentages,' Daskalos insisted, 'but part of the nature of things.

'Suppose,' Daskalos went on, 'someone who has killed a lot of people through several of his incarnations has been loved by another person. A loving bond has been established between them through the centuries. That person may willingly, whether consciously or unconsciously, accept some of the Karma of the loved person, assuming again that most of the debt has already been paid off by the other person who, in the meantime, has received the necessary lesson. Otherwise it will not be permitted.

'Whatever happens to us,' Daskalos said slowly and emphatically, 'which in this life causes us pain, is either the result of our own debts or the result of our readiness to pay off the debts of loved ones whose Karma may be too burdensome to carry by themselves. When you become masters and are able to coordinate yourselves with the universal Good, you will be in a position to assume the Karma, not only of loved ones, but also of persons who are considered to be your enemies. As masters you may be in a position to stop the pain in your own body but you will do nothing because by narcotizing the pain in your body you will automatically return the pain to the person for whom you have assumed the Karma. Christ showed us the way when he was crucified and suffered on the Cross like an ordinary person.

'When you reach a higher point in your evolution,' Daskalos continued, 'the Logos may require from you that you do just that, bear the Karma of others, even your enemies. You *are* the channel of the Logos and you *should* consider it an honor to be so burdened. You may ask, "And what is my reward for this?" The moment you ask such a question it means that your egotism is alive and very dangerous. The honor that is being offered to you, to put your shoulders under those of the Logos, is the greatest reward.'

'Daskale,' I asked, 'can you give us an example from your own personal experience of how you have assumed someone else's Karma?'

'Karma is the most difficult thing to understand,' Daskalos replied. 'It always puzzles me.' Then he proceeded to narrate a personal experience.

'Several years ago a nephew of mine asked my opinion as to whether he should marry a certain widow. I told him, "You will have my blessings assuming that you genuinely love not only the widow but also her daughter who was seven years old at the time." He said he did love the girl and I realized that he meant it. I was best man at their wedding. In a year's time they had a son but with a serious birth defect which the doctors were unable to correct. The baby was born with his two legs glued to his chest. They came to me. I took the child in my arms and I immediately realized who he was. Theophanis was with me that day and he also understood. I asked him not to mention anything to the others. I told the parents that I would take up the cure of their child. Slowly, slowly I managed to free the legs and put them in a cast. Every few weeks we would take the cast off, massage the legs and then put on a new cast. The boy was getting well and the father asked me to baptize him. He was three months old then.

'In the meantime one morning as I was walking from my house to the Sanctum I stepped on something and felt pain. When I went to my room I took off my shoe to find out what had happened. My granddaughter was with me. She said, "Grandpa, look. Your foot is black." I then realized what had happened. I was paying off the Karma of the little child. My granddaughter ran to her mother. She came right away and drove me to the hospital. The chief surgeon looked at my leg and his diagnosis was gangrene. The leg had to be amputated. I gave my consent. The gangrene had already reached my knee. The operation was to take place the following day. I checked into the hospital in a room facing the river. I told the doctor the day before the operation that I needed about an hour and a half to be alone in the room because every afternoon I meditate. The doctor did not object. So I was left alone. I sat on my bed gazing at the door facing the river. I smiled and addressed myself to the Logos: "If you think I am going to beg you to save my leg, get it out of your mind. This is my leg and this is your leg," ' and Daskalos pointed at his right leg. ' "If you think that it should be cured, let it be cured. If you think it should be cut, let it be cut. Thy Will be done, my Love." At that moment when I finished my sentence I felt something like a breeze kissing my cheek. Suddenly I saw an angel sitting at the edge of the bed holding my injured leg in one hand and stroking it with the other.'

'Had there been anybody else in that room,' I interjected, 'do you think he could have seen the same angel?'

'I don't know,' Daskalos replied, shrugging his shoulders. 'Perhaps yes, perhaps no. I certainly saw him. He appeared to me like a very handsome lad dressed in white. No wings or feathers. He was not paying any attention to me. He just kept stroking my leg. After he was finished, he disappeared, and so did the gangrene. The next morning the doctors came, ready for the operation. They looked at my leg in surprise. There was only a small black spot left at the top of my toe. In one more day all the gangrene was gone.'

Daskalos then proceeded to explain the karmic connection between himself and the baby whose baptism had to be postponed for a week until Daskalos had recovered from his ordeal.

'Several centuries ago,' Daskalos began, 'this baby was a sailor in the Byzantine navy. He was a poor man who had to spend months and sometimes even years away from his wife, a very beautiful woman. During one of his voyages a Byzantine aristocrat set his eyes on his wife and started having an affair with her. When the sailor returned she abandoned him for her lover. In his bitterness and rage he joined a group of pirates who eventually made him their leader. With their three boats they became a menace to Byzantium and other ships.

'At that time I was Italian, the son of the chargé d'affaires of Venice to Constantinople. I lived in Venice with my mother who was estranged from my father. So every two years I would make the trip from Venice to Byzantium to see my father. In all my travels to Constantinople I was always escorted by my governess, a fat old woman. During one of these trips, on our return home, just as our boat was passing by Sicily we were attacked by these pirates. I was then sixteen years old. The Byzantine pirates took off my clothes, which were embroidered with gold, and dressed me in rags. My governess was put to death along with other older passengers. They had no use for them. They took the rest of us who appeared young and strong to their stronghold in order to sell us as slaves. Their base was a town on the Moroccan coast. They had their tower there. It was a slave market for both men and women. A black Arab bought me after he checked my teeth to see whether I was fit. As I was being led away I looked back and felt affection for that Byzantine pirate. I can't explain why.

'I was in slavery for three years. The living conditions were deplorable. My hair was falling out. I turned yellow and lost many of my teeth. I got very sick. When the pirate boats arrived again, my Arab master took me to the Byzantine pirate and demanded his money back. The pirate protested. He said, "This is not the way I sold him to you. I expected you to use him as your personal servant and not to let him get sick like this." They quarreled for awhile and then the Byzantine pirate gave something to the Arab and took me back. I sat on a rock and let my body rest on a low wall. I looked into the eyes of the pirate and said, "How could you do this to me, a fellow Christian? Why couldn't you at least have taken me as your personal servant? How could a Christian like you sell me, a Christian?" He shouted angrily at me, "You are not a Christian. You are a Frank [Catholic]," and struck me on the face. In his rage he signaled his men to finish me off. As they jumped on me, piercing their swords into my belly, he changed his mind. Apparently his conscience awakened after what I had said to him. He rushed to stop the others from what they were doing but it was too late. I departed. He then took my body, folded the rag in which I had been dressed, kissed it and put it into his chest. After that he wrapped me in clean white clothes and took me to an Orthodox priest for burial. Byzantine pirates,' Daskalos went on to explain, 'used to set up colonies of their own along the Moroccan coast and had among them priests who had either been defrocked by the Church or were rebels of one sort or another.

'This priest refused to carry out the burial rites because I was a "Frank." The pirate then buried me himself and read all the appropriate prayers. He put a cross on my tomb and stood vigil all night long. Then he decided to give up piracy. He gathered whatever jewelry and money he could carry and asked one of his men to take over the leadership. He told them he was tired of piracy and had decided to settle down. I could see him from the psychic worlds and felt compassion for him. He then went to another Orthodox priest in Sicily and confessed. He asked the priest to give him a robe because he had decided to become a hermit. He took the robe and went off. Every night he would use my clothes as his pillow. A year and a half later he got sick. His belly expanded and he died. I have never met him since.

'As far as I know that was the first time I met him. The second time is now, as this baby. God only knows how much Karma he must have paid along the way, with all the murders and plunders he had committed as a pirate.

'When I went to baptize him,' Daskalos continued, 'the baby behaved in a rather strange way. He took my finger and wouldn't let go. He kept crying and looking into my eyes. He even pressed his lips against my cheek as I was holding him close to me. His father said it was the first time his baby had kissed anyone.

'Notice how Karma worked in this case,' Daskalos said in concluding his story. 'He once shouted at me that I was not a Christian and ordered his men to kill me. In this life I assumed part of his Karma, I cured him and became his Godfather in Christ.'

'Some poetic justice!' I exclaimed.

'You bear the Karma of your fellow man only when you want to,' Daskalos repeated.

Then in his characteristic manner Daskalos began to recount another experience he had had as an illustration on how a master can assume the Karma of another.

'Six years ago a relative of mine was to have his hand amputated. He had a wife and four children. Just before he was about to have the operation I experienced a strange pain in my arm. Theophanis, who was in Paphos, felt my pain, got into his car and came to see me. Again I had gangrene, this time in my hand. Following the blood tests the doctor concluded that it had to be cut. Theophanis left his job and sat by my bedside day and night. I remember one day, when the wife of the British High Commissioner was at my house (she used to come because of the case of one of her relatives), and while I was lying in my bed, there was a knock on the door. A Turkish woman came dragging in her body, she could not walk properly. She said, "I heard Spyro Efendi [master in Turkish] very sick and came here to have him cure me before he dies." They tried to send her away but when I was told about it I asked them to let her in. She climbed the steps with difficulty and came to my room. I put my hand over her and asked her to stand up and walk. She did as I told her and started walking upright. "Efendi," she said, "now I am fine. Now you can die if you wish," ' and Daskalos roared with laughter as he was reminiscing over the incident.

'As soon as the Turkish woman left,' Daskalos continued, 'I asked Theophanis to cover my hand with the white sheet. Then I placed the good hand over the sick and began my own cure. First I prayed to the Logos. Then I kept passing the good hand over the sick one, over and over.' Daskalos demonstrated to us how he did it by passing his left hand over his right hand.

'I kept dematerializing and rematerializing tissue after tissue until I created an entirely new hand. Then I removed the sheet and showed the hand to Theophanis. My hand was completely cured. Theophanis began to cry, he knelt down and kissed my arm. The next morning the doctor came. He looked at my hand and shook his head. "You've done it again," he said, not knowing what to make of me. My hand was not cut. The Karma had been paid off and my relative's arm was saved.'

After Daskalos finished telling us these stories he mentioned that he was planning to take up another Karma that may cost his life. I protested. He said to me, 'Were you to know who that person is, you would understand. I'll tell you later,' he said, inferring that he did not wish to talk to me about it in front of the others.

We stood up to leave, thanked Daskalos for the lesson, and began walking toward the door. As we were coming out he asked me to stay behind because he had something to tell me. I did. The others were already in the car waiting for me. Daskalos said the person he was talking about was his son-in-law. The doctors discovered a liver ailment that could cost his life. His son-in-law, Daskalos went on, got this illness from a friend of his. This friend, who was living in London, called him on the phone and begged him to help him because he was having a serious liver disease. His son-in-law, Daskalos said, told his friend reassuringly on the phone, 'Don't worry. We'll do everything we can to save you and if we can't, then I'll take up your Karma!'

'I was listening to their conversation,' Daskalos said, 'and when I heard him say this I yelled at him to shut up but it was too late. Now do you realize,' Daskalos continued, 'why I must take up his Karma? I can't allow my daughter to become a widow so young and let my grandchildren become orphans. My son-in-law is thirty-six years old. I am sixty-six. It makes more sense that I go should there be a choice.' Daskalos looked sad at the prospect of seeing his daughter a widow. He said he had already begun the prayers in the Sanctum.

'Hopefully,' he continued, 'Yohannan will take up this burden and I won't have to go as yet.' Then Daskalos implored me not to mention anything to Iacovos lest he try to stop me by assuming the Karma himself that had to be paid. 'But,' Daskalos went on, 'I am afraid he is beginning to suspect something.'

When Theophanis came in the following day I asked him to describe to me exactly what had happened the day Daskalos cured himself. He repeated the same story, including the incident with the Turkish woman. Daskalos was not present when I conversed with Theophanis about this incident.

6

Memories

Daskalos and Iacovos arrived at our home in the early evening to have supper with us. We had no agenda to discuss anything specific but I knew that with Daskalos there could be no dull moments. I remember how much I laughed one night when Daskalos narrated one hilarious incident after another. I was still laughing when I reached home and the laughter severely irritated my throat.

It was Friday, three weeks before Easter. I had completely forgotten that in the Greek Orthodox religion this was a period of fasting. Believers were expected to avoid meat, meat products, poultry, fish, even milk, cheese and eggs. I wondered whether Daskalos followed these nutritional guidelines of Orthodoxy as the dinner we prepared was hardly vegetarian.

'A priest eating chicken during Holy Week was caught by a bishop,' Daskalos mused as he worked on a crispy wing of the roasted chicken. ' "Your Grace," the priest said to the annoyed bishop, "each Sunday I transform bread and wine into the body and blood of Christ. Why can I not transform chicken into vegetables?" '

On that note Daskalos began to reminisce on his turbulent relationship with the Greek Orthodox hierarchy. Twenty-five years ago Daskalos, at the instigation of several Greek theologians, was labeled by the Cypriot bishops as an instrument of the devil and was brought in front of a religious tribunal for his excommunication. The tribunal was composed of the bishops and six theologians from Greece. The Archbishop was on an extended tour of the United States and Europe.

'They accused me of using satanic powers to perform acts of magic. They even claimed that I forced my daughter to dance on a rope! These bishops and a few archimandrites knelt in front of the Holy Altar day and night anathematizing my name. During the proceedings one of the bishops asked me whether I was in contact with spirits. "Yes. What is wrong with that?" I replied. "Had you known your Bible well, you should have known that there is nothing wrong in contacting the spirits." Then he asked me to raise my right arm and repeat after him, "I believe in one God, Father Almighty, Maker of Heaven and Earth and of all things visible and invisible. . . ." They assumed that had I been the devil I would not be able to recite the prayer and mention God's name. I raised my arm as he instructed me and said the prayer. After I finished I lost my patience. "These fools," I exploded, and pointed my finger at the stern faces of the six theologians, "are poisoning our church. You had better send them back where they came from because what happened today is a disgrace to the church." '

Fortunately for Daskalos Archbishop Makarios cancelled the proceedings. When he learned about what his bishops were doing in his absence (he was in America at the time), he sent a cable instructing that they should 'stop the nonsense' until his return.

'The Archbishop told me later not to be bothered by those "half-crazed illiterate bishops." '

'Why would the Archbishop interfere on your behalf?' I wondered.

'He was my friend,' Daskalos said with a foxy smile. He then revealed to us that the Archbishop regularly received taped talks and messages from Daskalos.

After our conversation on Daskalos' adventure with the local clergy the conversation shifted to Daskalos' early life. His father, I was somewhat surprised to find out, was half Scot and half Greek. After a successful career as an admiral in the British navy his father was knighted by the king. Daskalos inherited this aristocratic title but repudiated it and returned it to the British throne in protest against the maltreatment of Greek Cypriots by the British colonial authorities during the underground guerrilla war of the 1950s.

'My father was a tough rigid man who showed little outward affection towards me. He wished to make a British military officer out of me and demanded that all of us in the family speak English instead of Greek. I resented this pressure, but, desperately craving my father's affection and approval, I joined the British army and became an officer. I remember the day I completed my training and returned home dressed up in my uniform. Everyone remarked how tall and handsome an officer I was. I looked at myself in the mirror and all I could see was a belted mule,' Daskalos concluded, roaring with laughter.

'When I completed my training I visited my father in his office. I expected a warm welcome but received, instead, cool instructions from his secretary to wait for him. When I entered his office an hour later he was as distant and aloof as ever. He asked me to have a seat and then offered me a cigarette. I was terribly distressed when he began to address me as "Captain." "Have a cigarette, Captain." "No thank you. I do not smoke in front of my father," I replied. After I returned home I informed my mother that as far as I was concerned, my father was dead. I locked myself into my room, took off my uniform and belts, threw everything on the floor and stepped over them with rage. When my father returned home he came to my room. "Here is your Captain," I said, sobbing and pointing at the mess on the floor. "Behave yourself, Captain," he said, without any trace of emotion. What an English iceberg, I thought to myself. In spite of everything I still loved him. To have him as a father was like going through six incarnations,' Daskalos added, laughing.

'It is difficult for me to identify any traces of English upbringing in your personality,' I marvelled.

'This shows,' Daskalos responded quickly, 'that environment does not play the determining role in the formation of personality as most of you social scientists assume.'

He then went on to point out that he particularly objected to his parents' aristocratic pretenses. His mother, although Greek herself, behaved like an English lady, and his parents' circle of friends revolved around the British governor's mansion. To escape the suffocating atmosphere of his home he spent the summers during his teenage years at the Stavrovouni monastery, an ancient citadel renowned for its austerity and located at the very top of a precipitous mountain. According to legend, Saint Helena, Emperor Constantine's mother, left a piece of the Holy Cross behind her during a visit to the island. Daskalos had access to the monastery because the abbot was his uncle.

'One day in July my parents came to visit me there. They wanted to know how I was spending my time. That day I was out in the fields working with other monks. I was dressed in a worn-out black robe, sweat mixed with dust covering my body. My parents were instructed where to find me. I was working with a plow pulled by two oxen when I saw them coming towards me. At first they failed to recognize me as I wore a hat and my face was hidden. They were both impeccably dressed. My mother wore an expensive hat and high heels. They expected to find me sitting comfortably under the shade of an olive tree reading a book. When I raised my head and my mother realized who I was, she fainted in my father's arms. Right then I explained that I could no longer follow their lifestyle which I considered meaningless. Fortunately I had the good sense not to join the monastery. I could not cope with so much filth.'

An old tradition at Stavrovouni required of the monks never to wash themselves lest they wipe away the holy oil by which they were anointed at their baptism. Any washing of their bodies was done through excessive sweating and subsequent rubbing with towels. It is said that the Archbishop refused to pay a formal visit to the monastery until all the monks had a good wash. The abbot promised to carry out his wish. When the Archbishop arrived he greeted him at the gate. 'Behold your Beatitude, I am now clean,' the abbot said. He then placed his fingers in a bowl of water carried by an attendant and sparingly sprinkled his face.

When we finished dinner we moved to our balcony covered with jasmine bushes and overlooking a small forest of eucalyptus trees. In the meantime I put a Beethoven symphony on the record player, Daskalos' favorite composer, while Iacovos volunteered to prepare Turkish coffee.

'Daskale,' I began, in anticipation of further revelations about Daskalos' life, 'I was quite surprised to learn that you took part in the anti-colonialist movement against the British. I suppose a psychologist would say that it was an expression of a latent hostility against your father who after all tried his best to transform you into a proper Englishman. But I am really puzzled that a healer and a man of God like yourself could participate in an underground movement labeled by the British as terroristic.'

'Do you think I joined the movement for patriotic reasons?' Daskalos responded with irony. He then reminded me that a

Researcher of Truth can only be involved in politics for the sake of serving a higher cause. He should never participate in political life for either personal gain or for what ordinary people call patriotism.

'My involvement with EOKA [the underground guerrilla organization supported by the Church, that fought the British in 1955-9] was in reality play-acting. I joined to save as many lives as possible. More Englishmen, Greeks and Turks would have been killed had I remained aloof.' Daskalos then narrated the various ways he intervened to save lives. It was an extremely difficult and risky task that often created deep anxiety and moral dilemmas for him. A particular incident caused so much anguish that for a while Daskalos became confused on the question of right and wrong. These categories became blurred in his mind, he claimed.

'When I learned that several underground chiefs known to me were plotting the assassination of a man considered to be an informer, I intervened vigorously and changed their minds. Several years later just after the attainment of independence this same person killed several people, was arrested and hanged. I was in a psychic turmoil for twenty days, not knowing whether I had acted correctly when I saved his life. Finally, one afternoon while I was meditating in the Sanctum, I heard the voice of Yohannan. "When you do good to a human being," he said, "you are not negotiating with him on his future behavior. He alone is totally responsible for his actions. Your intentions were good. You did good. It is not for you to judge the future. This belongs to God and to Karma." '

When ethnic strife between Greeks and Turks broke out in 1963, three years after the declaration of independence, Daskalos again found himself in the midst of the turmoil.

'Because I had military training I was assigned to a small contingent of militiamen that made up part of the Greek defenses. I was with Pashie [fat] Kostes, the late police chief, at Omorphita [a Nicosia suburb where severe clashes took place during the Christmas period of 1963]. I carried a pistol in my belt and had a machine gun inside the car.'

'You mean to say you would have used those guns against the Turks?' I inquired, without trying to hide my incredulity. Somehow the image of Daskalos roaming the streets of

Omorphita with a pistol in his hand did not seem very likely.

'I would never use guns against anyone,' Daskalos replied laughing.

'What if you were attacked?'

'In fact at one point I was alone with Pashie Kostes and we were surrounded by forty Turkish lads. We were chased for a while and, to save ourselves, we had to jump over a high wall trying to hide from a river of bullets. Pashie Kostes had a hard time going over the wall because he was so fat. We used to joke and call each other "Captain." It was such a tragic farce! "Well, Captain, what do we do now?" I said to him when it seemed that we were trapped behind that wall. We began shooting in the air in the hope of scaring the Turks away. I would never fire at them. We were finally rescued by Anastasia, a wild woman from the village of Kythrea. She came along with her "boys" and chased the Turks away.'

'How come you did not use your special powers to defend yourself?' I asked.

'Psychic powers should not be used for such mundane reasons. The invisible masters will not permit it. I used clairvoyance only once during those troubled days in order to save lives. I gave strict orders to my men never to attack and never to fire against anybody unless their lives were in imminent danger.

'A pompous Greek officer came to our positions and ordered my men to attack a Turkish stronghold because he believed, the fool, that the Turks were either asleep or they were not there. I quarreled with him for a while and told him that what he suggested was lunacy. I threatened that I was going to report him to his superiors because he was endangering the lives of those men. In my own way I saw that the Turks were on full alert and had the Greeks moved they · would have been butchered. "Why don't you throw a few stones against those positions and see what happens?" I suggested. He did. The Turks, thinking that we were attacking, began a barrage of fire. They threw everything they had at us. Later on they abandoned their position and retreated. I then said to the Greek officer, "Now you can capture the fort and get the credit. We are not interested."

'When the troubles ended, Makarios, in a formal gathering

at which I was present, praised me for being a "true Greek patriot and a Cypriot." "Just a minute, your Beatitude," I interrupted in protest, "I am neither a patriot nor a Greek, least of all a Cypriot. The only reason I was at the front line was for the protection of your mothers and sisters. Nothing else." That is another form of craziness,' Daskalos said laughing, 'but at least it is not as stupid as patriotism.

'That same night,' Daskalos went on, 'a well-known woman philologist who played a role in the struggle against the British stood up and very proudly announced, "We women, your Beatitude, have also shed our blood for our country." I just could not resist the temptation. I leaned towards Makarios and murmured in his ear, "Yes, your Beatitude, they shed their blood once a month," and the Archbishop burst with laughter and spilled the wine he was sipping.' Daskalos leaned back in his armchair and held his hands over his stomach as if to prevent it from bursting as he roared with laughter. 'The philologist refused to talk to me for the next five years. We are now good friends and her sister is a member of my circles.

'I have had problems with patriotism,' Daskalos went on, 'ever since I was a child. I remember one day our teacher was lecturing on Greek history. He described how the Byzantine emperor, Vasilios Vulgaroktonos, pulled out the eye of a thousand Bulgarian prisoners except one whom he left with one eye to guide his compatriots back home. We were told it was a way to terrorize the Bulgarians so that they would stop their attacks on Byzantium. When I heard that story I stood up and shouted, "Shame." "Are you saying Greek history is shameful?" my teacher said angrily. "Shame, shame!" I shouted again at the top of my voice. He grabbed me by the ear and sent me out of the room. When the principal heard of the incident, he gave instructions that I was to be excused from that course. He tutored me on the subject himself and spared me from Greek history. I could not tolerate hearing such horrible deeds presented as acts of patriotism.'

Daskalos then stood up, pulled his shirt upwards and showed us an old wound on his back that he suffered during the critical days of 1963. The bullet was still inside the flesh. I touched the spot of the wound and felt it. Daskalos did not bother to have it extracted because it did not bother him. There was fat all around the bullet and there was no danger of an infection. 'Besides,' he added with humor, 'when I die I would like to take this bullet as a gift to God. I will tell Him, "God, here is a token of man's craziness."

'The late Muftizate, a Turkish Cypriot notable,' Daskalos went on, 'called me up one day. "Spyro, let's go to the Tekke [a Moslem shrine]. The hojah claims that he is able to make beans dance all by themselves." We drove to Larnaca, to the Tekke, together. The hojah was very excited. He made a circle in the middle of the yard and placed inside it a handful of beans. Then he recited certain prayers. The beans began dancing. He didn't know, of course, what was happening. They were nature spirits from the garden playing with the beans. I communicated with these spirits and asked them to come to me. The beans came and moved around my face. The hojah was terrified. "Stay away from this Giavour [derogatory Turkish term for Greek]," he told my friend, "he has satanic powers," ' and Daskalos giggled.

'What are the nature spirits doing there?' I asked.

'They were the nature spirits from the garden.'

Daskalos explained that every plant has an angel which is a projection of an archangelic source. It is a spirit that keeps the plant alive. When the plant dies this angel transfers the experience of the plant to the archangel. This is how information passes on from one generation of species to another.

'Nature spirits are playful, like little children. If you don't know how to handle them they can harm you but not out of malice. Like little children, they can harm you in an innocent way. When one communicates with a plant or an animal, one actually communicates with the angel in charge of that plant or animal.

'I had such great times with my Turkish friends,' Daskalos said sadly. In fact, before the outbreak of inter-communal violence, Daskalos held a circle of students on the Turkish side. He knew Turkish and even passed the entrance examinations of Istanbul University, just for the fun of it. The lessons for his Turkish students were based on Sufi traditions and Daskalos, instead of the New Testament, used the Koran extensively. On several occasions he told me how much he cherished his

friendships with many Turks, including some of their leaders. It
was rumored by many Turkish folk that 'Spyro Efendi'
was in reality a Moslem prophet whom God had sent to the
infidel Greeks for their salvation. In better times many Turkish
Cypriots would come to Daskalos for healing.

He proceeded to narrate several more episodes of his
entanglement with the ethnic conflict on the island. I had long
realized that whenever Daskalos was describing a personal
experience, either of a serious or comic nature, or both, he was
simultaneously trying to give a lesson to his listeners. There was
always a moral behind each story.

'While I was with my men watching over the Turkish sector,'
Daskalos went on, 'I heard the cry of an infant which
continued for almost two days. I discovered that a Turkish
mother was trapped with her baby inside a house somewhere
between the two sides. They were out of food and the baby had
no milk. I grabbed a loud speaker, raised a white flag and tried
to contact the Turks on the other side. "Is that you, Daskale?"
I heard someone shouting. I recognized the voice. It was Fikret,
one of my Turkish students. "Fikret," I shouted back, "is that
you?" "Yes, yes, Daskale. Do you see what the bigwigs have
done to us?" I discovered that Fikret was the leader of that
group of Turks opposite to our position. "Fikret," I said, "I am
going to get some milk for the Turkish mother. Tell your men
to hold fire." Fikret shouted back, "Daskale, you will come
alone, Okay?" "Okay, Fikret." I bought three cans of
concentrated milk, took a white flag and went under the
balcony of the house where the woman was stranded with her
infant. I heard Fikret giving orders to his men that if anybody
shot at me he was going to kill him himself. The Turkish
woman came on the balcony and I threw the cans of milk to
her. "Thank you, thank you, Daskale," she said, "God be with
you." Apparently she must have learned of my name when I
was conversing with Fikret. As I was getting ready to return to
our positions a huge Turk appeared on the corner holding a
shotgun. The woman screamed at me to watch out. I tried to
hide but he had already fired and several small-shots hit me. I
fell on the ground and I immediately heard another shot. It was
Fikret who shot and wounded his compatriot. He ran towards
me and asked whether I was all right. He suggested taking me

to their hospital. I said no. I preferred to be taken to a hospital on the Greek side. Fikret then volunteered to escort me back to our lines. I called on my men to hold their fire. Fikret helped me walk. My wounds were not serious. When we reached the Greek line I introduced Fikret to the others and asked them to shake hands with him. I introduced him as one of my students. At that moment crazy Sampson [a notorious gunman] came by. He was upset that I was friendly to a Turk and murmured nasty words. I demanded that he shake hands with Fikret. He refused. "Shake hands, you jackass," I shouted at him. With a heavy face he offered his hand. Then I said to everybody present to hold their fire and let Fikret return to his post. Before he left we made a pact that no matter what happened in other sectors of the city we would not fire at each other. Neither a Greek nor a Turk died in that area.'

Ten years after the above episode took place, when the Turkish army invaded Cyprus, Daskalos was again in the midst of events. His house was filled with refugees for several weeks, and mothers would flock to Strovolos with pictures of their missing sons.

'One day,' Daskalos reminisced, 'a woman came to me with the picture of her son. The moment I took it in my hand, I realized he was dead. I did not want to tell her so because she appeared extremely distressed. I just said, "Lady, I am really tired today and I cannot concentrate." She broke down and began crying. "You are lying, Daskale," she said. "My son is dead. Last night I saw him in my dream and he was waving goodbye to me. Farewell, Mother. I am going on a long journey and I am not sure when I will see you again." Her dead son visited her in her dream with his etheric body just before he was about to ascend into the psychic planes where he will rest until his next incarnation.

'On another occasion,' Daskalos continued, 'I managed, with the assistance of the United Nations, to contact a Turkish officer who I believed had information about the whereabouts of a missing Greek Cypriot.

'Several Turkish Cypriot soldiers who manned the barricade and could overhear our conversation asked me whether I was a Turk. They could not figure out what a Turk was doing in the Greek sector. I replied to them, "What is the difference whether

I am a Greek or a Turk?" "A Greek is a Greek and a Turk is a
Turk," someone shouted. "No," I said, "Greeks and Turks are
all angels." "Angels Efendi?" a Turkish soldier asked. "Yes,
angels," I replied. I grabbed his cheeks with my palms and said,
"You are an angel, my love." "Me? An angel?" "Yes, you."
They found out that I was "Spyro Efendi" and were excited.
One of them asked me to bless him. I recited a Moslem prayer,
placed my hand over his forehead and said, "Let no bullet ever
strike you." He kissed my hand. "Spyro Efendi," he said, "I
shall never fire against my Greek brothers. If I am ever ordered
to shoot I will aim over their heads." I then crossed the
barricades and returned to the Greek side,' Daskalos concluded
and leaned back in his chair.

'Some time ago,' Daskalos went on, as he began another
story, 'a twenty-year-old girl, a refugee from the village of
Vatili, sought my help. She was pregnant and the father was a
fellow-villager, a Turk. She said that during the invasion, just
before the Turkish tanks entered her village, all the Greeks got
into buses, cars and tractors and fled south. In the confusion
she was left behind. But Orchan, a Turkish Cypriot she knew,
took her to his home for protection. He lived with his parents
and the three of them were very kind to her. They kept her
hidden for several weeks. But their secret was beginning to be
known and they were afraid that she was bound to be molested
by the Turkish officers once she was discovered. Orchan
suggested that they get married, on paper, until they found a
way to send her south. It was assumed that if they were defined
as married the officers would not be able to harm her. The girl
accepted and they went through the Moslem wedding ceremony.
But they lived separately. Orchan kept his promise and never
laid hands on her. The arrangement, however, did not work.
The Turkish officer in charge of the village, who had his eyes
on the Greek girl, suspected that the marriage was fake. In the
meantime a strong bond of love grew between the Greek girl
and Orchan. One night she entered his room in her nightgown.
"I am your wife," she said to him, "make me yours." From
then on they lived like husband and wife. But in the meantime
an agreement had been reached between the Cyprus government
and the Turkish forces of occupation. It specified that all the
Greek women who were trapped in the north should be sent to

their relatives in the south. Armed with this pact the Turkish officer in charge forcefully separated the couple and sent the girl to the Greek sector. It was at this point that she visited me. After a lot of effort I managed to contact Orchan on the phone. He was in tears and pleaded with me to look after his wife and his unborn baby. He did not expect that he could have his wife back. I said to him that I would do everything in my power to bring them together again. Some people may think that what I did was treason. I told the girl, "Orchan is your husband. Go to him and live among the Turks. They are your people now." I realized that she was deeply in love with her husband. I managed to get a special permit and with a United Nations escort I sent her back to him.'

After ending his story Daskalos lamented on the sad predicament currently prevailing between the Greeks and Turks of the island. One day at a gathering with his students he urged them not to look towards the Turkish Cypriots as their enemies. 'Search inside yourselves,' he said, 'and there you shall find the real enemy.' Whatever happens to a people is not accidental but the result of collective Karma. If a tribe, for example, in its history has been warlike and plundered other nations, the elementals of destructiveness that were generated at that time will sooner or later catch up with that tribe under different historical circumstances. Just as there is individual Karma there is also collective Karma, and the people living within a group or a nation are under the karmic debts of that nation. It is imperative,' he admonished, 'to break the vicious cycle of creating destructive elementals. Of primary importance, therefore, for Greek Cypriots is to foster no ill will towards their Turkish compatriots, but extend to them a genuine hand of friendship.'

'Daskale, can you tell us who has influenced you most in this life?' I asked just after we had ended a short discussion on local politics and Greco-Turkish relations.

Daskalos thought for a moment and then repeated that throughout his life he had been guided by invisible masters like Father Yohannan, Father Hilarion and Father Dominico. Nevertheless there was one man that Daskalos met in his twenties who apparently helped him in his spiritual path. He was an Indian colonel, a surgeon who served in Cyprus during the Second World War years. Daskalos claimed that it was the masters from the 'other side' who literally guided him to meet this Indian doctor and become, for a while, his assistant in the operating room.

The relationship that Daskalos cherished most, however, in his present life, was with a boyhood friend killed by the Germans in Casablanca during the Second World War. Their friendship was established while Daskalos was in junior high school at the American Academy in Larnaca, a secondary school set up by American missionaries. Phivos, his friend, was three years his senior and played the role of protector for his younger and less robust friend. Daskalos described how, on many occasions, Phivos would rescue him from being beaten up and abused by other boys.

At the invitation of an expatriate uncle, Phivos eventually migrated to the United States to study literature. So strong was their friendship that Daskalos was making plans to migrate to the United States himself. 'We joked,' he said, 'about how we would marry two sisters so that we could always be near each other. But it was not to be. Phivos was drafted into the American army and was sent to Casablanca where he met his death. The moment his friend died, Daskalos said he felt it. In a vision he saw him lying on the ground smeared with blood. Then Phivos came to Daskalos with his etheric body.

'He came and stood next to my bed. "Spyro," he said, "I came to say goodbye to you. We will not see each other for a long time." He then disappeared. I sat in my bed and began crying and wailing for my lost friend. To relieve my pain I composed a poem right at that very moment.'

'Do you remember it?' I asked earnestly.

'I remember it as vividly as when I composed it even though I never put it down on paper.' At my instigation Daskalos started slowly to recite the poem, a homage to his boyhood friend. It was as if he relived the pain he experienced four decades ago.

> Winter night, sad and dreary,
> let the tempest and the gale
> overflow your leaden sky.
> A love is dying tonight

the glow of the flame
weak and trembling,
the time to expire has come.
Winds and thunder strike the sky,
rain drops linger
at the corners of the eye.
Inside me a storm, a quivering despair
quenches dreams and hopes.
Night depart!
The darkness heavy and oppressive
stifles me with threads of death.
A love is dying tonight
at his side, a mourning candle burns.

'Are you now in contact with your dead friend?' I asked after a few moments of silence.

'Yes. He is in this room,' Daskalos replied with a smile. I assumed he meant that Phivos, as spirit living in the psychonoetic worlds, was somehow attuned to and in communication with Daskalos. I immediately realized, however, that Daskalos was pointing at Iacovos who had a difficult time hiding some traces of tears in his eyes, left over from the emotional thrust of Daskalos' poem.

'This is Phivos?' I asked in disbelief, as I looked at Iacovos.

'Yes, that is Phivos,' Daskalos nodded without hesitation. 'When I look at him it is not just Iacovos that I see. For me he is also Phivos, Giovanni, Omar, Rasadat and many others.'

Daskalos claimed that he has been with Iacovos for over twenty incarnations. On several occasions he had hinted about a time in ancient Egypt when Daskalos, along with Iacovos, were hierophants. I had no doubt that in Daskalos' mind there was no question about the reality of his reincarnational memories. He said to me once that he can read his past lives as if they were leaves from a personal diary.

'Perhaps we can speak of ancient Egypt some other night,' Daskalos replied to my request. 'But it is already late and we have work to do.'

7

From Death to Rebirth

It was around three in the afternoon when Iacovos and I boarded a bus for Larnaca, the southeastern seaport of the island. Daskalos was to have his monthly meeting there with a circle of disciples. They planned to meet at seven in the evening at 'sister Theano's' house, the 'witch of Larnaca' as Daskalos affectionately referred to her, a member of his exclusive inner circle. Daskalos had already gone to Larnaca early in the morning to visit several patients at the local hospital.

Light rain began to fall when we boarded the bus at Liberty Square, the center of Nicosia. I felt tired from the day's activities and not wishing to arrive at Larnaca exhausted, I closed my eyes and practiced a 'concentration-relaxation' technique taught to me by Daskalos. Iacovos silently sat next to me as I tried to block out of my mind the external world.

I made myself as comfortable as possible and brought to mind Daskalos' instructions. I concentrated on my entire body as I inhaled and exhaled deeply. I began to feel and loosen up every single muscle of my body from the top of my head to the toes of my feet. I tried to shut out any other thought from entering my mind. After about three minutes of deep breathing I focused my attention exclusively at my toes and began slowly to move my concentration up my body until I reached my navel, and solar plexus. There I envisioned a large white-blue ball of light covering my abdominal region inside and around my body. I tried to keep my thoughts fixed on that region for about three minutes. With ease I inhaled deeply a few times and without losing the image of the white-blue sphere I moved further up inside my chest near the heart. I imagined another ball of light smaller in size radiating white-rose color, the center of which was a spot near the heart. The two spheres interpenetrated each other at the edges but maintained their distinct color. I remained in that state for

another three minutes, perceiving white-blue light covering the
lower part of my body and white-rose light the upper part close
to my neck. Then I transferred my consciousness to the center
of my skull and perceived a golden sphere, smaller than the
other two, enveloping my head and extending about six inches
beyond it in every direction. I concentrated at each part of my
head, as well as inside it, for another three minutes. I then
envisioned my entire body within a white aura in the shape of a
luminous egg. After feeling every part of my body again, I
made, with my mind, the following auto-suggestion: 'May
peace reign inside my entire material body, and harmony
within my psychic body. May absolute tranquility prevail in my
thoughts.' Before coming out of my meditation I spent three
more minutes breathing deeply.

Daskalos claims that this meditation exercise when practiced
regularly, preferably in the morning, will have benign effects on
the personality. The white-blue color can keep our material
body in good health, whereas the white-rose and golden colour
can purify and keep in harmony our psychic and noetic bodies
respectively. From my own experience this exercise and similar
other meditation practices that Daskalos taught me have the
effect of immediate relaxation. When I opened my eyes, on this
occasion, my fatigue was gone and I felt refreshed. The rain
had stopped and a rainbow decorated the horizon in front of us
like a majestic ornament. It was mid-March and the Cypriot
countryside was at its loveliest, filled with myriads of red and
yellow wild flowers.

In about an hour we arrived at Larnaca. Theano's house was
an old two-storey house facing the waterfront. She was an
affectionate elderly woman in her late sixties who welcomed us
with a grandmotherly hug and kiss. The fact that I was with
Iacovos and had the support of Daskalos in what I was doing
was sufficient to make me automatically a 'brother.' Theano,
Daskalos mentioned to me earlier, had been his mother in four
previous incarnations. 'That's why she is so motherly to me
every time she sees me,' Daskalos said, laughing. In fact Theano
used to address Daskalos in the same way that adoring mothers
address their little ones: 'my golden one.'

We sat in the living room waiting for Daskalos and the other
students to arrive. Over a piece of cake and lemonade Theano

talked primarily of Pavlos, her late husband, and how, through him, she had become Daskalos' disciple and a member of his 'inner circle.'

Pavlos was a poet who had spent most of his life in Paris. There he became interested in mysticism. One day he visited a famous medium and asked for information about certain metaphysical questions. The medium allegedly told him that the questions would one day be answered by his future master. He will be born, the medium told Pavlos, on the twelfth day of December 1913, the date Daskalos was born. She drew a sketch of Daskalos as a grown man, wrote Daskalos' initials on it and gave the sketch to Pavlos.

Many years passed. Pavlos left Paris, returned to Cyprus and married Theano, twenty years his junior. He kept the sketch the medium had made for him decades back. When he accidentally met Daskalos at a social gathering, Pavlos, according to his wife, became breathless. Daskalos' features matched the portrait drawn by the medium. The two of them had a private conversation and when Pavlos found out about Daskalos' birthday and other details, he embraced him with tears in his eyes. 'You are the master I have been waiting for for so many years,' he said. 'You are a master, too,' Daskalos is said to have replied. Pavlos, two decades older than Daskalos, was initiated into the inner circle the same year and remained, until his death, one of Daskalos' most devoted associates. Pavlos, I was told later, was more of an intellectual mystic. Unlike Iacovos, Kostas and Theophanis, his psychic abilities remained dormant. He was, however, a man of high spiritual stature and of a developed sense of humor. One day, Theano said, her husband was sitting with a friend on a bench under the palm trees gazing at the sea. Suddenly Pavlos stood up, took his hat off, bowed a bit, and said, 'Good morning, Daskale.' His puzzled friend asked for an explanation. 'Oh,' Pavlos remarked casually, 'I just saw Daskalos out of his body on his way to visit some patients.' In a while the friend stood up, took off his hat, and said, 'Goodbye, Daskale.' When Pavlos asked for an explanation, his companion replied, 'Oh, I just saw Daskalos running back to his body.'

Theano claimed that she was in constant communication with her late husband and I was told by others that she had healing powers as well. She confided to me that she had to be very cautious lest the local clergy launch a war against her. For that reason she tried to maintain good relations with the local bishop. 'What can we do?' she exclaimed, throwing her hands upwards. 'People can easily misunderstand us.'

Theano was very proud of her husband and handed me, as a gift, several volumes of his collected poems, some written in Greek, but mostly in French, and heavily influenced by French romanticism. Daskalos said to me later that Theano and Pavlos were one of the most harmonious couples he had ever known and the reason was their long association through the centuries. They were very old souls, he said, and had repeatedly come together as a couple through the aeons. One lifetime, Daskalos said to me on several occasions, is usually not sufficient to build a good marriage. People must come together repeatedly as a couple before they become compatible through experience and love.

One after another Daskalos' students arrived, a total of about twenty-five, ranging in age from twenty-five to seventy and evenly representing the sexes. Like the Nicosia circle, they came from the more educated segments of society. Daskalos arrived last, along with Kostas, who drove from Limassol to attend the meeting. Iacovos and Kostas regularly attended all the lectures that Daskalos offered at various parts of the island. They would always sit next to their master as if to offer emotional support during the lesson.

Before the formal meeting began Daskalos sat in the living room, had coffee and cracked a few jokes. He then moved to another room and had private conversations with some of those in attendance. Daskalos was not only a teacher to these people, but also a confessor and advisor for their personal problems.

After everybody had gathered in a larger room, Kostas lit within a container some incense, the type used in Greek churches. Daskalos stood up and everyone followed suit. He held high the container with the burning incense and with it made the sign of the cross. He then recited a short prayer.

'We will spend the period today,' Daskalos said after he completed the short prayer, 'reexamining some issues concerning the psychonoetic worlds. I have noticed that some of you have many questions about the nature of these realms. You may proceed with your questions. Father Yohannan is ready to answer them.'

Kostas, who was sitting on Daskalos' left side, served as moderator. The first question from the audience was sweeping. 'What happens to a person from the moment of his death to the moment of reincarnation?' Kostas repeated the question so that everyone would hear it clearly.

Daskalos began to answer by first giving a definition of death and by explaining the transformation of the self-conscious personality after death.

'We have said before that the gross material body cannot maintain itself without its corresponding etheric-double. Death, therefore, means the separation and disintegration of the etheric-double from the gross material body. Normally it takes forty days for the dissolution of the etheric-double of a deceased person. It is for this reason that in our religion a candle is lit for forty days over the grave of the dead. Fire accelerates the process of dissolution of the etheric-double.'

Daskalos pointed out that the etheric-double of a dead person is highly malleable and can be snatched by a black sorcerer who can use it for evil purposes. The custom in India, therefore, of burning the bodies of the dead is preferable.

'Ordinary people assume that death is a frightful and painful experience. In reality it is the opposite. The process of death is no different than a pleasant sleep after the exhaustion from a day's work. One may suffer from a serious illness but at the moment of death no pain is experienced. A great mystic once said, "Never have human lips tasted a sweeter kiss than the one given by the angel of death." I know this from personal experience. The moment a person begins to abandon his body his face acquires a serene stillness and he no longer experiences any pain.

'An individual will, after death, begin to live fully conscious within one of the subplanes of the psychonoetic world, carrying along with him his virtues and vices, his goals and his aspirations. His personality undergoes no change. Only the reality of space changes. The individual enters into a situation where space as we know it in the gross material plane does not exist. He perceives space as meaning, as conception.' Daskalos' last remarks provoked several questions for clarification.

'Suppose,' he went on, 'I bring you into this room while you are asleep and give you a certain lesson. You will have the impression of the space as you have at this moment. When you see me the next day you will probably tell me, "Daskale, we came to the Stoa, and each one of us sat at the spot of our preference." The question I pose to you is the following. Will you have really come to this room to listen to my talk? In the state you will be in anybody living within the psychic world, regardless of distance, may be able to hear the same lesson through coordination. In the psychic world we are like television stations that others can tune into and receive whatever we monitor. When we leave our bodies, either through death or through exomatosis, we actually enter within ourselves. Communication, then, as well as all other experiences, takes place from within. Everything is there. Some time ago our master mentioned to us a great truth. "The abyss within us," he said, "is in no way less than the abyss without."

'Perhaps it will be easier to understand what I have been saying if I offer you the following concrete case. Three brothers in their wish to communicate with their father decided to carry out a psychic experiment after his death. One of them was in Australia, one in London, and the third in America. Working through three different powerful mediums they managed to contact their father simultaneously. They wanted to bring their father "down" they said. They actually assumed that their father was somewhere "up." He talked to them about certain family matters that none of them was aware of and which later they confirmed to be true. They reached the conclusion, however, that it was not their father they conversed with, but the devil. How could it be their father, they reasoned, since they were at three different spots on the planet while communicating with him at the same time? They assumed that their father was in a similar condition after death as that of the material world.

'They came to Cyprus and through me contacted their father again. He reassured them that it was he who had spoken to them earlier. "I did not pay attention to your surroundings but I did speak to all three of you. I even touched you," he told them. "How could you do that, Father, since we were so far away from each other?" his three sons asked.

'I warned them that had they persisted in doubting him they could create confusion in his mind. Just because he was on the other side did not mean that he had transcended the phenomenal reality. I reassured them that it was not the devil's doing but that it was indeed their father who talked to them. I pointed out that in the psychic realm communication takes place through vibrations at similar frequencies. "Let us suppose," I told them, "that I have several powerful radios that can get any station anywhere on the planet. Now, if I place these radios at different parts of the Earth and then tune them in to the same frequency, would not all of them receive the same broadcasting?" Communication on the psychic plane is something analogous. No human consciousness will ever be mixed up and be confused with another. Ever since the discovery of radio and television it is much easier for ordinary human beings to understand the nature of the psychic worlds.

'You must realize that the planes and subplanes of the psychic and noetic worlds occupy the same space. And this space is the center of the Earth, everywhere on the planet, the periphery of the planet and the space around the planet. Do not imagine that these psychonoetic planes and subplanes are juxtaposed one on top of the other. At this very moment inside the head of a pin, in this space and everywhere there exist all the planes and subplanes of the psychonoetic worlds. It is a state of being, of vibrations and a method of tuning into them.

'Within the psychic world you, as a self-conscious personality, will be wherever you choose to focus your attention. That is why whenever you see a vivid dream and you perceive yourself moving instantly over vast distances, you conclude that such experiences are unreal, that they are illusions. They are not. When, some day, you find yourself in the psychic world, you will realize that those worlds are more concrete than gross matter. You will begin to live with greater intensity with greater ease. Yet the world that you will find yourself in will be in many ways similar to the one you now know. It is a matter of your ability of receiving impressions and psychonoetic vibrations. On the basis of your interests and predispositions, you will enter after death into an analogous psychic state. You will find yourselves in a hell, a purgatory or a paradise, the same one you are in right now at this very moment.

'There is, however, one important difference between the material and the psychic realms. When we find ourselves in the psychic environment, feelings acquire a greater intensity. For example, feelings of hatred and jealousy can become like fire that burns. In this life such sentiments can be tempered by the limitations of the material brain. On the psychic plane limits do not exist. That is why in the psychic worlds life is experienced with such intensity. But you should never assume that the so-called hells are some kind of psychic torture chambers. The hells and purgatories are schools and workshops for the acquisition of experiences so that human entities may ascend towards their perfection. In reality there is no punishment. There is only experience. If there is suffering it is not because the Absolute wishes to punish us for our transgressions but so that we can find out who we really are. The purpose of such experiences is to help us shake off our illusions and ignorance.

'Hell and paradise are relative terms. One person's hell may be another person's paradise. To help someone in the psychic plane move out of his hell, for example, you must show him an alternative condition to the one he is in. If he was a querulous person during his life on Earth, he will find himself in a similar situation after he leaves his body. To help him you will have to expose him to the immediately better condition that he can move into. If he is not receptive to your suggestions, let him remain where he is. He lives in his paradise even though it may be the most tortuous hell. Let me give you an example. I have tried to help someone who during his life was a gambler and a very quarrelsome person. He died from tuberculosis forty-five years ago. He has been living in the psychic world exactly the same way as he did when he was in the gross material plane. He has created with others the same environment analogous to the one they knew on Earth; dirty windows, dirty clothes and tables, fights, arguments, just like the environment of the coffee houses they knew before. They did not even have the imagination to build them any better. One day I said to him, "Come, my friend, let's go somewhere." I took him away from his situation and created the vibrations of a Beethoven symphony that I like very much, specifically that of Joy. I told him. "Charilae," that was his name, "look!" And I showed him a beautiful forest, with colors, water, flowers, everything. I harmonized the sounds with the sights and created for him what I considered to be a paradise. He gazed at me for some time and then he said, "Aren't you tired? Let's go back and play some poker with my friends. How long are you going to keep me here listening to these tin drums of yours?" What could I tell him? He lived in his paradise which for me was an intolerable hell. How could I explain to that man the difference between hell and paradise?

'Here is another case. A peevish woman spent her entire life accusing, gossiping and cursing her neighbors. When she died she continued the same kind of life, only more intensely. Instead of the real human beings she left behind, she created and quarreled with their elementals which she brought along with her; the elementals of Maria, of Eleni, of Efterbe. We tried in vain to show her that she lived in a hell and that she ought to dissolve those elementals so that she could see more clearly. Only after she is exhausted from her condition will she voluntarily ask for change. Those of you who will one day become invisible helpers will encounter such difficulties. You must know that unless a person seeks change himself you cannot help him. Each person will develop gradually. The most we can do under such circumstances is to create a benign elemental and place it on the aura of the person to work. When he is ready for change, that elemental will be there to assist him.'

'Daskale,' I asked, 'do the psychonoetic planes and subplanes have an objective existence independent of the individual's subjective perception of them?'

'I have said before that the psychic worlds have trees, mountains, oceans, rivers, everything that exists on the planet, everything that has ever existed and everything that can exist. What you consider as the real world is actually the shadow or the reflection of other more luminous worlds within which everything material that is considered real exists. In the various planes and subplanes of the psychic worlds there exist not only whatever exists on this planet which was created by archangelic forces, such as water, mountains, forests, but also whatever humans have created either while they are still alive or after they depart. The psychic world is a much richer world.

However, most persons who live there perceive it through the elementals that they themselves create. In the psychic worlds, for example, there is no sun that rises and sets every day, unless we create one ourselves. But the sun we create will be within our individual subjective psychic world, not the external one. Therefore, when a human being abandons his gross material body, he begins to live simultaneously within two planes of existence, the real psychic plane and his own subjective psychic world. Most human beings are so engrossed within their own subjective shell that they are unaware of the nature of the psychic plane within which they vibrate. It is as if, for example, we are on a journey but because of our passions and psychic turmoil, we are oblivious to the beauty of the countryside outside. And let me say something that may seem blasphemous. On the basis of my own personal experience what may be considered an intolerable hell is, in reality, a most beautiful space, assuming that you can coordinate your consciousness with the real psychic plane. It is our predisposition that will let us or prevent us from perceiving that beauty.' Daskalos went on to say that the evolution of the Researcher of Truth implies the development of the ability to distinguish between the real psychic world and the subjective psychic environment that people build around them with the elementals they bring along when they enter there. What is ugly in these psychonoetic planes is what each individual hides within his subjective shell, his own psychic world, which gives him vibrations of evil, hatred and vulgarity.

'Where is this shell?' someone interjected.

'You mean in terms of space? Again, everywhere and nowhere. But a person who constructs his own shell and lives in it, perceives it as having clear limits within which he is confined and is allowed to act. People build their villages, their churches, their fields, just as they had them on the gross material plane. We can enter into their psychic shells when we coordinate ourselves with them and understand how they perceive their psychic world from within.'

On a different occasion Iacovos had mentioned to me that he regularly meets with his grandfather who died several years back. His grandfather, he said, is still preoccupied with the same concerns as when he was alive. He looks after his citrus orchard, cultivates it, sells the fruit and worries about the rainfall!

'In the lower levels of the psychic world that we call hells and purgatories there is less light than in the higher planes. Divine Mercy places within beautiful landscapes those vibrations of light that make these subplanes equivalent to convalescent homes. It is similar to what we normally do when we attend to the needs of an ailing person. We keep the windows shut and the room dimly lit so that the nervous system of the patient may calm down. In a comparable manner the Absolute dressed all those magnificent landscapes of the lower psychic planes within a twilight. It is an appropriate environment for those sickly personalities who find themselves there so that they can recuperate and evolve. As we move from the lower planes towards the higher, we observe that there is increasingly more light in a similar manner to the way that a landscape is illumined as the Sun rises over the horizon. Paradises, which are the higher psychonoetic planes, are swimming in light of vibrating intensity.

'Notice,' Daskalos continued, 'that a key attribute of the psychic world is that every atom of matter emanates its own light. It is unlike the three-dimensional world where light comes from a Sun or some artificial source.'

Daskalos' last remark brought to mind Castaneda's description of an experience he had during his apprenticeship with Don Juan. Castaneda claimed that one moonless night while walking in the desert with Don Juan, having difficulty in moving about because of the darkness, he suddenly perceived the entire landscape lighting up as if the Sun had come out. He could see, he said, everything clearly and could walk forward, as if it were daytime, with great ease. In addition, he said, he was able to carry on a dialogue with a coyote that happened to be there. Did Castaneda, I wondered, enter at that moment into a state of what Daskalos would have called the psychic counterpart of that place? When I posed the question to him later on, he said that probably this is what must have happened.

'Let me now ask you this question,' Daskalos went on. 'Can one communicate with a flower or a plant? Ordinary people, no matter how much they may love plants and flowers, cannot consciously communicate with them. They appear as objects to them, outside of themselves. A poet may be inspired by the beauty of a flower, but can he incorporate into his consciousness the semi-consciousness of the flower? In the psychic world it is very different. When you advance you will be able to communicate with all forms of life. All things are alive and have their own language, vibrations, and luminosity that you can feel on your psychic body.

'In the psychic world,' Daskalos said further, 'we do not think with our brains. We have them but we do not need them. Every cell of the psychic body is a center of consciousness receiving impressions. We have eyes but we do not need them for the same reason. Within the psychic world there is no separation between us and an object outside of us. When we coordinate ourselves and focus on something we are simultaneously one with that object. We are within it and around it. But we can do this assuming that we are in fact within the real psychic world and not within our shells which create for us our own psychic world. Under these conditions we color everything through our preconceptions and impressions.'

Responding to someone's query on the nature of movement within the psychic planes Daskalos went on to say that it is radically different from the way we are accustomed to moving on Earth. 'We do not move by walking, taking buses or driving. But we can perceive ourselves and others as walking or driving. This is only a perception, and an illusory one at that. When we are outside our bodies and we move here and there within the psychic world and the etheric of the gross material world, we may have the feeling that we are flying. Sometimes in your dreams you have this sensation. Have you ever wondered how this is possible? Are we birds that can fly? In the psychic world movement can take place instantly. It is a matter of transporting our consciousness through coordination. We can be in London, for example, in a split second without having to "fly" over Europe. Some day you will learn how to transport your consciousness over vast distances instantly while you are still within a gross material plane.'

'Can you tell us how this is done?' I asked.

'I can tell you but it will not mean anything to you at this stage. You have to create in your mind the image of the place you want to go to, live intensely within that image, hold it in your mind without distraction, coordinate yourself with that place, then you will be there. And if at that moment there happens to be a clairvoyant at the place where you transported your consciousness, he will be able to see you. When you develop further you may be able to actually materialize yourself at that place and be seen by people who do not have clairvoyant abilities.'

'When you do that,' I probed further, 'what happens to your material body?'

'Again it depends on how advanced a master you are. Your body may be in a state of deep sleep. But one can reach a point at which he can do all that while at the same time being fully awake. With time you can develop a superconscious self-awareness and be at several spots of the Earth fully conscious and focused.'

I confessed that I had a hard time understanding what he was talking about. To be at several places at the same time!

'These are difficult issues,' Daskalos proceeded, 'but your question was such that I had to give you a general answer. Do not torment yourself for the time being. These are great truths that are very difficult for you to understand because you are familiar with conditions within time and space.'

Daskalos then mentioned that the worlds of 'separateness' are the poorest kinds even though they give us the greatest paradises and the greatest hells. 'The worlds of separateness include not only the material world but also the psychic and the noetic. These are worlds of forms, images, impressions. We call them worlds of separateness because one sees oneself as a separate entity which gets impressions and interprets them. It is something other than the real self. There are, however, other worlds where separateness is transcended. There are, for example, the higher noetic worlds, the worlds of ideas – laws that are beyond concrete thought forms. There is also the world of eternal light, of the seven heavens. We have talked of only three, the gross material, the psychic, and the noetic. Beyond that there is what our religion calls the kingdom of heaven which is within us.

'These lessons,' Daskalos proceeded slowly after pausing for a few seconds, 'were given by the Most Beloved One to his disciples under the olive trees in the Garden of Gethsemane. He taught them exomatosis, materialization, dematerialization, and many other secrets. In the essence of Christianity there are no barriers to knowledge even though black-robed priests have imposed limits and restrictions. We, as Researchers of Truth, want to know through reason, inquiry and concentration. We take seriously Christ's admonition, "And the Truth shall make you free." This is why Christ came to this world, to give us a few lessons and show us the road away from the hells that we find ourselves in, and to lead us to His paradise, and ours. Unfortunately very few men have learned from His teachings.'

Daskalos stopped his monologue and waited a few seconds for further questions. He then stressed once more that the psychic planes are schools where human beings enter to receive the necessary lessons and draw appropriate conclusions based on their experiences on Earth. 'The individual will then move to higher, more luminous planes, and after he reaches a certain point he will be ordered by the great masters of Karma to return to Earth in order to receive further lessons. In short, the psychic planes are resting homes for the self-conscious personality until the new school year begins. Unless of course one flunks the exams and has to repeat the year all over again.' With these remarks Daskalos laughed heartily and everyone else joined him.

'Is it possible to enter a lower class?' someone joked.

'Never. It is possible to remain in the same class where one becomes a more experienced student. A self-conscious entity will incarnate within an environment analogous with other kindred spirits that vibrate on the same frequency. People call it heredity. There is no such thing. Instead of heredity I would say there is the omniscience of the Absolute which brings together those that must be brought together in order to advance together towards love. Hatred, in reality, does not exist. It is an illusion based on ignorance. Of course these issues require deep contemplation and study.'

'Does the soul know its destiny and the experiences that it will acquire from a future incarnation?' a black-clad middle-aged woman asked.

'Not in detail. Subconsciously, however, the permanent self-conscious soul knows. But it does not bring this knowledge to the conscious level of the present personality. For example, a little child touches fire and burns his finger. He will forget the detail of the accident but when he is near fire again he will pull his hand away. It is not necessary to remember the details of his earlier experience.'

'Should we assume, therefore, that the experiences acquired in a given incarnation are predetermined?'

'No. The self-conscious soul knows only possibilities and probabilities. The present personality has freedom of action. Otherwise human beings would be nothing more than robots. How an individual pays off his debts is his own choice. It is as if at this very moment I am ordered to embark on a vessel headed for New York. My destination is preordained. The kind of life I lead on the boat is my own concern. What is predetermined is my destination, New York.'

'Then everything is based on a Divine Plan,' the woman insisted.

'The Divine Plan means birth and death, that is all,' Daskalos said in a loud severe voice betraying impatience. 'Everything else is your affair. Let us not misunderstand this question and assume that what happens to us is unavoidable. Otherwise we become absurd fatalists and we cease to be Researchers of Truth. What is predetermined is that you descend to be born, complete a life cycle, and then die. This you cannot avoid. Everything else within life is based on what you bring from previous lives and how you choose in the present life to develop or express it.

'I repeat, what is predetermined is our descent into matter after passing for the first time through the Idea of Man. Then, through repeated incarnations, our destiny is to return to where we came from. This is the general law of incarnations. One descends into matter with the ultimate aim of ascending back to the source. How long it will take you to do that is your problem.'

'Why is it necessary for a soul to incarnate and then return?' I asked.

'To realize, perhaps, who one is and acquire self-consciousness.'

'Are you saying that inside the Holy Monad there is no self-consciousness?'

'There is, but one does not recognize it. Let me give you a simple example. Suppose you were born into a luminous room and I asked you, "Do you know what light is?" Do you think you would know? On the other hand if I turn the lights off or take you outside the luminous space you will be able to know what light is. As eternal entities we do not become something which we are not already. However, my permanent self-conscious personality, which is the sum total of all the incarnations that I go through, develops around my eternal beingness my distinct individuality. Beingness and individuality are not identical. I exist even before I pass through the Idea of Man. Once I do pass through and acquire the experiences of gross matter, I am in a position to realize that I exist. Therefore, what we gain is individuality within beingness. We become conscious of our beingness. Had this not been the ultimate goal, descent into gross matter, followed by the incarnational cycles, would be pointless. In the Parable of the Prodigal Son, Christ cryptically revealed to Mankind the purpose of its existence.

'Christ narrates how one of two sons decided to leave the palace of his father. He asked for his share of the wealth so that he might go and experience the world. Had it not been part of the Divine Plan, the all-wise father could have refused. But the plan was to let him go, suffer hardships, acquire knowledge and then return. The son was given what he asked, in reality reason, sentiment and a material body, that is, his present personality. He took his share and went off. Some may call the departure from the palace and descent into matter a fall or sin. I choose to call it experience. In this new condition the son abused his inheritance and consequently was transformed into a swineherd. In reality he created elementals, pastured them and nourished himself with the same food, that is, with the lowest expression of the mind. The pigs in the parable symbolize the elementals that men create ceaselessly.

'One day he rebelled and questioned the life he was leading among the pigs, that is, within the world of elementals. He decided to return to his father's palace where even the servants were so blissful. He asked, "Father, I have sinned. Make me one of your servants." The son took one step forward, the father took ten. Where is the punishment? Have you noticed any reproach or punishment in the parable? The father opened his arms, embraced his son and brought him back into the palace. Instead of punishment he rewarded him by placing on his finger a ring, that is, the symbol of eternity. Life is movement. When we move on the ring in any direction, we cannot stop. There is no beginning and no end. There is only eternal movement, symbolizing eternity. The other brother who never left the palace lives in the eternal present. He is not aware of eternity. Man, on the other hand, through the experiences of the swineherd, has tasted time as past, present and future. The father, according to the parable, ornamented the Prodigal Son with the costume of his brother, that is the Prodigal Son lost nothing of what he had had. The father then killed the fatted calf, a symbol of the material body. The other son protested. "What have you done for me who has been loyal to you all along?" But that son, the archangel, never entered inside a material body. "Everything I have is yours, my son," the father responded. I am asking you now, who is in a better position? The archangel who never stepped outside of the palace, who is good but knows nothing else? Or the Prodigal Son who returned and has whatever the other brother has plus self-awareness? Consider it as an axiom that in Theosis (return to the palace), the condition of man is much superior to all the archangelic systems. Therefore, in the final analysis there is no eternal punishment. There is only the acquisition of experience within matter that develops for us our self-consciousness. In the words of Saint Paul, "O death, where is thy sting? O grave, where is thy victory?" '

When Daskalos ended his analysis of Christ's parable, there were further questions from the audience about reincarnation, a topic of apparently great interest to those in attendance. Someone raised the issue of population increase and reincarnation. He wanted to know where the new souls come from. Daskalos replied briefly that there is continued communication between the noetic, psychic and gross material level. Humans who are born now may come from other dimensions of existence. Those who die move to these other universes. We should not consider this a problem, he said, since we know how a first incarnation takes place. That is, by the passage through the Idea of Man of an emanation springing from a Holy Monad. This is an eternal and continuous process.

'How long does a human being stay within the psychic worlds before he reincarnates again?' I asked.

'The Rosicrucians claim one hundred and forty-four years. Others say fifty years, some others five hundred. Still others insist that it takes one thousand years before one is reborn. I say nonsense. There is no fixed time. It is a personal matter. I know of a mystic, for example, who stayed within the psychic world for only ten months before he reincarnated.'

'Who decides,' someone asked, 'when one will return to Earth?'

Daskalos replied that after a period of time within the psychic world, when the individual has assimilated the experiences of the previous life, he will reach a point when the appetite for more experiences on Earth will be rekindled. The person then will search for a kindred spirit to have him incarnated. Daskalos mentioned that a clairvoyant can see the spirit of the entity to be incarnated attached either to the aura of the prospective father or mother, awaiting the opportunity to be conceived. It often oscillates between the auras of the father and mother.

'Are you suggesting, Daskale,' I probed, 'that when you are on the psychic level you will voluntarily search around to find someone to incarnate you?'

'Naturally.'

'But I thought that these matters were determined by the Masters in charge of incarnations?'

'The Masters will shut you up with others in a pen. Then it will be up to you to find a house to enter. Suppose that through the centuries you established close relationships with forty or fifty persons whose aura is like yours. You love them, they love you. They could make you their child. Wherever you can accommodate yourself you can enter. There are beings that are so close that whenever they are herded together they will find one another. But there are those who come together blindly, because like attracts like. Do you understand now what is happening? Suppose we have a basket like a sieve, full of holes of different sizes. When we pour various objects through and shake them well, those that are bigger than a given hole will stay on top, others will pass through. Those which remain will try to find another hole to pass through. It is possible that there may be fifty similar holes through which an object can pass. Which one it will choose does not matter. It is possible that great love between individuals which developed through the centuries will create strong magnetic attractions so that two souls will pass through the same hole. This process of incarnation is a very complex matter that requires careful study.'

'It seems from what you are saying that to an extent it is up to you to find the appropriate hole so that you can pass through,' I added.

'Of course, with the understanding that Karma will permit you to do so. The choice is given to you to decide to pass through wherever you can fit. Pay attention to this point. From all the thousands of holes, you can pass through from, say, only two hundred. It is natural that I will pass through a hole of the two hundred that is nearest to me during the shaking of the sieve, a hole through which I can fit, for which I have similarities, where the vibrations are alike, the Karma is alike.'

'But the hole you have chosen may create problems for you. . . .' I began to say.

'That is a different issue. We certainly do have problems. But the vibrations fit. We have to pay our debts together. We cannot avoid the problems. The Divine Plan is similar. All the incarnations that I have studied show that the Law works mercilessly. You cannot transcend it. Why do we fit? We fit in terms of give and take. We may have certain unfinished tasks from the past that must come forward in order to torment us so that we can evolve. Or to torment others involuntarily in order for others, as well as ourselves, to evolve. You may say, for example, "What do I have in common with this parent who is depressing and oppressing me?" Or if you are a parent, "Why did he have to come into our family and tyrannize us, such nice people that we are?" Do you understand now? It is the give and take within Karma. It is also possible for the Masters of Karma to take hold of someone and place him at the right hole because it may be better for the person to pay his debts that way. Now how these four Masters of Karma work, I do not know.'

'Four?'

'They are the Masters of the four elements. They are eternal archangelic entities, laws. They are a certain class of Michael, a certain class of Raphael, a certain class of Ouriel and a class of Siamael. The Siamael are those who give us the meaning of Evil. Through them we have Satan. All four cooperate in terms of where an individual will go to incarnate. They weave his psychonoetic body. It is very difficult for us to understand how they work through the cells, through magnetism, through energy. It is a complex question how a being becomes entrapped in this whirlpool which brings him down to Earth.'

'What rational arguments can you offer in support of reincarnation and what proof do you have that it is not an illusion but a reality?' I probed further.

'First, there are historical and religious arguments that, although not proofs in themselves, support the idea of reincarnation. Second, there are cases that clearly show that reincarnation is a reality and not fantasy. And the third and best proof of the reality of reincarnation for an individual is when he awakens to the memories of past lives. But let us take one argument at a time.

'In our world a great number of people, if not the majority, accept reincarnation as a fact of life. In most of the religions of the planet reincarnation is either clearly stated or implied. In the esoteric traditions of Buddhism, Taoism, and Hinduism reincarnation is taken for granted. For those who understand Islam, I mean the Sufis, reincarnation is also a reality. In Christianity, too, reincarnation is implied. In the Eastern religions, of course, the idea of reincarnation is much more easily accepted because in these religions there is more direct contact with the psychic spheres. Unlike Western societies, there is a continuous contact in the East with the departed and of entities living within other dimensions. Therefore they are more aware of the reality of these dimensions. In Christianity reincarnation was widely accepted until the fathers of the Church removed it from the scriptures.'

Daskalos went on to elaborate that the idea of eternal damnation is a cruel and tyrannical doctrine cooked up by the priests to terrorize the faithful into submission. A person now had only one chance to attain the kingdom of God and could do so only by submitting to the authority of the Church and the clergy.

'This doctrine is both foolish and an insult to the "most merciful God" that the priests eulogize in their churches. We know that even Orthodox Christians accepted reincarnation. We can find these ideas in the works of Origen and many others. In the New Testament itself, of the things that survived the censorship of the clergy, we hear Jesus Himself asking his disciples, "Who do men say is the son of man?" And they reply, "Elias or one of the prophets that came from the dead," that is, reincarnation. Christ could have told them that "What you are talking about is nonsense, there is no such thing." Instead He responded that indeed it was Elias but they did not recognize him. They asked John the Baptist whether he was Elias. He replied very correctly, "I am not Elias. Now I am John." "And who are you?" they asked. "I am a voice crying in the wilderness," that is, a situation similar to the one in which Elias found himself, in the desert. We can observe in John the Baptist the characteristics of Elias, with the same virtues and the same weaknesses.

'And what about Paul's epistle to the Corinthians when he said that "Your sons have preceded you."? Does that not imply the idea of reincarnation? However, there is better evidence about the reality of reincarnation than resorting to the Scriptures. Is it not proof when a child suddenly begins to speak a foreign language fluently without any prior training? Furthermore, is it not proof when he claims that he was a certain person whose relatives have been located? There are many such well documented cases.

'An even more powerful evidence for a Researcher of Truth is when he finally manages to enter into his subconscious and becomes aware of his own past lives. Believe me there is no greater proof than this.'

'Why don't we all remember our past lives?' someone asked.

'You do not remember for your own sake. It is part of Divine Mercy so that you will have a chance to progress in your path without remaining attached to old habits and desires. Suppose, for example, that an individual in his present life is a good missionary. He has reached a certain point in his evolution where alcohol no longer poses a problem for him as it did in previous incarnations. Within Universal Memory, however, the alcoholic part of him is alive. If such memories reawaken in him in his present incarnation, he may regress to his old habit and become an alcoholic again. Christ Himself made the point when he said that whoever puts his hands to the plow should look forward at the furrow to be created rather than focusing his gaze on the one already plowed.'

'Daskale, when you say that the alcoholic part is still alive, are you suggesting that it exists as an elemental? And is it possible for a master to make contact with such an elemental?' I said.

'Whatever has been imprinted on the Universal Mind will always exist. Suppose, for example, I wish to contact a master who lived four thousand years ago, let us say he lived in Egypt as Rasadat. Since that time the entity that manifested as Rasadat has incarnated over twenty-five times. Is Rasadat at this moment alive or is he a dead entity? Both Rasadat, as well as all his other incarnations, are alive within the Universal Memory. Subconsciously we are linked to all our incarnations and whatever incarnation we bring to consciousness is a living entity. Rasadat is alive because the entity that emanated him is alive. Socrates may have incarnated many times. Perhaps he is alive today in another body, in a different culture, with a different name. It is possible, however, to bring up Socrates from the pool of Universal Memory and even semi-materialize him in front of us and converse with him irrespective of the fact that today the entity that incarnated as Socrates may be in another body.'

'Is it possible,' I asked, 'that Socrates would act and talk in the same way as the entity who was once Socrates but is presently somebody else?'

'No. You must bear in mind that Socrates within the Universal Memory is a living elemental and not a human being. The self-consciousness that was Socrates is no longer there. If I bring Socrates and converse with him, he will have the intelligence and knowledge of the Socrates of that period. He will not be able to offer more than Socrates knew during his life.

' "The God of Abraham, of Isaac and of Jacob is not a God of the dead but of the living," said Christ. How many do you think understood what He meant? He was not talking of the self-conscious soul of the patriarchs, but of the then self-conscious personalities.'

'Daskale,' I persisted, 'who can awaken the elemental of a past incarnation?'

'Either the person himself or a master. However, masters as a rule are reluctant to tell you of your past lives lest they awaken in you old weaknesses and habits.'

Daskalos then explained that it is possible for a master to read one's past lives like pages from a book. He can do so by 'coordinating' his consciousness with the elemental of a person's past life and experience the sentiments and thoughts of that elemental. Unless past incarnations are still alive, such a feat would be impossible. 'The pages in our book of incarnations are not dead leaves but living elementals,' Daskalos said.

'When, then, can we have memories of past lives without a disturbance on the present self-conscious personality?' I asked.

'Each Researcher of Truth will learn the way slowly and patiently. At first we will feel our past incarnations intuitively until full memory is recovered. The memories will come as the present self-conscious personality is more closely in atunement with the permanent personality. Then, like good actors, we will be able to remember the roles we have performed. The Earth is the theater within which every one of us plays his various roles in order to learn and progress towards perfection. When we look back without being disturbed at what we see, it is time and safe to remember. Before we can safely remember, we must first transcend the idea of Good and Evil. In the meantime Divine Mercy has shut the door of past memories in order to give us a chance to proceed in our path without the interference of past imperfections and weaknesses.'

'You said that our past incarnations are living elementals within the Universal Memory. If so is it also possible to contact a past incarnation-elemental and effect changes on its behavior?'

'Let me answer your question by telling you of a personal experience in this life. A few months ago I wanted to observe myself giving a talk in the psychic world. I remember my Master (Yohannan) saying to me, "You shall give a talk and yet it will not be you." So I withdrew, sat back, so to speak, and listened to my talk. As I was observing myself I detected certain mistakes I made. The Master brought to me, with mathematical precision, the elemental of myself as I had given the talk in the psychic world months in the past. It was like a recording of myself on a video tape. Could I intervene and make corrections at the moment I realized my errors? No. I did not have the right or power to add or subtract anything. At that moment I was simply coordinated with the one who was giving the lesson, the elemental of myself. I relived the lesson as an observer. Someone other than myself could have listened to the same talk had he coordinated himself with that elemental.

'It is possible, however, that I can create a new elemental of myself and make the appropriate corrections. This is different. But whatever has been imprinted cannot be erased, and what is imprinted is alive. Perhaps this could offer us an explanation of the meaning of hell and paradise. An elemental of myself may exist in a hell of its own making which can affect and tyrannize the present personality when the latter has not transcended its past problems. That is again the reason why Divine Mercy has shut the door towards the past, so that we will not be adversely influenced from the life of ourselves as elementals which we have left behind in a hell or a paradise. However, we should keep in mind that the present personality is always linked through the law of Karma to the living shadows of its past.

'The subject you have raised today,' Daskalos concluded, 'is inexhaustible. I hope our discussion has given you some basic ideas on the nature of the psychonoetic worlds.'

8

Encountering the Logos

'Brothers and Sisters,' Daskalos said just after we had finished the short prayer. 'Father Yohannan is waiting for your questions.'

There were a few moments of silence and then someone asked about the relationship between Judas and Jesus.

'What,' he asked, 'is the truth about the events that led to the betrayal of Christ by Judas? What was his relationship with the Divine and why did he commit suicide?'

The question was timely as the meeting took place on the Friday before Holy Week, the most important and festive period of Greek Orthodoxy. After various opinions had been expressed by other members in the group and more questions raised, Daskalos began to describe the relationship of Judas to Jesus.

'The other disciples knew Judas as an ambitious aristocrat, a Hebrew patriot, a zealot one might say, who wished to expel the Romans from Judaea. He was enchanted with Jesus and dreamt about the liberation of Israel from Roman rule.

'Judas the Iscariot was influenced by circumstances that made him behave in an irrational manner. Some called it betrayal, yet others applauded his actions. Let me explain.

'Judas, along with the other disciples, sought and competed for the Love of the Most Beloved One. On many occasions he even pushed aside the others in order to embrace the Master who often reciprocated with a kiss.

'Pay attention to the fact that Judas kissed the Master and expressed his love to him. Only John and the more genteel disciples expressed their love to Jesus in this manner. For example, Peter never kissed the Master. It was awkward for a tough man like Peter to exchange embraces and kisses with Jesus.

'Judas was close to Jesus daily. He was perhaps closer to

Jesus than any of the other disciples with the exception of John. Consequently he witnessed most of Jesus' miracles.

'What was Judas' ambition? To enthrone Jesus as King of Israel and stand beside Him. Judas had money and ordered a golden crown. Who do you think set up the refrain, "Blessed be the Kingdom of our father David, that cometh in the name of the Lord"? Who do you think urged the masses to give Jesus that tumultuous reception into Jerusalem? Judas the Iscariot. When Jesus was in the middle of a group of Pharisees, one of them challenged Him to state whether he was the Son of God. Jesus responded, "You said it." Judas was there with two other disciples and witnessed what followed. The Pharisees accused Jesus of blasphemy and took rocks and began throwing them at the Master. But just before the first stone reached Jesus He disappeared from their midst and the stones fell in an empty space right at the spot where Jesus had been standing.

'Judas witnessed this phenomenon and he began thinking of a plan on how to crown Jesus King of Israel. He once gathered the disciples and the crowds together and raised the crown he had brought with him in order to place it on the head of the Beloved One. At that very moment Jesus disappeared again, and the royal crown remained in the hands of Judas the Iscariot. It was the second time that Jesus disappeared in that manner. Judas then thought, "I will force you to accept. When they begin to abuse and curse you, you will change your mind. When they attack you, what else can you do? You will be forced to raise your hand and show your Glory, your Power. You will be tired of the affectations of the sinful and the beastly, and you shall become the King."

'So the aim of Judas the Iscariot was not to betray Christ but to force Him to become leader of the Jews in order to expel the Romans. And yet Jesus explained Himself clearly. "My kingdom, Judas, is not of this world. Understand this." That is what Judas did not want to understand, that Christ was not interested in worldly power.

'Judas was not a traitor, he was an imprudent beloved. Jesus washed and kissed Judas' feet just as he washed and kissed the feet of the other disciples. Then he told Judas to go and do what he was supposed to do. Christ loved Judas. But Judas could not understand Jesus' teachings. In fact only very few of

His disciples understood Him, specifically John, Philip and James. Philip understood Jesus because he had been previously involved with the Greek mysteries at Delphi. The others understood Jesus only after the descent of the Holy Spirit.

'Jesus expected His Crucifixion and prophesied his Resurrection in front of Judas by saying, "I can destroy the temple and in three days I shall rebuild it." What did He mean by this? He was speaking in parables. Judas was hearing only those things he wanted to hear and that he could interpret as benefitting his patriotic plans and ways of thinking.

'When Judas realized that the Master was about to be crucified, to be put to death, he began doubting Christ. He thought the Master had lost His powers and could not prevent Himself from being slapped, insulted and kicked. When he saw Jesus carrying the Cross with a thorny wreath on His head, blood dripping from His forehead, Judas began doubting the Resurrection. He became desperate and in his anguish he committed suicide.

'It is too harsh a term to call Judas a traitor. I would call the condition that led him to act the way he did a state of unreason or confusion. Judas loved Jesus pathologically, foolishly and egotistically. He also loved an imaginary country. The world is full of such nationalist zealots. Do you realize that the confusion and troubles in Israel today that have led to the spilling of so much blood between Arabs and Israelis are to a large extent the product of the thoughts and desires of the zealots and other patriots of the time? Those of them who have come to their senses by now are beginning to be able to see the evil that they themselves have caused.

'So we are facing such conditions that must be dissolved, and obliterated because there are personalities that are sensitive and receptive to such conditions. Judas the Iscariot was such a person. We must not call him a traitor. When one of Jesus' disciples sighed once and said harsh words about the Iscariot, Jesus said, "Be aware, because every time you say the word traitor for some Judas, at that moment you are crucifying me."

'Judas has incarnated many times since then, as a rich man, as a poor man, as a troubled man, as a common man, just like every other human being. Today he is incarnated within a Jewish body and he is a great mystic.'

There followed a few moments of silence. Then someone asked whether it could be argued that for Judas the betrayal of Christ was an experience that he had to go through.

'It was a bitter experience,' Daskalos replied, 'and a tragic role he played, for which, nevertheless, he was responsible since he vibrated on that level. The role of Judas is something within the Divine Plan because it facilitates its unfolding.'

'Was it necessary,' someone else asked, 'for Jesus to be betrayed or was it possible for Him to be arrested in some other way?'

'Perhaps,' Daskalos replied, 'it was necessary in order to attract the attention of mankind, to stimulate involvement, to create the rifts and conflicts between the two sides, those who called Him Holy and those who denied His Divinity. Perhaps things had to be that way, to create the controversies in order for the appropriate conditions to mature.'

'After Pentecost,' someone mentioned, 'the disciples received the Light. How did they behave in the Acts of the Apostles?'

'When we compare their behaviour with their behaviour two years earlier or even a month before the Descent of the Holy Spirit upon them, we would notice that the change was great. But when we say that they received enlightenment, what does that mean? Were they transformed from one moment to the next into bright suns? That would have been a cacophony in both Nature and society. And it would have been impossible for them to endure such an experience. Their enlightenment proceeded gradually. They received as much light at a time as they could endure. They did have their imperfections. Light was given to them so that they could advance in their spiritual path. Nevertheless, in the Descent of the Holy Spirit, Grace was offered them immediately so that they were enabled to perform miracles. This is not a small matter. They began to reason with more wisdom. Let us not forget that the Apostles were mostly illiterate fishermen who suddenly started behaving and sounding like philosophers. Let us take Peter again, as an example. He was a fisherman who, had we compared him with the intellectuals of his time, we would have considered coarse and boorish. But suddenly he was transformed into a great Master. Those who had known Peter before, as a fisherman, and met him later, after the Descent of the Holy Spirit, noticed the difference in spite of all his imperfections. What were these imperfections? His Hebrew fanaticism. He began to resist the Hellenistic Jews and the Gentile Disciples. He opposed Neoplatonic philosophy. He began to oppose John. Later on he started a war against Paul who had Greek relatives. Peter had strong Hebrew sentiments and he could not tolerate any Greek influence within the new religion. When the other Apostles tried to explain to him that circumcision should be abolished, he accused them of losing their wits. I would not call his fanaticism evil. It was just his way of thinking, of wanting to preserve traditions that he thought were important. These disagreements persisted among the Apostles even after their enlightenment. They received as much light as they were capable of handling. There is nothing more dangerous for the eyes than too much light. It is like gazing at the Sun. One goes blind. So it is not a question of giving more light to someone but, rather, of providing as much light as will be beneficial to him.

'Christ revealed to His students enough of His Glory, as much as they were capable of coping with. I have in mind the Transfiguration. John was with Him, and so were Peter and another disciple. Did they endure the Light of the Transfiguration at Mount Tabor? They fell down and covered their eyes.'

'What was the purpose of the Transfiguration, Daskale?' someone asked.

'It was certainly not for the sake of demonstrating His power in creating phenomena. He wished to enter into His Divine condition. The Pan-universal Logos wanted to initiate Himself into the Divine state. The Transfiguration at Mount Tabor was the initiation of Jesus as God-Man in order to endure the Crucifixion and be able, as God and Man, to resurrect Himself. After the Resurrection, when Jesus was completely attuned with His Divine state, He materialized in front of His students in the image of Jesus the Man, within a body that still bore the scars on His hands from the nails, saying to them, "All authority has been accorded me in Heaven and on Earth." '

'When Jesus was resurrected, Daskale,' someone asked, "did He dematerialize Himself?'

'Certainly! He dematerialized His body completely. You may ask, had He not dematerialized Himself before? No. He put His body in a state of sleep somewhere and then carried out His exomatosis. He would then collect etheric matter and materialize a new body which became visible. After the Resurrection it was something quite different. He dissolved every cell of His material body. He became Spirit, Absolute Spirit, and could at any moment, as a complete self-conscious personality, reconstruct a body identical to the gross material body He had before, even with the marks of the wounds from the Crucifixion. This is different from exomatosis. An advanced Master will be able to know this when he materializes himself while he is still in a gross material body. When such a Master dies he may be able to materialize his body anywhere on the planet. There is a great difference.

'We shall continue. May the Love of the Most Beloved One be with you and in your homes and with the whole world.'

After the meeting was over and most of the students had gone, I made arrangements with Iacovos, Kostas and Daskalos to meet at the latter's place and spend the night chatting. We had no particular plan on what to discuss. Usually a topic would come up spontaneously and then Daskalos would begin to speak. Daskalos enjoyed talking, particularly when he was in the presence of his close students, and no matter how tired he may have appeared to be, the moment he began to talk on an issue he would regain his energy and become totally transformed.

It was about eight o'clock in the evening when Iacovos and I, after having dinner at a *souvlaki* café, went to Daskalos'. Kostas was already there chatting with him. Daskalos was brooding about how tired he was because of problems with relatives and some difficult cases that he had handled during the day.

'They don't let me rest for a single moment,' he complained.

'Your problem,' Iacovos said, half seriously, half jokingly, 'is that you are too innocent and people take advantage of you.'

'Yes, you're right,' Daskalos responded playfully. 'I heard the One who told me "Blessed be the meek in spirit." '

I was puzzled. I wondered whether Daskalos was serious or whether he was joking. I promptly asked for clarification. Daskalos shook his head affirmatively and changed the tone of his voice from humorous to soft and serious.

'Yes, yes,' he murmured, 'I met Him!'

'Could you tell me about it?' I asked as I prepared to put my tape recorder on.

'I will, on condition that you do not tape what I say.' I complied with his wish and took, instead, my pad and pen which Daskalos never considered objectionable. When I was ready Daskalos began.

'It was one of my most intense and tragic incarnations. My name was Jason and my parents were Hellenistic Jews. Our house was at the foothills of the Golgotha. It was a *makrinari* with an enclosed yard where we kept a few goats. At the edge of our yard there was a room, detached from the rest of the house, where an uncle of mine was living by himself and was preoccupied with the study of religion and philosophy, or so he pretended. My mother and sister knew Jesus' mother who was called Miriam. They often listened to Jesus preaching. Jesus was actually called Jeshoua. Yohannan [John], Jesus' student, knew our family and he used to take me to listen to Jesus talk. Even though I was a young boy at the time, I understood what Jesus was saying. These truths were not new to me. It was the result of my experiences as hierophant in Egypt. Yes, I was one of the children that Yohannan used to take to Jesus.'

'Was that the beginning of your relationship with Yohannan?' I interjected.

'No, it goes further back,' Daskalos replied and continued his story. 'Yohannan was twenty years old at the time. My father was unaware of my mother's and sister's relationship with Miriam and Jeshoua or about my own involvement with Him. My uncle, who had a great influence on my father, considered Jesus an evil-doer. They were both part of the crowd that was screaming for His Crucifixion. We insisted that Jesus was innocent but Father was adamant. So we kept our contacts secret.

'When Jesus was about to be crucified I ran to see what was happening. I saw a procession of people moving toward the top of the Golgotha. In front of the procession were the judges who had passed the death sentence. Pontius Pilate, in order to punish them for their decision, demanded that they wear their official garments and lead the procession. About ten to twenty feet behind them came Jesus carrying the Cross, surrounded by soldiers who kept the people from coming near Him with their spears.' Daskalos stood up and demonstrated with his hands how the Roman soldiers were holding their spears in such a formation as to prevent the crowds from coming near Jesus.

'Being a youngster, I sneaked under the spears, stood in front of Jesus, and gazed into His face. Blood was coming from His forehead. He saw me and smiled. I tried to smile back but the tears overwhelmed me.'

As Daskalos was describing the scene I noticed that his eyes were watering. It was the first time that I had ever seen Daskalos coming so near to tears.

'I said to Him "I love you" and He kept smiling at me. The soldiers became angry and chased me out of their enclave. But I tried again. I ran ahead and attempted to go under their spears once more. A kind-looking soldier, when realizing that I was trying to get in, raised his spear so that I could more easily go under. Again I was face-to-face with Jesus. He tried to smile at me but there was a sadness in His face. Perhaps He knew what was coming. Another soldier saw me and with sadistic mania stepped on one of my feet with his shoe. I was wearing sandals and had no protection for my feet. The Roman soldiers had tough nails attached to the soles of their shoes. The pain was excruciating. The soldier literally destroyed my toes. I couldn't walk. I crawled outside the soldiers' enclave and tried to get home. At that moment I could only think of myself. The pain was extreme. I must have crawled for about half a mile when there was an earthquake and the sky became full of clouds. Houses were falling, walls were falling. When I reached my house it was the only one standing in the area. My uncle's room was decimated. I said to myself, "Now I can tell my father that it was the earthquake that hurt my foot." I was still afraid of my father. When I arrived home and my mother saw my condition, she rushed to get wine and some herbs. She cleansed my wound with the wine and put on the herbs. Then she tightened my leg with some rugs. I heard my father quarreling with my uncle. He blamed my uncle for misleading him. Then he came to my mother and sister, embraced them, and apologized. He murmured to them that Jesus was indeed the Son of God. My uncle was still insisting that the earthquake and the rest were natural phenomena and had nothing to do with the Crucifixion. My father literally forced him out of the house.

'In the meantime my situation deteriorated. I felt that my body was being paralyzed. I must have caught tetanus, I guess. As I was lying in bed I saw Jesus coming through the wall like a bright light. This took place just after the Resurrection. Apparently the rest of the family saw Him too because my mother, sister and father knelt down. He spread his hands and told me, "Come." My mother began crying and begged Jesus not to take me away from her because I was her only son. But I went with Him. I don't remember where, but I did.'

As incredible as Daskalos' story appeared to me, he himself had no doubt about the authenticity of his experience. Since I had no way of 'testing' the reality of Daskalos' story, I preferred instead to pursue further questioning to get as full a picture as possible of Daskalos' experience.

'Daskale,' I asked, 'do you remember Jesus' teachings?'

'I was too young at the time to remember details. But I vividly remember that His teachings were not unfamiliar to me. As I told you, I had had similar experiences as a hierophant in Egypt. I remember Peter was rough-looking, blondish, with heavy arms. He always held a stick, chasing people away from Jesus. Peter was envious of Yohannan because of his education. He apparently had an inferiority complex because he was illiterate. I remember that Yohannan would smile and shake his head whenever he would see Peter with the stick in his hand driving people and children away from the Master. But when Yohannan would arrive, his glance alone was sufficient to calm Peter down.

'I remember one time when Jesus was sitting on a rock, very tired, with one leg stretched out in front of him. I fell on the ground, and kissed His feet. He said, "Why are you doing this? Don't you see, my child, that my legs are dusty?" I replied, "But I am dust, myself, my Christ." He took me by the hand and I stood on my feet. He then embraced me and kissed me on the forehead saying, "Never say this again. You are not dust," and He blessed me. I love Jesus so much,' Daskalos murmured. 'No, He is not a theosized man, as some mystics would argue. He is the incarnation of the Logos Itself, I tell you. Whenever I need to call on Him, I raise my elbows up in the direction of an unfinished triangle,' and Daskalos raised his two arms to demonstrate how he did it, 'and call on the Logos "Come my

Love." This is what I call Him when I want to bring Him to me. And He completes the triangle.'

'How many times have you done this so far, Daskale?' I asked.

'Four times in this life. It is not easy to do. It is very painful to come back to a normal state after you have brought Him to you. When I call on Him I immediately feel bright rays emanating from my belly and my head, and the room becomes very hot. One time when Theophanis was with me in the Sanctum, the candles in the room bent from the generated heat.'

I asked Theophanis about this later on and he confirmed what Daskalos had said. Iacovos also mentioned that he too had inspected the melted candles.

'I tell you,' and Daskalos touched my knee to emphasize what he was about to say, 'I rarely do it because it is shattering to the body. The energy generated is too much for a weak body. The pleasure is so intense that coming back is very painful. You want to stay there with Him. It is like being an astronaut and then ending up in a prison cell. To be able to call on the Logos and not get burned, you have to reach a certain level of spiritual development. It is the same with Yohannan. You cannot be a cable for Yohannan, who is the planetic Logos, if you vibrate low. He will burn you.'

'Daskale,' I asked, 'since it is so painful to you to enter into these ecstatic states, are you planning never to do it again?'

'I will do it, again and again. I don't care what will happen to my body,' Daskalos replied with a determined tone in his voice. From what Daskalos had been saying before, I assumed that in order to be able to coordinate yourself with the Logos without being 'burned,' you had to be in a state of what Daskalos called superconscious self-awareness. So I wanted to ask him what is specifically the meaning of this term. He said it implies first that you are constantly aware of your permanent Self, which often includes being aware of previous incarnations. Second, you are a master of materialization and dematerialization, and third, your consciousness can be simultaneously at seven and even more different places, and be able to get impressions and experiences from all of these places.

'But are these not,' I asked, 'attributes of a theosized human being?'

'Yes, they are,' Daskalos replied. 'These are attributes, but it is not Theosis itself.'

'And you,' I said, 'claim that you can do all these things?'

'Yes.'

'Then are you a theosized human being?' I inquired. Daskalos' reply was that he can enter into a state of Theosis but cannot remain there. He can be there only momentarily, he said.

'You cannot live in the material world,' Daskalos continued, 'and be a theosized human at the same time.'

I then asked him whether the concept of Theosis is similar to what is called by other mystics, God Consciousness.

'Yes,' he said. 'You have consciousness of God but you do not live continuously in God Consciousness or Theosis.'

'Daskale,' I asked, changing the subject, 'what is your reason for being on this Earth?'

'Love. It is love that keeps a master bound to matter. You bear the Karma of others and return in order to help them. When you are freed from your own, you may choose to help others. This will keep you bound to Earth.

'I don't know about you,' Daskalos said abruptly as he turned toward Iacovos and Kostas who so far had been listening quietly, 'but I am getting hungry.'

I put my pad and pen on the chair on which I'd been sitting and followed the other three into the kitchen. We quickly fixed plates of fruits, cucumbers, tomatoes, bread and cheese. Our menu somehow seemed to be appropriate to our conversation on Jesus. We indulged.

9

Cosmology

I discreetly stood up, said goodbye, and walked out of the house towards my car. It was Wednesday afternoon, the day the inner circle met. Since I was not a member of this group, I assumed that the appropriate thing for me to do was to leave. The meeting was to take place within a quarter of an hour and already most of Daskalos' students were present.

I was about to enter my car when Iacovos rushed to the door and waved at me. He was followed by Daskalos who signaled me to wait. 'Let us see if we can get permission from Yohannan so that you can attend today's meeting,' he said as I walked back towards them. I was very pleased. Several days earlier I had expressed my desire to Iacovos to attend a few of the meetings of the inner circle. I assumed it was he who conveyed the message to Daskalos.

'Iacovos and Kostas will meditate in the Sanctum together and request permission so that you can attend the meeting,' Daskalos repeated as we walked in.

Not long after, word came from Iacovos that Father Yohannan consented. I was pleased, not only because I was being given the opportunity to explore the workings of the inner circle, but because that particular Wednesday Loizos, one of Daskalos' students, was to become initiated.

I already knew most of the members of the inner circle. They gathered in the Sanctum, put on their white robes, and waited for Daskalos. It was the first time I had seen them wearing white robes, a practice reserved for the inner circle.

'Come on, you Tibetan,' Daskalos said jokingly as he pulled me by the elbow and led me into the Sanctum. 'Father Yohannan,' Daskalos announced, 'having recognized Kyriacos' thirst for knowledge, gave his permission so that he may attend a few of our meetings.' He then explained that I had been a Tibetan in several incarnations and I was, therefore, not a stranger to esoteric teachings. In fact the quickness with which I was able to absorb the teachings, he said, was due to the hard work I had applied in previous incarnations. Daskalos then asked whether there were any objections to my temporary participation in the proceedings of the inner circle. Nobody objected. He then placed a long piece of white cloth about my neck and put on his own white robe.

Loizos stood in front of the altar facing a large picture of Christ. On the altar there was a folded white robe upon which rested the Unpointed Sword. Kostas lit a white candle and some incense while Iacovos turned on a switch and two powerful bulbs, one on the left, the other on the right hand side of the icon, lit up Christ's image.

Daskalos knelt and placed his right hand over the Unpointed Sword. For a few moments he kept his eyes closed and murmured a prayer. He then stood up.

'I want you to tell us,' Daskalos addressed Loizos, 'whether you agree with the following seven statements that Iacovos will recite. These are promises that you must make to yourself if you wish to wear the white robe. It is not an oath but a promise.'

Daskalos said earlier that an oath bears heavy responsibility. The breaking of an oath can have tragic consequences. On the other hand, if one falls short of a promise, then one is accountable only to oneself. The seven promises, Daskalos went on, are the keys to spiritual perfection. They were given by Yohannan when he was seven years old. He categorically insisted that the seven promises are absolute, unalterable and valid for all times.

'I promise to myself,' Iacovos began.

'I promise to myself,' Loizos repeated in a low voice.

'To serve at all times and in all places the Absolute to which I wholeheartedly belong,' Iacovos went on as Loizos repeated after him each sentence.

'To be ready at all times and in all places to serve the Divine Plan.

'To make good use of the divine gifts of thought and word, at all times, in all places, and under all circumstances.

'To endure patiently without complaining all forms of trials and tribulations which the most wise divine law may bestow on me.

'To love and serve my fellow human beings sincerely from the depths of my heart and soul no matter what their behavior may be towards me.

'To meditate and contemplate daily the Absolute with the objective of total coordination of my thoughts, desires and actions with its divine will.

'To investigate and check every night whether all my thoughts, desires, words and actions are in absolute harmony with the divine law.'

When Loizos finished with the recitation of the seven promises, Daskalos held his right hand and as everyone else listened he proceeded in a serious tone: 'The white robe is neither a reward nor a privilege. It is a heavy cross to carry. It is a promise and a commitment to be always of service to your fellow human beings. Your brothers here agree that you deserve to put on the white robe. It symbolizes the necessity to keep your soul white. Love must be the dominant force in your life. Hate no one, even those who do you harm. Be firm when need be but do so with love and always bearing in mind what is best for your fellow human beings.'

Daskalos then asked whether anybody had any objections to Loizos becoming 'a white-robed brother.' Everyone in unison declared that he was 'Axios,' that he was truly worthy. Theophanis and Kostas took the white robe from the altar and helped Loizos put it on. Following Daskalos, each one of the other brothers kissed Loizos on the forehead. Then he knelt and Daskalos crossed him over the head by using the Unpointed Sword. The neophyte kissed the Unpointed Sword right at the point where a six-pointed star was inscribed.

'We shall now proceed with the Communion of Love,' Daskalos announced and gave the floor to Theophanis. The latter mixed water with wine and poured it into a silver communion cup which was on the altar. Theophanis, eyes closed, both hands stretched upwards, firmly held the communion cup in front of Christ's icon. The rest of us knelt as he remained in that position for several minutes. There was total silence. When Theophanis turned around everybody stood up. He gave communion to each one of the brothers, starting with Daskalos who kissed Theophanis' hand after he drank from the cup. Everybody, with the exception of myself, drank from the communion cup three times, 'In the name of the Father, and of the Son, and of the Holy Spirit.' Theophanis then poured some of the 'blessed wine' into an ordinary plastic cup, and repeating the ritual, he offered it to me to drink, 'In the name of the Father,' and I drank once, 'and of the Son,' and I drank twice, 'and of the Holy Spirit,' and I emptied the cup.

'Let me explain to you some of the symbolism of the ritual you have just witnessed,' Daskalos told me as the others left the Sanctum and went into the main room of the Stoa. 'The Communion of Love is not a substitute for the Holy Communion in Church which I always urge my students to take.'

'What is the purpose of the Communion of Love?' I asked.

'Before we begin the lesson of the inner circle we need the blessing of the Christ Logos. Whoever carries on the Communion of Love must be very advanced in the construction of noetic images. When Theophanis held the cup with his eyes closed, he first made a prayer and then envisioned a powerful sun inside the cup radiating light. He then proceeded to dissolve it. When the sun continued to shine with greater intensity, it was a sign that the Logos had taken over. The water and the wine inside the cup had been blessed.'

'Is it only Theophanis who carries on this ritual?' I asked.

'No, not always. We take turns. But only those of us who have psychonoetic powers are capable of intense concentration and can accomplish this feat.'

'What is the meaning of the inscription on the Unpointed Sword?' I asked and looked at the sacred object lying on the altar. On its short and broken blade I read 'Στούς 'Αχράντους Σου Πόδας Λόγε Πάσα 'Εξουσία' (At Thy Immaculate Feet, O Lord, All Authority Rests).

'Let's talk about that after the lesson. The others are waiting and we must proceed,' Daskalos said quickly as we walked into the other room.

Daskalos sat in the front chair facing his small audience while Kostas sat next to him looking pensive.

'Kyriaco,' Kostas said severely, 'what you hear today you cannot tape or discuss with outsiders.' I realized that Kostas, with whom I had already established a close friendship, was uncomfortable that I was given permission to attend. Unlike

Daskalos and Iacovos, he was much more cautious in revealing the 'mysteries.' I reassured him that I would neither tape nor take notes on the lessons of the inner circle.

'Children of the Spirit, of Light and of Fire . . . ,' Daskalos began in a low voice. It was the first time I heard him address his students with these words. Before the lesson was over Daskalos asked me to leave the room because, he said, Father Yohannan was about to give a meditation exercise that only the members of the inner circle must practice.

I waited in Daskalos' living room. In about half an hour I heard noises coming from the Stoa. I assumed the meditation exercise was over. Daskalos came out first, thirsty for coffee. He apologized for sending me out of the room but it was Father Yohannan's wish, he explained. I reassured him I was not the least offended and volunteered to make Turkish coffee.

'Can you now explain to me the meaning of the Unpointed Sword?' I asked Daskalos as I handed him a cup of steaming coffee.

'You don't forget, do you?' Daskalos said jokingly as Iacovos and Kostas joined us.

'The Unpointed Sword,' he began, 'is the symbol of our circles. We are part of a wider circle called the "White Brotherhood." However, our invisible masters asked us to call our groups "Circles for the Research of Truth" in order to differentiate ourselves from certain circles in Europe because of abuses.'

'When did the White Brotherhood start?' I asked.

'The very moment man turned his eyes upward and asked the question, "Who am I?" And then knelt down and wondered about the great power that governs the universe.'

'I suppose,' I added, 'all religions of this planet are qualified to be part of this White Brotherhood.'

'Yes, as long as the central characteristic of these religions is universal love. Nevertheless our particular system for the Research of Truth began in the year when Christ was born just after he was visited by the three wise men.' Daskalos then proceeded to briefly chronicle the events that led to the creation of this branch of the White Brotherhood.

'The Maharajah Ram, with his friend the wise Tsekinata, through clairvoyance, monitored from India the events that led to the birth of Christ. Imagine that Ram was able to calculate the exact time that Christ was to be born. With Tsekinata he traveled by camel all that distance and arrived at Jerusalem at the appropriate time.

'Ram left his kingdom to his brother and traveled without an entourage. They were able to protect themselves from bandits with the power of their thought. On their journey to Jerusalem they passed by Armenia which was divided in two. One part was ruled by King Ntikran and the other by his brother Gaspar, a great mystic. Gaspar reconciled himself with Ntikran, making the latter king of the whole of Armenia. He then joined the other two wise men on their pilgrimage. The three of them encountered Valtasassour, the Arab king of the desert. The rest of the story is known through the gospels.

'When they arrived at the cave the Maharajah Ram took off his royal golden robe and placed it at the feet of the Godman. He then took out his sword, broke it in two, placed it in front of Jesus and said, "At Thy Immaculate Feet, O Lord, All Authority Rests." Then he knelt down, kissed Jesus, and said, "Cham el chior" which in the ancient Indian language meant, "I saw God."

'When the three wise men returned to their countries they set up the circles for the Research of Truth. As you noticed the brothers of the inner circle wear only a white robe without any insignia. It symbolizes the under robe of "Chamelchior" after he took off his royal robe and placed it at the feet of Christ.'

'That's quite a story!' I exclaimed and before I finished my sentence little Marios, Daskalos' three-year-old grandson, appeared at the door holding triumphantly the bottle of wine Theophanis had used for the Communion of Love. The child, who was present at Loizos' initiation, apparently took the bottle from the altar and spilled its contents all over the Stoa.

'Don't worry,' Daskalos reassured the others, 'we can buy another bottle. Now Marios will know the difference between the blessed wine in the communion cup and the wine in the bottle.'

'How is he going to see the difference?' I wondered.

'Marios is clairvoyant. He can see the blessed wine radiating light. The wine he spilled did not radiate light. Spilling the wine was his way of testing the difference between the two.'

'That is a very healthy way of explaining Marios' mischief,' I marveled and the rest joined me laughing.

'I wonder, Daskale,' I said after Kostas and Iacovos left, 'whether you would care to elaborate a little on the lesson you have just given? I am not clear on what you exactly mean by the "self-sufficiency" and "Divine Expressiveness" of the Absolute.'

'It is not possible with our human brains,' Daskalos began while I pressed the button on my tape recorder, 'to comprehend the nature of the Absolute. As I have told you repeatedly, we cannot know God unless we get to know ourselves. When we reach that point our own self will become the mirror which, through reflection, will enable us to know God. Our small consciousness will become awakened inside the superconsciousness.

'However, even though our earthly brains are inherently limited in comprehending the Absolute, we can still have a faint notion of some of its characteristics. Now, I speak on the basis of my personal experience, based on my investigations within universal memory. I know that the Absolute Is. Do not imagine, however, that this Absolute is some strange God that the various religions have given us. The Absolute is everything, a multidiversified entity in One.

'A basic attribute of the Absolute is its self-sufficiency or autarchy. By that I mean it has everything within it. It lacks nothing and it needs nothing.'

'Had the nature of the Absolute been only autarchy,' I added, 'the creation of the worlds would have been impossible.'

'Good. But another attribute of the Absolute is the urge, call it Divine Expressiveness if you will, to manifest itself. It vibrates within itself. It has life, motion. Can you imagine life without the phenomenon of motion? No. Based on this observation various mystics concluded that God is movement. This is a mistake. Life as movement is the nature of the Absolute. It is not the Absolute.

'Now, pay attention because this is a difficult point to grasp. Suppose within the boundlessness of the infinite there were no phenomena. What could we possibly know about the infinite?'

'But who would be the knower in this case, since we would not exist?' I pointed out.

'Fine. We would not exist but we would still Be.'

'You mean we would be as Holy Monads, as eternal souls?'

'Yes. If we assume that the Infinite has within it life, movement, vibration, without anyone or anything vibrating or moving, we would have simply been in absolute self-sufficiency. We would not exist. However, it is the nature of the Absolute to express itself, to create the universes. Mind was created. When? Since it is part of the Absolute it has always been.'

'What do you mean by Mind, Daskale?'

'Mind is that supersubstance that makes possible the Divine Expressiveness of the Absolute.'

'It must include the gross material universe,' I added.

'Of course. Not only the gross material universe, but all the universes, the psychic, noetic, higher noetic and beyond. Everything is Mind but Mind is not the Absolute. It is the means by which the Absolute manifests itself. The Absolute is beyond all manifestations. Just think for a moment. Everything we see around us is the product of Divine Thought which becomes materialized.'

'Daskale,' I asked, 'what is the difference between the Christ Logos and the Holy Spirit?'

'I am glad you asked. The Christ Logos and the Holy Spirit are the two ways by which the Absolute manifests itself through Mind. The Holy Spirit represents the impersonal superconsciousness which expresses the power of the Absolute, making the creation of the universes possible. It is the dynamic part of the Absolute. The Christ Logos is that part of the Absolute that makes possible the existence of self-consciousness. We, as eternal entities, are both Logoic and Holyspiritual. Animals are only Holyspiritual. Do you follow me? Let us assume that the Absolute is the head, the Holy Spirit the left hand and the Logos the right hand. It is the Trinity in One. Do you understand now why they chant in church, "In the name of the Father, the Son and the Holy Spirit"?'

'When you say Christ Logos do you mean Jesus Christ?'

'No. Jesus Himself said, "Before the mountains and the hills I Am." The Christ Logos has always been within the Absolute before the appearance of Jesus. We call Jesus of Nazareth "Christ" because He was the most perfect and most complete expression of the Pan-universal Logos. It is the light that enlightens every man descending upon the Earth. Let me illustrate what I mean. Suppose Christ is the Sun whose light is reflected on the surface of our planet. A black stone will hardly reflect that light. Another stone of a different color will reflect more light. A white marble will reflect even more light. The light that each stone reflects depends on its quality and color.'

'We are, I suppose, these stones.'

'Exactly. The amount of Logoic light reflected within us will depend on how evolved as self-consciousness we are, how developed our psychonoetic body is. But every stone, no matter how dark it is at the present, will one day through the impact of the Sun become as bright as alabaster. Do you understand? We speak now of existence as distinct from beingness.'

'How are the two different?'

'Whatever exists Is, beyond evolution, beyond expression. It is within the eternal present, inside the Absolute.'

'Now I am really confused,' I said with exasperation.

'Look! We Are, as Holy Monads, as souls, before we exist. We acquire existence when we pass through the Idea of Man and enter into the world of separateness, of existence. What exists has a beginning and an end which in turn becomes a new beginning for another cycle of existence. As eternal entities we simply are. We have always been. It is through the cycles of existence that we shall acquire our self-consciousness. This is the meaning of Christ's parable of the prodigal son as I explained it to you before. When Christ said, "I am the Way and the Truth and the Life," what do you suppose he meant? "I am Time. I am the wisdom of the Absolute behind the evolution of phenomena in space and time." How many do you think can grasp the meaning of Jesus' words? Believe me the Christian religion has substance. But we have remained on the surface of the ocean. We have yet to explore its depths.

'So,' Daskalos said and clapped his hands on his knees, 'the mind of man can conceive two natures of the Absolute and three attributes. The two natures as we have seen are the Logoic and Holyspiritual. By studying Nature we can also comprehend the three attributes of the triadic God, namely Omniscience, Omnipotence and absolute Goodness. We can perceive these attributes in the smallest particle of matter as well as in the greatest of galaxies. What is true on the microcosm is also true on the macrocosm.

'Everything,' Daskalos continued, 'is within Divine Autarchy, unexpressed, unmanifested. Within Divine Autarchy there is also Divine Expressiveness through which the manifestation of what is begins.'

'Daskale,' I asked, 'I wonder whether you care to elaborate a little more on the difference between existence and beingness?'

'Common people assume there is nothing beyond existence. If you ask the question, "Does God exist?" my answer will be a categorical, "No." God simply is. Existence is the manifestation of God through the supersubstance we call Mind. Whatever exists has a beginning and an end. God as the Absolute has no beginning and no end.'

'In the King James version of John's Gospel,' I noted, 'we read "In the beginning was the Word. . . ." '

'It is a mistranslation from the Greek original,' Daskalos snapped. 'As you know, the word *arché* in Greek means both beginning and authority. In the English translation the first meaning was mistakenly chosen. It should have read, "In authority is the Logos. . . ." '

'I would like to ask you one more question on the distinction between beingness and existence. I suppose we can say that beingness is the reality whereas existence refers to the world of phenomena which includes the gross material, psychic and noetic worlds. From this point of view entering reality means transcending existence and receding into beingness, into a form of non-existence.'

'Very good. It is not easy to transcend the various dimensional worlds and fearlessly enter into our beingness. I now speak of my own personal experience. Though we feel we are part of the One Reality, Life, we enter into a conception of non-existence. This is probably what must have confused even the Buddha who said that Nirvana is a state of nothingness. In reality it is not nothingness. You still know that you are you. As a present personality you reflect yourself in three mirrors, the mirror of matter, the mirror of psychic existence, and the mirror of noetic existence, of concrete thoughts. Suppose I hand you a hammer and tell you, "Look! There is so much distortion of yourself in these three mirrors. Break them." And you break them. What are you now? You can see no reflection of yourself as thought, as sentiment or as a material being. Who are you now? You are still you, no less and no more than what you were before the smashing of the mirrors. However, unless you are reflected you cannot become a phenomenon of life. Suppose I boldly enter into that sense of non-existence, yet beingness within the Absolute Beingness. Can I come out of it any time I wish and re-reflect myself within matter, that is become incarnated? Definitely yes. We are eternal beings.'

'That must have been the state we were in before we passed through the Idea of Man to get incarnated,' I remarked.

'Good. You can enter into that state any time you wish, assuming that you are an experienced master of the metaphysical world.'

'It must be a frightful state to be in, Daskale,' I added.

'Well, to tell you the truth, I experienced it long long ago in centuries past and at first I felt a great fear. But I was helped by my masters. Entering that state of being, without feeling I am the reflection of myself, gave me such happiness, such self-abundance, autarchy. Is there any other word for autarchy, of self-sufficiency? But even in that state you have the desire to return. Yet I cannot really call it desire because the moment I do that I automatically find myself in the psychic dimension. Nor can I call it thought, obligation, because when I say that, it is implied that I am within the noetic world. What is it then, this state of non-existence, yet self-sufficient beingness, which impels me to return? It is perhaps the nature of Beingness to reflect itself by itself. Masters have done it. Christ has done it.

'When entering within myself, which from the human point of view is nothingness, and from the point of view of beingness self-abundance, I know that it is my nature to re-enter the world of matter. I now speak strictly on the basis of my own experience. Suppose you ask me, "Where do you prefer to be, within the self-abundance of non-conceiving being, where we find what we call happiness, or within the trials and tribulations of our phenomenal existence?" Believe me if I have a beloved person near me, to gaze into the eyes of, to smell and caress the loved one's feet, I would say I prefer that. Call it weakness, call it whatever you like, still it is an attribute of our beingness not of our existence. Maybe this is the same urge within the Absolute Beingness itself that brought about the creation of the worlds. To touch and caress lovingly with the rays of its Sun even the dullest, the most stagnant waters.

'Perhaps,' Daskalos went on after a few seconds' pause, 'what I am saying is blasphemous. This is how I feel. The material world with all its torments and imperfections is beautiful! Do you find that I am wrong?'

Daskalos' question took me by surprise. The tone of his voice and the intensity of his glance gave me the impression that he actually expected an answer, as if, in fact, I were in a position to give him one.

'I wish,' I mumbled clumsily, 'I could give you an answer.' In fact I was moved with Daskalos' earthly yearnings. It reminded me of a story about a Zen master. All his life he preached of the unimportance and the illusory nature of the material world. When he was about to die his disciples gathered around his deathbed eager to hear some final words of wisdom. All he could utter was, 'I want to live, I want to live.' His adepts were dismayed. 'But master, how can you say that?' they protested. 'Really, really, I want to live,' he repeated and closed his eyes. That was the master's final lesson.

It was early evening when I left Daskalos' home. We agreed to meet again and continue our discussion on the nature of the Absolute and man's place in the universe. In the meantime I had already made arrangements to meet with Kostas on Saturday. He was to be back in Nicosia that day. I planned to ride back to Limassol with him and attend a meeting with his circle of students scheduled for that afternoon.

Kostas was a master in his own right. I had already attended several of his meetings and was impressed by the high quality of the discussions that followed the formal presentation. Unlike Iacovos, whose father was a laborer, Kostas came from a wealthy family of Famagusta, the leading port city of the island before it was overrun by the Turkish troops in 1974. After that tragedy he found refuge in Limassol with his wife and two children where he managed a large garage for auto repairs. Before the Turkish invasion Kostas had spent five years in England and earned a degree in mechanical engineering.

After I got to know his students I realized that most of them joined his circle after they witnessed healing performed either by him or by Daskalos. A woman in her middle forties told me that she joined Kostas' group when he cured her from excruciating headaches she had suffered for over twelve years. Kostas' most advanced disciple, a government employee, joined his group after Daskalos cured his young daughter who had a walking disability.

'When I went to Daskalos,' he told me, 'my daughter was three years old. I was sitting on a chair holding her on my lap. Daskalos was talking to me about her condition. Suddenly he extended his hands and said to my daughter, "Come, my love." Before I realized what was happening and to my great astonishment, she slipped from my lap and walked towards him. He picked her up and put her on his lap. For a moment I was terrified. "What is he doing to my daughter?" I thought. Up to that point she could hardly walk. She was also afraid of strangers. When I saw her sitting on Daskalos' lap, smiling, I felt at ease and realized that a miracle had taken place. He took off her shoes, put her down, and said, "Walk, my love." She has been walking normally ever since.'

Another student of Kostas was a former member in Daskalos' circle but when he moved to Limassol he joined Kostas' group. 'I once,' he said, 'suffered from my kidneys and planned to have an operation to remove the stones that caused me extreme pains. The day of the operation I tried to get out of bed and put on my pants. I felt such extreme pains that I fell back in bed. As I lay there Daskalos' image came to my mind. Then I began concentrating on my kidneys, sending with my mind rays of certain colors that Daskalos had taught us. In a few minutes of concentration the stones on my kidneys fell off and the pain was gone. I cured myself without the need for an operation.'

'How long have you known Daskalos?' I asked Kostas as we drove off towards Limassol.

'Ever since I can remember. He used to hold me on his knees,' Kostas replied with laughter. 'My parents were his students. I was exposed to his teachings very early in my life. I remember one day when I was a small child Daskalos was in our home when I got a spanking from my father. Daskalos said to my father, "Do you realize, my dear, that you are spanking a master?" At that time I could not understand what he meant.'

Kostas then said to me that it was only five years ago that he was 'awakened' to the reality of who he was. Memories of past lives were beginning to come back to him. He claimed that in one of his incarnations he was a knight in the court of Richard the Lionheart and took part in the crusades.

'When I was studying in England I had a strong feeling that the countryside was very familiar. But the actual memories have come to me only recently. Believe me these are not dreams,' Kostas said, and looked at me as if to check my reaction on what he was saying. 'The intensity of that incarnation must have been very strong,' Kostas went on. 'One time when I was out of my body I encountered, for the first time, a threatening black elemental. Instinctively I reached for my sword. I thought I was a knight fighting an evil enemy. I immediately realized that that was not the way to fight elementals,' Kostas said laughing.

'Well, how did you fight that monster?' I said smiling.

'I created with my mind an elemental radiating white light and directed it against the black elemental. You never fail if you know how to do that.' Kostas then went on to say that whenever he feels that an elemental is too powerful for him, he just runs back to his body for safety.

'Our bodies are like castles. They protect us from outside enemies,' Kostas said as we passed a large lorry that had slowed us down for several miles.

'What do you understand by the term "awakening"?' I asked. 'Are there any steps that one must follow before one becomes "awakened"?'

' "Awakening" to us means realizing who we actually are which is something other than our present personality. It implies remembering past incarnations. It usually happens in three stages. First you subconsciously feel that you have lived before. This is what happened to me when I was studying in Glasgow. The second step was when I began to have images coming to my mind in the form of dreams. The third step is when you begin consciously to relive certain experiences of the past.'

'Can't you skip the first two steps?'

'As a rule, no. I am speaking now for the ordinary person on his path in the Research for Truth. For an advanced master the first two steps may not be necessary. Perhaps Daskalos was born awakened, or almost so. But don't assume that Daskalos is not also researching for the truth. He, too, is a disciple. You never stop being a student until you re-awaken as a god.

'The moment that you enter the path of knowledge,' Kostas continued, 'you begin to consciously carry your own cross. You may also consciously begin to lift the cross of your fellow man.'

'You mean you begin to take up his Karma?'

'Yes. You do that through love. When you carry on a therapy, you absorb consciously or subconsciously the pain of the other. Believe me this is not masochistic. You enjoy life more fully. You come close to so-called happiness. Of course, within gross matter there is no happiness. There are only pleasure and contentment.'

'Where, then, is happiness?' I asked.

'Real happiness exists only within the noetic worlds. Naturally at every stage of reality the meaning of happiness is different. When you enter the path of knowledge life is more meaningful. Do you think it is a small thing to realize,' Kostas said with exuberance, 'that you are not lost?'

'Perhaps it is wishful thinking that leads you to this belief,' I added wryly.

'No. When you have the experience nothing can shake up your feeling of certainty,' Kostas replied. It was the standard response that I had heard Daskalos and Iacovos make repeatedly. They had the certitude that they were bearers of enlightenment and that their mission in life was to help their fellow men to come out of the darkness of ignorance and despair.

'Kosta,' I said, 'I noticed that you are very reluctant in revealing information about the teachings. Why are you so cautious? Why the need for secrecy?'

'Listen, Kyriaco,' Kostas replied as he kept his eyes fixed on the road, 'it is not wise to expose someone abruptly to too much light. He can be blinded. You can harm a person if you reveal to him certain truths that he is not as yet ready to absorb.'

'In what way can the truth harm anybody? Can you give me an example?'

'I will tell you,' Kostas said with determination, after pondering my question for a few seconds. 'Several months ago

we had to expel a brother from our circle because once he
learned how to carry out exomatosis he abused it.'

'How?' I asked, and I noticed Kostas smiling.

'He was the principal of a high school and the rascal used to
visit the bedrooms of his female students while out of his body,'
Kostas replied, and joined me in laughter. 'In spite of his pleas
to be accepted back into the circles, I was adamant against it. I
could see on his aura a lot of egotism. If we had let him
continue, he would have been tempted to misuse such powers,
not only to the detriment of others, but primarily to himself.

'You see,' Kostas went on, 'when you involve yourself with
mysticism a mistake of this type can keep you bound to the
same condition for several incarnations. The higher you climb
on the mystical path, the more painful your fall can be. That is
why mysticism is secretive. Don't forget that if through certain
meditation exercises that you learn in the inner circle, you
manage to prematurely open up your sacred discs, you can be
overwhelmed by feelings of terror. When such experiences take
place, one's receptivity to spiritual matters may be stunted for
several incarnations.'

'Or one may end up in the asylum,' I added.

'Very true. That is why it is wise to always have a mentor to
guide you in this path. It is the safest route. Believe me,
whenever a person is ready for these truths, a master will
always appear in his life.

'To tell you the truth,' Kostas went on, 'it is very difficult to
judge whether a specific information about mystical issues will
have a benign or a catastrophic effect on someone. These
matters can lead minds that are too attached to earthly interests
to confusion. What may benefit one may harm another.'

'Is it possible to get the information given within the circles
by reading books?' I asked.

'No. The teachings of Father Yohannan as given to us are
not recorded anywhere.'

'I have noticed that Daskalos, yourself and the others are
absolutely certain that the knowledge you acquire on spiritual
matters is second to none. How can you be so confident since
there are some discrepancies between different mystical systems?'

'Our information comes from the very source itself.
Yohannan is not just a master who lives on the other side. He is

Christ's most beloved disciple and the entity that oversees the evolution of our planet.'

'Does that mean that Daskalos is infallible? Do you accept everything he tells you as the truth?'

'Not at all, not at all. We do have disagreements between us as you must have noticed, particularly on issues pertaining to worldly matters.'

Kostas argued that it is natural to have disagreements at the lower levels of existence since the material brain is always an obstacle in the absorption of wisdom. Therefore the way to resolve spatial-temporal issues is through discussion and agreement, and never through the imposition of Daskalos' will or that of the invisible masters. 'In the higher levels of existence, however, knowledge is such that it is pure light and wisdom. Whoever enters there absorbs it.

'The masters do not dictatorially tell us what to do. They show us the way and it is up to us to proceed on our path. Yes, we will make mistakes in the process, but this is how one learns.

'Our views on politics and social questions may differ,' Kostas continued, 'but we all know that these issues are of no ultimate validity. We do not therefore accord them more value than they deserve. To give you an example, I have in my circles people who belong to various political parties. In fact in my circle I had a leading member of the communist party.'

'I find that difficult to believe,' I said laughing. 'A communist mystic?'

'Oh yes!' Kostas retorted emphatically. 'But I must say he eventually had difficulty reconciling his political role with his spiritual activities. His wife threatened that unless he quit our circles, she planned to report him to the party.'

'What did you advise him to do?'

'Remain in the party and quit the circles temporarily until he sorted out his marital difficulties. He could be of service to his fellow human beings from where he was, as a member of the communist party. Ironically, his wife suffered from cancer and during our meetings we tried to help her from a distance.'

We stopped for a rest at Skarinou, a village half way between Nicosia and Limassol. It was a traditional resting stop, a small oasis where one could indulge in some local delicacies, sweets made of raw walnuts, watermelon rind, and where one could sip the omnipresent Turkish coffee.

Kostas generously continued answering my relentless questions on his relationship with Daskalos and his personal involvement with the circles. So much of his time was absorbed with healing and the teachings of Yohannan that he hardly had any time to look after his own business.

'You know,' Kostas said as we got back to the car, 'we are like dwarfs in front of Daskalos. He is light years ahead of us on the spiritual path. But the public has no idea who he is or what he does. Most people assume he is just a psychic or a sorcerer and they come to him often for the most banal of reasons.'

'What, for example?'

'A man came last year demanding from Daskalos to "finish off" the husband of his sister-in-law. Daskalos was angry and asked him to leave at once. That fellow took a bundle of money from his pocket and waved it in front of his face. "You see this mister?" he shouted, "they are five pound bills. They are all yours if you do what I asked you to do."'

'I can imagine how angry Daskalos must have been,' I commented.

'His response was, "Roll up your five pound bills and. . . ."'

'I can guess the rest,' I said, and joined Kostas laughing.

'For a whole week,' Kostas continued, 'Daskalos tolerated another man who pestered him continuously. He sold lottery tickets and demanded that Daskalos pick up from the bunch of tickets the lucky numbers. Daskalos explained that he could do no such thing and asked the man, in vain, to leave him in peace. He sat in the hallway for hours. Finally Daskalos lost his patience when a couple of young women visited Daskalos and this fellow began making lewd remarks. Daskalos took him by the ear, pulled him out of the house and sent him away with two slaps on his nape. "What the devil!" the man mumbled as he ran away holding his head. "You're crazier than I am!"

'Sometimes people come to Daskalos,' Kostas went on, 'with the intention of poking fun at him. I was there when a couple brought him a picture of their dead brother. The moment Daskalos touched it he realized the "deceased" was alive and well, waiting outside in the car. He sent them away in disgust.'

'It is hard for me to imagine how it is possible to tell whether one is dead or alive by simply touching his picture.'

'Believe me,' Kostas said confidently, 'it is the easiest thing in the world. The picture is the means by which you coordinate yourself with the magnetism and the vibrations of the person. If you perceive that his silver cord is intact, it means the person is alive.'

'Sounds simple,' I retorted as I smiled and raised my eyebrows.

The silver cord, Kostas explained, is that which connects the psychonoetic body with the gross material. If you meet a person on the psychic plane and that person has a silver cord, it means that he also lives within the gross material plane. In the absence of a silver cord, it means that one resides only within the psychonoetic worlds.

We were approaching Limassol when Kostas, responding to my question, began describing how he personally feels in exomatosis.

'Intense concentration is necessary before you can leave your body. Your material brain must stop vibrating completely. You must first learn how to shut the doors of your subconscious so that thoughts do not interfere with your concentration. Then, through a special meditation technique that you will learn after you advance in your research, you will find yourself outside your body.

'At the first step of my exomatosis I am in a state of hypertension. I feel both inside my material body and outside of it. It is a factor that sometimes does not permit me to leave my body. When you are outside your body and your consciousness is near it, there is a great temptation to think of and look at it. The moment you do that you are back inside.

'When we are outside of our bodies,' Kostas continued, 'we absorb etheric energy from the universe and through this energy we can carry out healing.'

'How do you feel when you return to your body?' I asked.

'I am fully alert and incredibly energized. I feel full of life. In exomatosis you absorb so much etheric energy that it revitalizes you. Every particle of your body is charged with vitality. It is something you will know yourself when you first experience that state.'

'I doubt that I ever will,' I murmured.

'Don't despair,' Kostas said reassuringly. 'I know of a brother who tried for twenty years unsuccessfully to leave his body. When he decided to quit the exercises he found himself out of his body. You should always keep in mind the principle of limits that we find in Nature.'

'What's that?'

'Ice will remain ice until a certain critical point in temperature which will transform it into water. Water will remain in its liquid form until a certain point in temperature which will transform it into vapor. It is the same with the exercises. You may struggle for years to accomplish a certain psychonoetic feat and you may get desperate that you are not progressing. Yet you are progressing towards the critical limit without being aware of it. Some day, unexpectedly, you will wake up and begin to live consciously within the psychonoetic worlds. But unless you persist and persevere you cannot go very far.'

Without realizing the passing of time, we found ourselves inside Limassol. There was pandemonium in the streets. Leftist organizations had set up an anti-war rally against the British bases nearby. The demonstration ended up at the city park near the apartment of my in-laws. We could hear, over the loud speaker, political speeches and slogans, followed by protest songs of Mikis Theodorakis. The famous Greek composer flew to the island for the purpose of attending the rally and his hoarse voice could be heard leading an impromptu and cacophonous choir.

With great difficulty we managed to maneuver through the crowds and reach on time the apartment of one of Kostas' students where the meeting was to take place. Most of his associates were present except a few who took part in the rally.

After the short prayer Kostas read slowly a mimeographed lesson previously given by Daskalos. It was on the Absolute and the nature of holy monads. Individuals who are emanations of the same holy monad, Kostas said, have a particular affinity for one another. With these individuals we are telepathically connected and affect one another. In the 'realms of separateness' we have brothers who may even be considered our enemies yet with whom we are psychically linked.

When we evolve spiritually we subconsciously assist our brethren to rise up as well. 'The spiritual development of each leads towards the spiritual development of all.' Our own ascent therefore will depend on the spiritual development of our brethren.

On several occasions Kostas had mentioned to me that Daskalos, Iacovos, Theophanis and he were part of the same holy monad. Hence they were in continuous telepathic communication. Whatever happened to one, the others felt it. When Daskalos had a minor accident Kostas claimed to have automatically felt the pain right at the spot where Daskalos was hurt. Kostas had to quit his job and lie in bed all day. There was no evident medical reason for his pains.

When the formal presentation ended there followed a vigorous two-hour discussion about holy monads and man's relationship to the Absolute. I asked the last question.

'Since the Absolute, as you said, is all-knowing, It must know in advance what our choices and actions will be. Where, then, is our freedom of choice?'

My question created an uproar. It seemed as if almost all the members in the circle faced this dilemma. Kostas insisted that man is free and fully responsible for his actions and for the creation of his own karma. 'If we change the elementals we project,' he said, 'we can change our destiny.' Any projections about the future, Kostas went on, are nothing more than probabilities based on what has happened so far. 'Every moment that passes, we are rewriting the history of the future based on the choices we make.' Kostas went on to present argument after argument in support of the notion that man is fully responsible for his own actions and thoughts. Then in an earnest attempt to make us understand the notion of free will, he shared with us a psychic experience he had had sometime in the past when he was struggling with the same issue.

'Quite often there are no words to present certain truths. This is a problem even for Yohannan. One day, in order for him to give us a lesson on the nature of the relationship between the Absolute and the future, he took us inside the eternal present. We found ourselves within an enormous temple suspended by gigantic pillars. The floor of the temple, and the walls, were made of alabaster. The dome was made of silver.

We looked at the back of the temple and we saw no end to it. At the entrance new additions were constantly being created. It appeared as if the temple were continuously getting bigger at the entrance. As we proceeded inside the temple we went back into time. Yohannan was present but it was another master who was giving us a tour of the temple. On both sides of the walls there were bas-reliefs and we noticed that new ones were ceaselessly being engraved. Daskalos inquired to find out what they were. The answer was, "It is the Logos which records the details of whatever takes place within the universes, within the worlds of separateness." Daskalos was then given permission to touch one of the bas-reliefs and momentarily experience the events as they were recorded there.

'Within this temple of time we saw nothing engraved in the future. We were given a lesson to understand that nothing is pre-recorded and that the future is constantly being created within the eternal present. We were given to understand experientially that man's freedom is a reality and not an abstract notion.'

10

The Guardians of Planet Earth

We were having lunch with Daskalos and Iacovos at our home when the radio announcer reported on the latest news about Skylab, the American space laboratory orbiting the Earth. It was July 11th, 1979, the expected date of its reentry into the atmosphere, and the world's media were on the alert. Even airlines cancelled flights during the expected hour of its fall, and there was a general feeling of uneasiness and apprehension. It was reported that the Americans lost control of Skylab and there was a possibility of its crashing over populated areas.

In a humorous mood Daskalos described how a few days ago a villager had knocked on his door very late at night asking whether Skylab was going to fall on his house. He was a poor man who had just built himself a three-room home. His wife, frightened of the news, had demanded that her husband visit the 'Magus of Strovolos' to find out what would happen. Daskalos was both amused and annoyed at being disturbed so late at night for such a triviality. 'If it is your kismet [fate] to have Skylab fall on you, it will fall on you!' he said to the villager. The peasant's fears were hardly eased. Daskalos was not always tolerant of people coming to him for what he considered foolish issues such as fortune telling. Poking fun at people was a habitual pastime for Daskalos. One day a man came looking for him while he was in his yard watering his plants. The visitor apparently took him for the gardener. 'I am looking for that fakirist,' he said. 'Do you know where he is?' 'Yes,' Daskalos replied. 'He is upstairs lying on his nails. Go find him there.' The incredulous man walked up the steps and in a few minutes returned stating that there was no one upstairs. 'Was the window open?' Daskalos asked, feigning seriousness.

'Yes.'

'Oh, well,' Daskalos shrugged, 'he must have flown away.'

145

I mentioned casually that in yesterday's newspaper I had read about an Indian yogi who claimed he was going to try to turn Skylab into ashes.

'That is very dangerous. It can burn his body,' Iacovos remarked.

'That Indian yogi,' Daskalos joined in as he finished his last bite, 'is not the only one who is working on Skylab. There are many mystics who are trying to divert its trajectory. I myself have been working on it all day.' Then he turned abruptly towards Iacovos and said, in a low voice, 'That rascal, Loizos, was in my house this morning and understood what I was doing. Sometimes he is so bright, sometimes he is like a log.'

I realized that something significant was about to take place and I searched for my notebook. Emily had already shut all doors and windows and spread the curtains in order to keep the July heat out of the house. The streets were quiet. It was the siesta period. All shops and offices were closed between one and four o'clock in the afternoon. There was hardly a trace of life in the streets.

Daskalos said it was time for him to check and see how Skylab was doing 'up there.'

He sat on the couch and leaned back in a semi-reclining position. I was facing him, pen and notebook at hand. Emily was sitting next to me with a look of puzzlement and bewilderment in her face. Iacovos was on Daskalos' other side, his face betraying signs of anxiety.

'Would you come up with me?' Daskalos asked him.

'No,' he replied wryly.

Daskalos closed his eyes as he was getting ready to leave his body. Iacovos, an intense expression on his face, focused at his master's navel as the latter appeared to be in a state of trance. We silently observed what was taking place. There was an eerie feeling in the air. In ten minutes Daskalos woke up.

'It is very dark up there,' he observed somberly. 'There are others also. I saw some Indians, Tibetans, and a black American. I was the only European. They seemed to be afraid of the darkness and they stayed far away from Skylab. I tried to get as close as I could. It vibrates demonically.' Daskalos demonstrated with his hand how Skylab moved.

'Daskale, what did you do up there?' I asked.

'I tried to push it to the southern hemisphere where there is more water and there are fewer people.'

'Just how did you try to push Skylab towards the southern hemisphere?'

'I created with my mind a moonlike disc and directed it towards Skylab so that it would bounce back and push it towards the south.' Daskalos then mentioned that his Silver Cord was pulling him back to his body.

'That was the reason,' Daskalos continued, 'that the space around my Solar Plexus was vibrating so much, as you probably noticed.' We had not. Only Iacovos had noticed.

'Why don't you join me this time, to help push it south?' Daskalos again urged him. Iacovos refused once more. He preferred, instead, to keep a watch over his master's body. He apparently considered Daskalos' adventure quite dangerous and could hardly hide his anxiety.

'As long as I am breathing,' Daskalos instructed him, 'do not disturb me. Don't repeat,' he said laughing, 'the slap you gave me on the face last time to force me to return.' He was referring to an incident when Iacovos had 'forced' him to come back to his body while in a state of exomatosis.

Daskalos closed his eyes. He appeared to be in a state of deep trance. Iacovos kept guard. Emily and I remained silent, passive spectators to the strange drama that was unfolding in front of our eyes. In a few minutes Daskalos opened his eyes again.

'Skylab is moving with tremendous speed and vibrates like a drunkard,' he reported and once more demonstrated its movements with his hand. He then closed his eyes and went into an even deeper trance. Several minutes went by and Iacovos appeared more anxious than before. He asked me whether Daskalos had been up for more than ten minutes.

'No, he has been up for just over seven minutes.' Then Iacovos took Daskalos' right wrist and checked his heart beat.

'It is time for him to return,' he murmured and looked at us as if we had a say. As soon as he finished his sentence, Daskalos opened his eyes. He was fully alert and very excited with the experience he had just had.

'It is as big as a minaret and it is ready to reenter the atmosphere.' I found the use of the minaret metaphor rather amusing and despite the gravity of the occasion, had a difficult time keeping a straight face.

Daskalos paused for a moment and looked at us. He must have perceived our incredulity. He smiled, saying that perhaps I should not talk publicly about what we had just witnessed. One can easily get 'scandalized.' Daskalos was concerned that the great messages and teachings coming through Yohannan may not be taken seriously if incidents that appear too 'fantastic' are reported. I confess that I have succumbed to the temptation to narrate this extraordinary experience during that hot day in July. I was certain that their experience was genuine and authentic, regardless of the fact that, to us, it appeared extraordinary, to say the least. Of course I had no way of testing the 'objective reality' of their experience since I could not 'go up' myself.

'Did you change your mind?' Daskalos urged Iacovos once more.

'No.' The apprentice preferred to monitor his master's physical condition like an attentive medic. Daskalos entered into a trance again. There were stillness and silence in the room as we waited for Daskalos' next move. When he opened his eyes he appeared more excited than ever.

'I just saw three flying saucers. The entities inside communicated with me and asked me to stop sending the moonlike discs against Skylab because they disturbed its balance. Their method was better, they said, and they invited me to move onto their side and observe their work.' He then explained that these beings beamed rays of light against Skylab and then moved south in an attempt to pull it along with them. Daskalos took Iacovos' hand and urged him once again to join him. Meanwhile I turned my transistor on softly to hear the latest BBC news. The announcer reported that the Americans hoped the spaceship would fall in the south Atlantic or in the Indian Ocean. They still had no control over it and worried that it might fall over populated areas. When Daskalos came out of his trance once more, he continued in an animated voice to narrate his experiences with the extraterrestrials.

'These entities are really advanced. They live in the higher noetic world and have no form. They asked me to abandon the image of myself and join them.'

'Must you really?' Iacovos muttered, knowing full well that it was hopeless to dissuade his master.

'Oh yes,' Daskalos said stubbornly, and explained what he was about to do.

'Now I must leave behind the image of myself and ascend formless with only my self-awareness.'

While he explained his new adventure, Emily hastily stepped out of the house to receive our two children whom my sister had just brought over. Constantine, my two-and-a-half-year-old son, moved to another room and played by himself whereas Vasia, our six-month-old daughter, crawled noisily on the floor in front of Daskalos. I asked whether the baby talk interfered with what he was doing. He reassured us that the noise was no problem and that we could even play music if we so wished. Then, after his brief rest, he got into his self-induced trance once more. I noticed that this time his hands were shaking violently and he was making spasmodic facial movements. Iacovos continued to be on the alert. Ten minutes later he checked Daskalos' pulse. In a whispering voice he reported that it had reached one hundred and ten beats per minute. Daskalos soon opened his eyes.

'They are having problems pushing it. It whistles demonically, making a deafening noise. These superintelligences are working very hard. We are so insignificant in comparison to them. If they fail to change its trajectory, it is going to fall over Canada.' He then got ready to 'go up' again.

'Let my heartbeat go as high as one hundred and forty. It will be easier for me,' he instructed his disciple.

'Are you sure what you are doing is not dangerous?' I remarked, as I noticed Iacovos' face drop in almost total despair.

'It will be more dangerous if we do not manage to push Skylab south. This is the first time I have done such a thing,' Daskalos added and then closed his eyes. Eight minutes passed while Iacovos monitored his master's pulse.

'It got to the desired trajectory,' Daskalos remarked as he came out of his trance, fully satisfied about a job well done.

'Daskale, could someone see those beings with naked eyes?'

'No, they live in the noetic world. They have no form.' Then he proceeded to relate his experience with the extraterrestrials in greater detail.

' "We are the guardians of garden Earth," they said. "Your Earth is like a nursery school of noisy infants." "It is a garden full of parasites and viruses," I replied. "No, it is an expression of Life," they answered back.

'They seemed as if they were working in groups which gave me the impression of flying saucers. I asked them whether they in fact were flying saucers but they seemed to ignore my question. Their response instead was that they are "space people." They live around our planet. The Earth looks a beautiful ball from up there.

'I communicated with these beings by coordinating myself with them. I was inside them and they were inside me. I expressed a wish to meet them again and invited them to come down to Earth. They refused. They preferred, they said, to watch us from afar. "You know the way, come and meet us here," they replied.

'Perhaps it is not pleasant for them to visit the Earth. When I was about to return to my body they advised me, "Come pass through us so that you may go down rested." I felt very relaxed after that. They truly love us.' Daskalos expressed his amazement and ruminated upon the nature of these superintelligences.

'I felt as if they were a form of light with vibrating intensity. They are innumerable.' There was a pause as Daskalos pondered over his experience. 'Thought is something so beautiful! I was receiving their thoughts and I could understand them. I had the impression that whatever I knew they knew. They are probably archangelic forces.'

'Do you think they have self-consciousness?'

'Apparently they do.'

'But is this not contrary to what you told us about archangelic forms which are Holyspiritual entities rather than Logoic?'

'Perhaps what is valid on Earth may not apply on higher levels of consciousness. Holyspiritual entities, therefore, may also have self-consciousness. I must study this.'

It was four-thirty in the afternoon and the streets were alive again. The heat had subsided and the afternoon breezes from the sea were bringing relief. Daskalos asked me to drive him home. On our way he marveled at this unique and exhilarating experience which he dearly cherished.

At nine in the evening I listened to the BBC. The announcer reported that the American scientists began to have limited control over Skylab. However, it could still crash over the northeast United States or over Canada. Later on that night the BBC announced that parts of Skylab had fallen in the Indian Ocean and in an uninhabited region of Australia. Everybody was relieved.

I met Iacovos the following day and chatted about the unusual event. I asked him whether he actually witnessed Daskalos coming out of his body. Iacovos explained that he saw Daskalos leave his body like a smoke going up through the top of his head. What appeared like a smoke was actually part of Daskalos' etheric. He used the etheric-double of his gross material body because he was working on the etheric-double of the material Earth. Skylab was not on the psychic but on the material Earth. Iacovos pointed out that Daskalos' heartbeat reached up to one hundred and forty. It was for this reason that he repeatedly refused to join him. He had to keep an eye on his physical condition because that kind of work was very dangerous.

Later in the day we met with Daskalos and continued our discussion about Skylab. He mentioned that as soon as he reached home he went 'up again' to keep a watch on Skylab. The moment it entered the atmosphere it began moving up and down like a fast speed boat over the surface of the sea.

'The Americans,' Iacovos remarked with irony, 'reported that they were unable to control Skylab and were worried that it was going to fall over Canada and Maine. Then all of a sudden they beamed a signal and moved it south.'

'Had it not been for these superintelligences,' Daskalos added, 'Skylab would most probably have crashed over Canada. I saw them three times trying to pull it south. They waited until it appeared on the horizon and then beamed rays of light towards it. The Americans should learn how to build Skylabs that disintegrate once they enter the atmosphere.'

It was early evening and Daskalos seemed to be in a relaxed and talkative mood. Uncharacteristically we had no telephone interruptions or visitations. After Iacovos brewed three cups of Turkish coffee we continued chatting until late in the evening.

I asked Daskalos whether he had any prior contacts with extraterrestrial beings other than those he encountered while working on Skylab.

'Yes,' he said, and began to narrate another encounter he had had with such a being some time in the past.

'I felt him somewhere near *Petra Tou Romiou* [a spot on the southern shore where, according to Homeric legend, Aphrodite was born. According to Daskalos it is one of the energy or magnetic centers of the planet]. I was in exomatosis with Iacovos and Theophanis. After I escorted them back to their bodies I returned to the same place in search of him. "But I have seen you," I muttered, "where are you?" "I am inside you," he whispered. "I am inside you so that we can have a common center for communication. How would you like me to give you some experiences? Spread out," he commanded me. "I can do this," I responded. "I know that you can do it, but now it is going to be through a different method." "What do you mean?" "Just wait and you will see." For a moment I felt everything was inside me and that I spread over a large area. "Become the pulsation of Life. Forget who you are." "No, I am afraid," I told him. "Forget that you are a separate entity. No matter how much you imagine you have stripped your personality, you are still bound to it." "What do you mean?" I asked. "Stop feeling that you are an entity." "Are you asking me to become annihilated inside God?" "Why? Do you think you get annihilated when you become the breath of Life, here, everywhere, inside everything?" "Yes," I said. "And yet you become more, you expand more, you do not become annihilated. Without losing your beingness you can emancipate yourself from its limitations, you are not transformed into zero. Take this space. Become the breath of this place, the breath of water, of Life, everywhere. You will see how beautiful it is!" "I am afraid." "Just a moment," he replied, "you will see that through me you will not be afraid." For a moment I turned around and I was able to see him. He was absolutely beautiful!'

'Did he have a human form?'

'The idea of man, not the form. He was a human idea.

' "I am confused," I said, "but I do know I exist." "Whenever you look at yourself in the mirror and say I exist," he replied, "it is an illusion. When you talk about the self, what do you understand?" "Love." "Now we are in perfect agreement. When you say Love you imply the image of persons you love. You become one with them. It is not you." "Do you know," I replied, "that I understand and feel what you say but that you are creating confusion in me?" "It is through confusion that you will enter into Knowledge. Because if you do not get confused you will not focus your attention toward discovering the Truth and you will not find it. You will be content with situations that are not the Truth." "I am not ready, for the time being Daskale, to follow you." He began laughing. "Ha, ha, ha. How much you are enchanted with this word and you pass it on to me like a lollypop that you give to your grandson to lick. This 'Daskale' . . ." '

Daskalos laughed heartily as he reminisced over the ironical comments of the extraterrestrial and continued.

' "I cannot understand you," I said to him. "In spite of everything you do understand me perfectly. But you get tired because you do not want to rid yourself of certain illusions. However, you are ready to overcome them without pain whenever you wish." "Are you perhaps guiding me to some form of annihilation, universalism?" I asked him. "Aren't you using nice words! What do you understand by universalism?" "Well, to feel everything and not feel that I am a separate entity." "How can that be? It simply means that instead of you being Iacovos, Marios [grandson], Nina, Yianna [grand-daughters] you become that and more. Do you understand? Vibrate less." "No, I will not vibrate less." "Go back. You are not ready yet." "Do you have a family?" I asked him. "Do you love your father, mother and children?" "What did your Master say, the Great and Most Beloved One? Whosoever abandons father, mother and children for my sake I shall give him one hundredfold from that, and father and mother and children. Christ said that in the New Testament did he not? Have you thought out the meaning of His words?" "I am tired," I replied. "We shall continue the lesson later." '

'He is powerful! And what jolts he was giving you!' Iacovos exclaimed in the midst of laughter.

'He looked at me,' Daskalos added, and said "Love, do you know that you are me?" "No. I don't want this," I said. "Whether you like it or not you are." "When you say me, which me are you talking about since you wish to annihilate myself?" I asked him. "I want to put you into the great Self into bigger frames." '

'Was this conversation carried on in Greek?' I interjected and immediately realized that my question was irrelevant.

'He talks to you the way you will understand. Besides, if I want him to draw me only with thoughts, communication is much easier. You lose the meaning of time and space and you enter into the Present inside Reality, into the Life of things.'

'Did you have this dialogue,' I continued, 'right at the *Petra Tou Romiou*?'

'That was the focal point, but we spread out within the psychic plane of the area. How much of Cyprus I am not sure. It is not easy to make you understand. How am I going to make you see all those infinite pictures?'

'Daskale, was he a theosized human being?'

'I don't know. I did not ask him.'

'Was he, perhaps, an archangel like Michael or Gabriel?' I persisted.

'Perhaps he is one of a higher class. A man is superior to those archangels that are so monolithic. They know their job and nothing else. They simply obey the command of the Lord.

'I am telling you,' Daskalos continued, 'it is not painless to give up what we hold onto.'

'I have thought about this before,' Iacovos remarked.

'And who told you that they don't work on you subconsciously without your realizing it?'

'Now that you mention it,' Iacovos added, 'I am beginning to suspect that it is so.'

'He talked to me a lot about him,' Daskalos said, pointing at Iacovos. 'At one moment he said "It is he that you are afraid you will lose." Then he revealed to me certain matters concerning my family that shook me up.'

'Did he tell you anything about Nicos [Daskalos' son-in-law]?' Iacovos asked.

' "If you withdraw yourself from him he is lost. He suffers when he is away from you. But now he is getting an experience." "I want to move away," I said. "What does move away mean?" he answered back. "The more you try to move yourself away from him, the more attached you become to him."

'Can you explain this to me?' Daskalos asked Iacovos with intense inquisitiveness. 'He talked to me about so many matters that I could not understand.'

'I wish you could think like him,' Iacovos remarked teasingly.

'But how could I think like him?' Daskalos responded apologetically. 'Do you know what else he said to me? "We shall discuss what Love is because you only imagine what it is." "What do you mean?" I asked. "You focus your attention on the molecules of Love and you think you know Love. The material body," he said, "no matter how perfect it is, and how much the very Beloved One sanctified it, is not absolute Love." "I know what you are driving at. But are you calling this evil?" I replied. "No. I would not call it evil. I would call it incompleteness. Can you see the beloved person from a higher perspective?" "But it is beautiful right from here," I pleaded. "I did not say it is not beautiful, but does it stop being an enchantment?" "It is Love," I replied. "Do you see that you do not know what Love is really all about? Suppose at this very moment the beloved person, because of Karma, loses his body and you are deprived of him," he said. "Karma caused that to happen and gave him [Iacovos] back to me." "Fine," he said, "Karma gave him back to you because you wanted him. But can you find Love beyond the form?" "Yes," I said. "Then why don't you focus your attention there? Why do you need the form?" "Because the form is beautiful," I replied. "I did not say that it is not beautiful, it is imperfect. You are too small for a God. You are too big for a man." "Thank God," I said, "I am not a small man," ' and Daskalos burst with laughter and continued narrating his psychoanalytic encounter with the extraterrestrial.

'He was sending me thoughts. "Abandon the image. Cease to be enamored by the image of the material body. Spread inside Love. When I show you those you love inside Love you will not care whether they have material bodies or not." "Why did you not show me when he left then?" "You were not mature enough and you would not have been able to understand at the time." '

'Who left when?' I asked quickly.

'That's who,' Daskalos said after pointing at Iacovos.

Daskalos referred to Iacovos' death in his previous life.

'He had such a fine sense of humor,' Daskalos remarked laughing.

'Did anything stay with you of what he had told you?' Iacovos chuckled.

'How can I know?' Daskalos replied shrugging his shoulders.

'I wish you thought about all the things he told you on your own,' Iacovos said.

'Have you thought about such matters yourself?' Daskalos fired back.

'Not about all of them,' Iacovos said laughing.

'And who told you that you actually came across such thoughts on your own? Perhaps you got them through reflection?'

'I cannot know that,' Iacovos continued, giggling. 'Perhaps I got them through you.'

'Next time,' Daskalos added playfully, 'I will not put you back in your body. I will tell him "grab this fellow from the hair and let him have some experiences." '

'I would love that,' Iacovos replied and his eyes sparkled.

'Daskale,' I asked, 'have you met any of these superintelligences here on Earth, among other human beings?'

'You mean while walking in the street?'

'Yes.'

'Several. They move and look like ordinary people. I can spot them through their aura and communicate with them through thought. One day I was walking on Ermou Street right in the heart of the bazaar. It was the first time I encountered such a being.'

'Did he have a name?'

'It is possible that when such a superintelligence comes down he acquires a name. The one I met is a great master. The Logos blinded him temporarily when he appeared in front of him like fire. Now do you understand who I am talking about?'

Iacovos nodded affirmatively but it required further probing on my part to realize to whom he was referring.

'Was he a Cypriot?' I asked rather naively.

'No,' Daskalos replied lowering his voice. 'He was Saint Paul who in his present incarnation lives as Father Hilarion down in the Sudan. Some friends of mine met him there. He materializes and dematerializes like a great master.

'He came with a material body,' Daskalos continued with a serious look in his face. 'It was at the time when my wife was still alive. I was at the market when I suddenly felt him. After a few moments I spotted him walking in the street and communicated with him by thought. "Master, is that you?" He turned around, smiled at me and continued walking. At that moment there was a cart coming from behind him. "Watch out you stupid idiot or I'll run you over," shouted the driver. He looked back and talked to him in impeccable Greek, "I am sorry, sir," and moved to the side of the street.' Daskalos laughed as he recounted the incident.

'Why did he materialize himself?' Iacovos asked.

'I have no idea. But I did see him with a material body, with clothes. I tried to come near him and suddenly I lost him. Kyrie Eleison, I muttered. On my return home I found him chatting with my wife. "Do you know who he is?" I asked, pointing at the visitor. "I saw him sitting on the side of your bed the day you were sick. That is Father Hilarion," she said. He joined us for dinner and we had a long talk. He was in a material body. He even ate beans and onions. As he was getting ready to leave he mentioned that he was on his way to various parts of the island to place talismans. I could not understand what the purpose of his visit was. He disappeared from our midst as my wife went to the kitchen to fetch something. A few days later I met him again. "Do not mention anything about what you have just experienced," he said to me.

'Now you may ask why is he doing all these things? I do not know. It is a Divine Plan that we cannot comprehend. At least I cannot comprehend. Other masters do not materialize themselves. They remain in the psychic world and work from up there. They work in different ways.' Daskalos suddenly stopped his narration and gazed at me in the eyes.

'Now we have completely confused you, Kyriaco,' he cracked and roared with laughter.

He was not far from the truth. These 'fantastic' stories were part of his daily reality. For my ordinary conventional mind they were not easy to digest. Yet what was puzzling to me was that Daskalos was neither trying to fool me nor was he trying to impress me. In every other respect he was like any mortal, yet a man extraordinarily gifted who could accomplish feats of healing that were truly miraculous and seemed to defy a conventional scientific explanation.

11
Tales of Possession

It was already midsummer. The thermometer showed 41 degrees Celsius and the weatherman threatened that the heat was to reach 43 degrees. The streets of Nicosia were deserted. The populace, in spite of the energy crisis, headed en masse towards the coast for a refreshing splash in the Mediterranean. But going to the sea on Sunday was a tortuous odyssey in itself as access to the northern shore was cut off by the Turkish forces of occupation. Only the southern coast was accessible and there was only one crowded highway left linking the capital with that part of the island.

I preferred to stay home, work on my notes and listen to the sad tunes of the radio. It was July 15th, an official day of mourning for Greek Cypriots. On that date in 1974 the military junta that ruled Greece at the time carried out a disastrous coup against the Cyprus government that provoked the Turkish invasion.

I made arrangements to meet Daskalos and Iacovos late in the afternoon. Kostas telephoned that he could not come. As a volunteer in civil defense he had to attend a special drill session.

Iacovos spent the day assisting his brother with the construction of his new house. When he came to our place he consumed large quantities of water. Laboring all day under a merciless sun had dehydrated him.

We arrived at Daskalos' at seven o'clock but found nobody there. The door was unlocked and we sat inside waiting. In a few minutes Daskalos arrived with Loizos. He was pleased to see us but looked tired. He went straight to the refrigerator for a glass of cool water. He had spent the entire day at Larnaca visiting patients and trying to help a couple who were facing marital problems. He was satisfied because he helped save the marriage and went on narrating the day's events. Iacovos seemed somewhat impatient and after a while interrupted Daskalos' monologue.

'This is not why we are here,' he said somberly. The inference was that we had come to continue a discussion we started earlier on mental illness.

'But I thought you came here just to see me!' Daskalos responded playfully, feigning disappointment. 'My dear Iacovo, please make me a cup of coffee.' Daskalos was in a teasing mood and Iacovos responded in kind.

'Iacovos,' Daskalos said to me after taking a sip of coffee, 'is not as tolerant as he ought to be. I noticed for example that he finds it hard to tolerate Niciforos.'

'That's right. I cannot tolerate him to the same extent that you do, going there night after night. . . .'

'But he needs me!' Daskalos pleaded. 'That idiot could commit suicide if I were to abandon him. I have to be very patient with him and not expect him to meet our standards. If he commits suicide I will have him on my neck day and night.'

'In what way?' I asked curiously.

Daskalos explained that those who commit suicide may find themselves in a difficult situation when they enter the psychic world. Occasionally such persons may be trapped in the etheric of the gross material world, unable to move to the higher psychic planes. The individual may vibrate too close to the material world which will not allow him to find rest.

'So,' Daskalos continued by turning to Iacovos, 'we have to watch Niciforos very carefully.' Apparently he felt that Niciforos was a potential victim. I mentioned that I was not sure whether I understood what he meant when he said that a person after death may continue living in the etheric world and be attached to the gross material plane.

'Perhaps,' Daskalos said thoughtfully, 'a better way to make you understand is to describe certain cases that I have encountered.' I started getting ready to set up my tape recorder. 'No taping for these stories,' Daskalos said categorically. I realized that the 'stories' which he was about to discuss must have been highly unusual or controversial and one way of protecting himself was to forbid taping. I picked up my writing pad instead and got ready to note down everything he was about to say.

'Many years ago,' he began slowly, 'an engaged couple lived together without being married for four years. Throughout this period the girl remained a virgin. She would not allow her fiancé to consummate their relationship. In the fourth year he got tuberculosis and the doctor isolated him in a tent outside of Nicosia. The girl promised him that they would get married as soon as he got well. His great torment was that during the four years of their relationship she would not allow him to have intercourse with her. He died with this unfulfilled craving. This overwhelming yearning for her kept him floating in the etheric world from where he began harassing her. The girl was going mad. Each night before she would go to bed he would semi-hypnotize her and induce her to keep the window of her room open. He would then enter inside a bat and would come to her. The bat would wedge on her neck and draw blood and etheric.'

'Why blood and etheric?' I asked.

'An individual in such a state needs etheric matter in order to sustain himself there. The girl was losing a lot of blood and became extremely weak. Her parents brought her to me in despair. "Daskale," they implored me, "our daughter is dying and the doctors cannot help us. Look at her and see how weak she is." I noticed that although it was high summer she had her neck covered. When I inquired about it she mentioned that it was due to some pimples that appeared there. I asked her to let me look at them. She opened her collar and I saw clearly the teeth of the bat in twos, right at the spots of her arteries. It was the first time that I had encountered such a case and, inexperienced as I was, I sought help from Father Dominico who lived on the other side. He explained to me that the dead man, by using the bat, lived more intensely in the etheric world. Father Dominico instructed me on how to treat such a case. "Stay in their home for awhile," he said. "The girl will wake up at night to open the window. Have a brasier with burning coals in it in the next room. When the bat arrives grab a broom, enter into her bedroom and then shut the window. Be careful because the bat will attack you. Hit it with the broom to make it dizzy. Then wrap it in a towel. You should then go to the next room and throw the bat inside the brasier. Shut the bat inside and let it burn." ' Daskalos leaned back in his chair and continued.

'Well, this is exactly what happened. When I closed the window the bat attacked me. At that moment the girl woke up and assaulted me. Her father, who was present, grabbed his daughter and held her tight. She was groaning and screaming hysterically while the bat was dying. Then she calmed down and became serene. "What are you doing to me?" she asked. "Were you trying to burn me?" I advised her parents to bring a priest in order to bless the house.'

'What happened to the fiancé?' I inquired.

'We helped him disentangle himself from the etheric worlds so that he could go higher. Do you understand now what it means when someone gets trapped in the etheric world?'

I had hardly finished writing Daskalos' last comments when he began to narrate another similar case.

'Thirty years ago I was on a journey to the Peloponnese in southern Greece. I spent a few days in a town where there was a girl suffering from a serious psychological problem. I was asked whether I could help. She was about twenty-five years old and single. A shepherd, twenty-five years older than the girl, fell in love with her and asked her parents for their daughter's hand. They refused. The shepherd, Loizos was his name, died in an auto accident. Five years passed after his death and nothing happened. But one day this girl claimed that while she was looking after her two goats she saw Loizos calling her. Frightened she began running to her house. He followed her. "You are dead. What do you want from me?" While saying this she started feeling very sleepy and sat under an olive tree. He hypnotized her. The girl confided to me that under that olive tree she experienced for the first time sexual pleasure. When examined she was found a virgin. Three days after this incident the dead man visited her at home. He came at night through the walls. She got used to him making love to her. When she was examined once more, she was no longer a virgin. The doctor, however, insisted that she was not deflowered by a penis but by her fingers. I noticed that on her neck there were two reddish spots. I asked about them. "He kisses me there but his kisses are strange. They are like sucking and I like them," she replied.

'I spent the night with them. He did not appear. Nor did he on the second night. But late in the afternoon of the third day I saw him coming from the orchard. When he entered the house and noticed me, he behaved as if he had known me for years. "Hey, friend Loizo," I said, "are you aware of your situation?" He explained that he had craved the girl for many years and that he had never experienced sexual relations with a woman before. The only sexual relations he had were with animals like donkeys, shegoats, and even with chickens which died after the act. Now that she had become his he wanted her and was not about to let her go. I tried to explain to him that he was not alive like the rest of us. He could not understand. "What are you talking about, mister?" he protested. "Here I am talking to you, I fuck, and you are telling me I am not alive?"

'Exorcism could not work on him because he was not afraid of the Cross. He was, let us say, an immoral believer. He accepted Jesus. Therefore, it was necessary to persuade him with logical arguments that he had to leave. Fortunately I succeeded. "I am leaving," he promised me, "and I will not return. But I do not want to die." "Should you continue bothering this girl you will remain in this narcotized state like a vampire," I warned him. He turned around and walked away. The dogs in the yard felt him and began barking. When the priest and the doctor asked me about what happened, I avoided telling them the truth because I assumed they were not likely to believe me anyway. I mentioned that the girl was under the influence of illusions and that through psychoanalysis I helped her overcome her problem. At night the doctor gave a lecture to the villagers, sitting in the coffeehouse, on psychoanalysis. He spoke about Freud, the unconscious, and so on. I was in a corner listening and laughing to myself.' And Daskalos roared with laughter as he recollected the incident with the doctor.

'I left the following day.' As if he anticipated what I was about to ask, Daskalos continued. 'I never found out whether it was the dead shepherd who deflowered the girl or whether he made her break the hymen with her fingers.

'People get possessed by elementals which they themselves create as a result of their weaknesses. Only in rare cases do I encounter possession by beings who reside in the etheric world. For example many young men in Cyprus end up in the asylum after creating powerful elementals from obsessive masturbation over the image of a woman. Such an elemental sucks from the etheric of the individual in order to prolong its life within the etheric counterpart of the gross material world. This may lead to insanity. The "sucking of blood" of the so-called vampires is in reality etheric matter. The same situation occurs more rarely when human entities behave as if they were vampires. One should not be hostile and narrow-minded with these beings. Even in cases of demonic elementals, one should also be tolerant. Demons also know how to love.'

I pointed out that I found Daskalos' last remark incomprehensible and I asked for clarification. In his customary manner he proceeded to answer my query by narrating another yarn.

'After the civil war in Lebanon, when many refugees came to Cyprus, there emerged an epidemic of black sorcery. Among the refugees there were several powerful sorcerers who made their living by offering their services. These black magicians posed a formidable challenge to us. My concern was that they were training local people in the secrets of their craft.

'One such sorcerer was asked to kill a young couple for the price of three hundred pounds. He knew how to carry out invocations of satanic powers and succeeded in trapping a demon inside a bottle. He used rubber from a tire to carve the image of the demon. He then managed to place the bottle with this demon-elemental under the mattress of the newlywed couple. On their wedding night both of them began to bleed from their ears and noses. They began to lose their strength. They came to see me but I was in Paphos that day with Theophanis. They left and returned the following day. Still I had not come back. Meanwhile I cut short my visit to Paphos because I felt somebody needing me desperately. I was back on the fifth day and found both of them sitting at my doorstep waiting. They held handkerchieves in front of their mouths to hide the bleeding. I knew what happened right away. They were both exhausted and showed me the bottle with the demon which they discovered under their bed. I immediately cut off the connection between the demon and this young couple and they both breathed with relief. The bleeding stopped and they could now lead a normal life.

'I deliberately kept the demon inside the bottle and waited for Iacovos and Theophanis to arrive so that we might discuss the matter and decide what to do. When they arrived I showed them the bottle and related the incident. I explained that my plan was to try to put him inside the Sanctum. As an emanation of Lucifer, the demon could not tolerate the Cross and the holiness of the altar. Therefore, as I tried to force him into the Sanctum, he broke his bonds and got away. There was an explosion like a small bomb.'

'I also heard this explosion,' Iacovos added. 'It was very loud.'

'I reassured both Theophanis and Iacovos that they should not worry and that the demon could do no further harm. He had escaped but I could bring him back any time. I was protected by Yohannan. Even if the demon were to attack me, I would experience some pains for a few days and nothing more. When Iacovos and Theophanis left, I became engrossed with other cases and forgot the episode with the demon. But he did not forget. The demon came back on his own. "Holy Virgin! You are so ugly. Why do you keep pestering people?" He replied, "Because I get great pleasure from it. I love people." He appeared to me like a mythological satyr. His color was dark green. His eyes were red and he had protrusions on his forehead that looked like horns. He gazed into my eyes and said, "I could have harmed you had I so wished. If I did not it is because I love you." "You really oblige me," I said.' And Daskalos burst with laughter as he was reporting his dialogue with the demon.

' "I love you, too," I said, "but you must promise me that no matter how intensely they invoke you, you shall never do any harm to anybody ever again." He gave me his word. After that I encountered him seven times. I noticed that he was gradually becoming less ugly and the protrusions on his forehead began to recede. He acquired a more tolerable appearance. I invited him to enter with me into the Sanctum so that he could get used to the holiness of the place. One day during a meeting I had in the Stoa with the members of the inner circle I felt him in the Sanctum. He entered with courage. "Come, I have something to offer you," he said. I excused myself from the other brothers and rushed to the Sanctum. As I entered he materialized an image of himself in the form of a small statue of baked clay. When I took it in my hands it was very hot.'

'The change from one dimension to another,' Iacovos

explained, 'always generates heat.'

'Using a towel, I took the statue,' Daskalos went on, 'and brought it to brother Theophanis. One of my students was so frightened,' Daskalos said laughing, 'that he refused to come near it. Some of the other brothers only touched it. I then took it back to the Sanctum and covered it with a black cloth.'

'Why the black cloth?' I interrupted.

'So that the statue would not dematerialize. When something dematerializes it gives away energy. The black color does not give away energy. It only absorbs it. I wanted to keep that statue for awhile in that state.

'As I walked into the Sanctum I saw the demon sitting cross-legged focusing his gaze on the Cross. He sat at the very spot where I found the statue. He was with his etheric body. "I did what you expected of me," he said to me, "but it was a hard fight. It was painful. I love you."

'I felt that he loved me like a faithful dog loves his master. It was not human love. A few days later I destroyed the statue.'

'I wish I had taken a picture of it,' Iacovos muttered.

'What are you talking about!' Daskalos said severely. 'To take a picture of him is to prolong his existence in that state. I had to destroy the statue so that he would not be able to use it and become fixated in that condition. Now I see him often. He has become quite good.'

Suddenly Daskalos turned abruptly towards Iacovos and gave him a cryptic signal. The latter responded with a similar excitement. I had no idea what was going on. Iacovos began to giggle. I nervously demanded that they let me know what was happening between them.

'He is sitting next to you,' Daskalos said slowly and with a wide smile on his face.

'Who is sitting next to me?' I asked with alarm as I turned around and saw nobody.

'The demon,' Daskalos said softly. 'He just entered the room and sat next to you.'

I felt butterflies at this unexpected turn of events. I became conscious that I was sweating heavily but I tried to reassure myself that my misery was from the high temperatures rather than from any fear of demonic powers. I found refuge in my scientific composure and detachment and kept furiously noting down what Daskalos was saying. Deep down I felt uneasy as well as intrigued.

'He even has a charming smile,' Iacovos added laughing.

'I hope I will be able to turn him into a benevolent spirit,' Daskalos went on. 'He can no longer do any harm. I asked him to adopt a name. He wants to be called Baalbook which in Assyrian language means "the purified from God." "Baal" means God and "Book" means someone who is being purified. I hope that some day he will become dissolved into the Absolute. Just as humans evolve, so do evil spirits. Consequently, one of our activities as Researchers of Truth is to be of assistance in all the realms of Creation. When this demon will evolve he will carry along with him many others of his kind towards holiness. He is still unable to differentiate between good and evil. He does no evil only because he wants to please me. I strictly forbade him to materialize himself or materialize objects. He promised not to. I also forbade him to descend into the vibrations of fire because he has the power to start one. I encouraged him to have as much contact with water as possible. He considers human sex as a game between children. His intelligence is very low. He can evolve, not in terms of human knowledge, but in habits and instincts. I don't think it is possible to do much more with him. Let him become dissolved within an archangel of a particular species. He already guards my flowers and assists animals like cats, dogs, and rabbits to give birth. Some time ago he said to me, "Should I strike those who bother your flowers?" "You do nothing of the kind," I ordered him.

'One day when you cut some flowers,' Daskalos addressed Iacovos, 'he came to me and said, "Why did he have to cut them?" He has speech but no intelligence. He has great powers but he is unaware of them. Humans are. afraid of demons because they are invisible. Had they not been so, men would have exploited them like other animals. This demon has no tail and he is very ugly. He is fat, short and has similarities with pigs. The time will come when he will dissolve within the Holy Spirit. Demons acquire the shape of human beings because they adapt themselves to whatever they see. They are the chameleons of forms. I have so much more to learn about them,' Daskalos concluded.

'I find the notion of demons evolving into the Holy Spirit quite consistent and in harmony with the view that only God exists,' I commented.

'Exactly. Had demons not evolved, it would have meant that there is evil inside the Absolute. This demon told me once, "You know you are not as handsome as I am." Another day he narcotized a snake. I ordered him to wake it up. He just laughed. He cannot differentiate my moods, whether I am angry or whether I am not. He perceives all of us as being part of the animal kingdom. Demons have no genitals. They are usually dark and sometimes even handsome. Do you know how he calls Iacovos? "The dark-complexioned beloved one." "What does he look like?" I asked the demon. He replied, "Like a worm that crawls on a leaf," ' and Daskalos chuckled.

Responding to my question on the difference between demons and angels Daskalos went on to say that they are both emanations of archangelic forces. In themselves neither demons nor angels are eternal beings. They are the elementals of the archangelic force which projects them. Humans are capable of creating both demonic and angelic elementals.

'Demons are archangelic emanations in the opposite side of existence in order to create the realms of separateness. Archangel Lucifer in the noetic world is no different than all the other archangelic systems. But his work down here is to create the opposite side of energy and power in order to bring the balance. I believe this must be part of the Divine Plan. It is that which we call Evil. The purpose of this Evil is to create for us more sharply the meaning of the Good.'

'How,' I asked, 'are demons different from the elementals that men create daily?'

'The elementals that human beings create are either angelic or demonic. Man is allowed to create both kinds. An archangel, on the other hand, can create only angelic elementals, with the exception of Lucifer who can only emanate demons.

'Demons,' said Daskalos, 'possess a form of subconsciousness that enables them to converse with humans. I am telling you,' he continued, 'you may reason with a demon but not with an angel because an angel is an unshakable law. An angel cannot deviate from his divine purpose. But, although a demon is something analogous to the angel, he opposes the work of the angel and can influence man. Once a demon attaches himself to a human being, he acts along with him, using the logic of man regardless of the fact that it may be a form of unreason. An angel cannot do that. He works monolithically within the realms of Creation. Do you understand now what is happening? An angel has no choice but to do good. A demon cooperates with man and therefore absorbs part of his experience, like the ability to logicalize. The angel expresses the love of his archangel uncolored. A demon expresses within the realm of separateness the love of his own archangel which is sentimentality. It is very similar to human sentimentality. That is why a demon can more easily get attached to a human than an angel. The only work of the angel in the plant and animal kingdom and in man is to create blindly and beautifully through the Holy Spirit cells and tissues and to assist in cures. The demon on the other hand does everything that man does. He lives fully with man's sentiments.'

'So,' I said, 'a demon is much more human than an angel.'

'Of course. You rarely see an angel assume a human form. They remain most of the time as powers, as a system. A demon takes up human form.'

'Therefore,' I said, 'in cases of schizophrenia and other mental disturbances it is usually the work of Lucifer.'

'Precisely. Cure, on the other hand, is the work of the angel. There is something else. Angels and demons are not in conflict. They appear to be so in human consciousness. I have noticed this but it is too bold to make such a statement openly. In Nature you do not see demons and angels fighting one another. They cooperate.'

'I have noticed the same thing,' Iacovos said thoughtfully, 'they work together.'

'I suppose,' I added, 'had it been otherwise, it would have implied that there are two Gods, one good and one evil.'

'Right,' Daskalos replied. 'However, I have observed that they take different positions within the subconscious of the individual in order to make possible for us the meaning of good and evil.'

Our discussion on demonology went on for some time. I almost forgot that what triggered it was our uninvited guest, the little satan sitting at my right side. I presumed he must have felt good with all the attention he had attracted.

'Iacovo,' Daskalos said suddenly, 'why do you suppose our little visitor is examining your toe? Do you think he is planning to imitate your leg?'

I never did find out whether Daskalos was serious, with that last remark, or whether he was joking. But I felt somewhat relieved that his sentimental friend left my side and moved on to examine Iacovos' feet!

12
Healing

My relationship with Daskalos was beginning to be known among friends and relatives in spite of my efforts to maintain a certain amount of secrecy about it. However, the growing awareness on the part of an expanding circle of people on the nature of my research had an unexpected positive effect. One such outcome was the role in which I was increasingly cast to act as liaison between Daskalos and persons who sought his services. I had played that role so often that I was beginning to accept it as part of my routine activities in Cyprus. I must confess I fully enjoyed it. Without others knowing what I was doing, perhaps my research itself might have suffered, since some of the most important occurrences that I witnessed might not have taken place.

One such case was the healing of a woman who was suffering from her spine and was completely paralysed for several weeks. It was in May of 1981 that this event took place. I had just returned to the island after a two-year absence, during which time I was trying, as much as my academic duties permitted, to work on my field notes. As in earlier instances, I was contacted by a friend who asked me whether I could approach Daskalos and inquire whether or not he would be willing to visit this patient in her home. I was told that it would be very difficult to bring her to his place as she had to lie in bed continuously. Moving about caused her excruciating pain. The patient had previously visited all the leading doctors on the island and found no relief. In addition, she had spent some time at an Israeli hospital but to no avail. Her spinal problems worsened. It was at that desperate point that Daskalos' services were sought.

When I telephoned Daskalos he expressed a readiness to visit the woman that very day. Without delay I drove to Strovolos, along with the patient's daughter-in-law. We picked Daskalos up and in fifteen minutes arrived at the patient's home. It was a pleasant house, with a yard and the usual vegetation that abounds in Cyprus, jasmine, rose bushes of all colors, lemon trees and a large shady grapevine. It appeared that the family was well off. I learned later that the patient's husband was a successful businessman, an importer of electronics equipment.

There were a couple of women relatives in the house, and the patient's son who was on a visit to the island. He was studying at a New England university. Daskalos seemed to be in a jovial mood, as he so often was, in spite of his own personal problems. Just before we entered the bedroom, he stood for a few seconds gazing at a painting hanging on the wall outside the patient's room. It was a reprint of El Greco's Saint Jerome. Daskalos identified the painting and expressed his admiration. He then entered the bedroom. The woman seemed to be in her fifties and distinguished looking. I learned later that she spoke fluent French and English.

'What is the matter with you?' Daskalos exclaimed feigning surprise. His playful tone 'broke the ice' right away and the woman, with a smile on her face, said that her vertebrae were constantly moving from their place and the doctors could not do anything to help her. We were told that she had undergone very painful treatments in both Cyprus and Israel where doctors would literally twist her spine in order to put the vertebrae back into place. Her situation, however, did not improve. In fact it got worse. We were told that a famous specialist in Israel had advised her that she had to learn to live with her pains as her case was incurable. It was the same advice she had heard from the local doctors.

Without hesitation and without any further questions Daskalos asked the two women who were present to turn her around and undress her from the waist up. I was standing near the door determined to witness the entire operation as closely as I could. Daskalos then placed his hands on the woman's back and began stroking and softly massaging her spine.

'Don't tighten up,' he commanded, 'just relax. It won't hurt.' While he was passing his hands up and down the woman's spine Daskalos looked at us and began offering his diagnosis of the problem.

'It is serious,' he said. 'Her whole spine is out of place. Her vertebrae are completely disjointed and there is a lot of porosity.' He said he was going to make the bones soft and malleable so that he could put them back in their right place and then resolidify them.

'Come and see,' he said, after a few minutes of continued stroking. 'Her bones are now completely soft. Come and test them with your own hands.' The two women who were next to Daskalos, including the patient's daughter-in-law, moved forward and pressed their fingers on her spine. Regretfully I declined to do likewise as I had never met the woman before and felt somewhat embarrassed at the thought of pushing my fingers on her bare back. But I noticed the astonishment in the faces of the others who had taken up Daskalos' invitation. Later they told me that her bones felt like a sponge.

'Now,' Daskalos announced, as if giving instructions to a group of interns in the operating room, 'I will put the bones in their proper places and resolidify them. I have already dematerialized the crystals.' With a few more minutes of gentle stroking, his treatment ended. The entire procedure had taken about twenty to twenty-five minutes.

'You are fine now,' he said to the woman, fully confident of what he had done. 'Turn around and get out of bed. You are completely cured. Your spine is straight and all the vertebrae are in their proper places.'

To the amazement of everyone present, the patient got out of bed and began walking without any help and without any pain. Her face lit up with excitement.

'Now,' Daskalos continued, 'bend down a few times.' She followed his instructions with great ease and without any apparent discomfort. She looked ecstatic, stretched her elbows, and sighed with relief. The atmosphere in the bedroom was euphoric. Daskalos looked pleased but not particularly impressed with his accomplishment. He took it matter-of-factly, just like an obstetrician after a successful delivery, a routine matter.

The patient was now walking about freely and offered to make us coffee. We accepted and sat in the living room. In a few minutes the coffee was ready and Daskalos, in between jokes, drank it with great pleasure. He was particularly fond of Turkish coffee.

Before we left, Daskalos instructed Mrs Katina, the patient, what foods to avoid. She listened attentively while he gave her a lecture on proper nutrition. 'You should also,' he said, 'get vitamin B complex on a daily basis. And you must do simple exercises like bending up and down a few minutes every day.'

As we were getting ready to leave, Mrs Katina rushed to the back of the house and in a few moments returned holding El Greco's Saint Jerome.

'Please,' she said to Daskalos, 'accept this as a token of my appreciation for what you have done.'

'No, no,' Daskalos said emphatically, waving his hands. 'Thank you but we are not allowed to take money or gifts.'

'Please take it,' Mrs Katina insisted, and tried to hand over the painting to Daskalos. 'It is not a gift, only a token of my appreciation.'

'Daskale,' I said, trying to rescue Mrs Katina from Daskalos' intransigence, 'the lady is right. You should consider it as a token and nothing more. After all it is only a reprint.'

Apparently my intervention worked. Daskalos shook his head and reluctantly took the painting. But seemingly uncertain whether he did the right thing, he murmured to himself that he was not supposed to accept gifts. Mrs Katina, meanwhile, beamed with pleasure.

Later on that day, just after the astonished husband and other relatives learned of the 'miracle,' a feast was held that lasted until the early hours of the morning. In the meantime Mrs Katina, incredulous herself over her cure, paid a visit to her radiologist that very afternoon. To the surprise of the doctor, the new X-ray plates showed marked differences from the ones taken only a week earlier. The new X-rays showed a normal spine.

I visited Mrs Katina again several days later. She appeared to me in excellent health, without any trace of her former ailment. It was hard to imagine that this woman could not even sit up in bed prior to Daskalos' arrival. Mrs Katina was more than eager to talk to me in detail about her medical history and her experience with Daskalos.

'What did you feel,' I asked, 'when Daskalos touched you?'

'I felt something very strange along my spine,' she said. 'It was like an electrical current, like little ants moving up and down my spine. At first I tightened up because, having in mind

how much pain I had suffered before with the twisting of my
spine, I was afraid that I was going to feel the same way again.
When Daskalos noticed my fears he asked me to let myself
loose.'

I was curious to find out to what extent Mrs Katina believed
that Daskalos could heal her. I wanted to know whether the
element of autosuggestion played any role in her miraculous
recovery. So I asked her whether she had had any contact with
Daskalos before.

'Yes I did,' she said, 'many years ago. I went to him when
my son, who at the time was two years old, was full of pimples
all over his body. We went to many specialists, we followed all
kinds of diets, we had all kinds of analyses done, we used all
kinds of ointments. Nothing. Until a friend of ours took us to
Daskalos. As soon as he looked at my son he said to me that
there was nothing wrong with him. He said the child was just
allergic to milk and the sweets he eats. Stop them both he said.'

'Did he say this by just looking at the child?' I asked.

'Yes, just by looking at him. I went back to the doctor and
told him about it. The doctor said, "Why don't we try it and
we'll see." We stopped the milk and sweets, and in four days all
the pimples were gone. On the fifth day the doctor said, "Let's
give him milk again and see what happens." In two days the
pimples returned. Then we stopped giving him milk for good
and the pimples disappeared.

'I went once more to Daskalos,' she continued, 'when my
mother got sick with leukemia. We were not even aware that it
was leukemia. She had had it for a long time. Her spleen
expanded so much that it caused a kidney to fail. They couldn't
do anything for her here in Cyprus because in those times there
were no specialists on the island. The doctors advised us that
we should send her either to Greece or to England. I went to
Daskalos after my mother was already in Greece. He said to me
the moment he touched my mother's picture, "Your mother
suffers from her spleen. It is her spleen that creates the white
blood corpuscles." He told me not to worry. Here in Cyprus
the doctors had given us no hope. They found that the white
blood corpuscles were 187,000. Normally they range between
8,000 to 10,000. Daskalos said, "Your mother will undergo
therapy in Athens and she will come back." And that was

exactly what happened. She lived eight more years. She then suffered a psychological shock when my brother-in-law got sick. Again her spleen expanded very quickly. We took her back to Greece for therapy but the doctors there told us that nothing could be done. I went to Daskalos again. He said to me, "I am sorry. I believe this will be her end." In two days she died. Whatever he told us came to be true.'

'So,' I said, 'when Daskalos came here that day did you believe that he had the power to cure you?' Mrs Katina hesitated for a moment as she pondered my question.

'Actually I can't say that I did believe completely because when they mentioned his name to me, I assumed that he was good only in diagnosing illnesses, but I did not know that he was also a healer. So I said to myself, "What do I have to lose? Let us try and see. Why, I said to myself, hadn't I thought of him before?" '

Mrs Katina brought the X-ray plates and we examined them together. I asked her whether I could keep them for a few days. She was so confident that her ordeal was over that she even let me keep them. She also gave me all the medical documents in regard to her illness. I promised to return them in case she ever needed them. As far as I know, Mrs Katina has had no relapse of her problem. The last time I saw her was at Daskalos' one month after her cure. She brought a friend of hers who also suffered from a spinal ailment. Although I was not a witness to that episode, I was told that Daskalos cured her, too. She was an English woman who was unable to coordinate her movements and could not walk straight. Again doctors had not helped, in spite of several operations.

I had witnessed earlier a similar impressive case of healing performed on a seventy-year-old woman. The doctors gave up on her as in the case of Mrs Katina. The contact with Daskalos was again made through me. As the patient was unable to walk we had to carry her in our arms. After her cure she began to move about freely without assistance. Although complete recovery, Daskalos stated, was impossible because of her advanced age, 80 percent of her problem was gone. From an almost total paralysis she now found herself able even to go swimming at the beach.

Such healing phenomena, although well documented, are

often ignored by scientists. There seems to be no available scientific theory to explain them, or to explain them away. I began to realize that what I had observed in Mrs Katina's case could not be understood within the existing scientific frameworks. For example, the element of autosuggestion did not seem to be a powerful and determining component in her sudden recovery.

Students of non-medical healing have argued that such phenomena could best be explained as a form of suggestion and autosuggestion, operating within a common cultural framework of understanding and belief shared by the therapist and his client. Most traditional or faith healers usually operate within a supportive cultural environment and healing ceremonies are charged with high drama and emotion. Daskalos acted more like a maverick within a cultural setting that was far from being supportive to his work or world view. Quite often the patients themselves would hide from their friends and relatives their visits to the 'Magus of Strovolos.' Daskalos once complained to me that sometimes he felt as if he were plowing on a barren rocky terrain.

From my point of view the case of Mrs Katina was exceptional, not only because of the circumstances of her sudden recovery, but most importantly because I had in my possession her case history and the X-rays. It was the type of empirical evidence that could undermine even the most devout skepticism. I thought Mrs Katina's case would qualify to be classified among those few instances that Jerome Frank, an authority on non-medical healing, calls 'truly miraculous.' In his *Persuasion and Healing* he argues that some individuals seem to have a gift of healing that defies scientific explanation. He goes on to say that one should not discount the possibility, as the evidence is ample, that some healers may serve as a kind of conduit for a healing force in the Universe sometimes called the 'life force.' For lack of a better term, he proposes that it must be called 'supernatural.'

I met Daskalos the day after I had the encounter with Mrs Katina during one of his regular meetings with his students. Coincidentally the topic was on healing and the role of the psychotherapist.

'All illnesses,' Daskalos began after he conducted the short prayer, 'are the result of psychonoetic conditions. You may wonder about the effects of viruses. As medical science shows, microorganisms and viruses exist in abundant supply within the body of every human being. Why then are some of us more immune to these organisms whereas others are so vulnerable? The etheric energy needed to keep the body in balance drops considerably when we vibrate improperly. A certain amount of etheric vibrations, say one hundred, is required for the Holy Spirit to create the cells, tissues and various organs of the material body. Our etheric energy is depleted when our desires and thoughts are such that create in us the vibrations of anxiety, depression, stubbornness, anger, hatred and similar morbid emotions. Therefore, we may only have eighty or sixty units out of the one hundred that we hypothetically need as etheric vitality to keep the body in balance. Automatically we notice that the most sensitive parts of our body begin to manifest the lack of an adequate supply of vitality. When an individual gets sufficient amounts of etheric energy through proper nutrition, breathing and way of living his personality should enjoy full health. The aura of such an individual radiates over a large area and gets absorbed often by those who need it. Such individuals benefit from the mere presence of a Researcher of Truth.

'You are probably aware that certain people generate in us positive vibrations whereas others may generate the exact opposite. The joy we experience in the presence of certain people is the result of an abundant supply of etheric vitality they emanate. Others who lack in vitality draw from our own reservoir or etheric energy. A Researcher of Truth who wants to be of service must keep his aura clear and radiating. Even when he feels drained by a fellow human being who absorbs from his vitality he should not reject him. These are the people that need our help most.

'It is etheric vitality that keeps us in good health and we must be ready to provide it for those in need. When we pray to God and ask for "our daily bread" in reality we are asking for life-giving ether. It is not bread we are praying for. Etheric vitality is required not only to keep the material body in good health but also to maintain our psychic and noetic bodies.' There was a moment's pause while Daskalos waited in anticipation of questions from the audience.

'What is the role of prayer,' someone asked, 'as a preparation for therapy?'

'I am not underestimating the importance of prayer. It could be a method of self-concentration in order for the therapist to enter into the state of mind which will permit him to be of help. As for myself it is sufficient to think, "Thy Will be done . . ." and proceed with the therapy. However, a Researcher of Truth must pray uninterruptedly. His every thought must be a continuous thanksgiving to the Absolute. Every one of his actions must be an expression of prayer. This is what Saint Paul had in mind when he admonished that we should "pray unceasingly." The psychotherapist, Researcher of Truth, must pray unceasingly through his actions, thoughts and feelings. When we are attuned to the Divine we need not spend time in prayer before therapy. Pay attention. Real prayer is not words. By themselves words mean nothing. It is actions and readiness to be of service that count. When we promise as Researchers of Truth to spend a few minutes each night in self-analysis is this not in essence a form of prayer? Our self-analysis, however, must not be accompanied by masochistic tendencies and feelings of guilt. The moment the Researcher of Truth feels guilty and sinful he is in no position to help others. I am telling you such masochistic tendencies that we see in many super-stitiously religious persons are nothing more than a form of mental malady. During our self-analysis we must be able to identify such tendencies and eradicate them. We must use our reason and fight such illusions and prejudices. For if you as present personalities do not reach a certain state of balance within life, how do you expect to help a troubled fellow human being who lives in a chaos of despair and illusion? Our work as therapists is not only on the etheric-double of the material body. We should also be ready to alleviate pain that exists on the psychonoetic level.

'Many healers assume that they can help only a certain number of people per day. They believe that their etheric energy is limited and could be depleted. This is an illusion. They simply create through autosuggestion an elemental which obstructs their road to healing. I assure you the more people you help, the more you fill up with vitality, assuming that you have love in your heart.'

Daskalos went on to say that a clairvoyant can 'see' on the aura of the person where the deficiency in vitality exists. Then with appropriate concentration the healer can fill up the space on the etheric-double of the patient that exemplifies the deficiency. He stated that it is possible for a healer to see such a deficiency on the etheric-double of the patient even though the problem has not as yet manifested itself on the gross material level. Consequently it becomes possible to foresee and prevent the manifestation of a physical ailment. A problem may appear on the aura of a prospective patient long before it expresses itself on the material body. Daskalos then recounted an experience he had with a sufi who was on a visit to Cyprus to see him.

'We were chatting in my living room when he stopped the conversation and mentioned that a cat was outside in the street. He concentrated and with his thought brought the cat next to my doorstep. Then with a sudden movement of his head he caused the cat to drop dead. I protested and demanded an explanation of why he had killed the poor animal. He explained that on the aura of the cat he saw a dangerous infectious disease. By killing it he prevented the spreading of an epidemic. What particularly impressed me was his power in foreseeing the evil potential resting on the aura of the cat. The body of the cat itself showed no signs of disease. I admired this sufi. We learned a lot from each other.'

I asked Daskalos whether he can ascertain in advance whether a specific case is amenable to cure or not. I asked this question because I was particularly impressed with his healing successes. I wondered whether he would claim that he was able to foresee whether the Karma of a patient would permit cure and then act accordingly. I do not recall any case when Daskalos intervened without at least partial success. In the case of Mrs Katina, for example, I was certain that he knew in advance that she would be on her feet that very morning. On other occasions Daskalos would flatly state that the case was hopeless but that he would still try anyway. As a rule his predictions were valid in both instances.

'You must always bear in mind that every feat of healing presupposes coordination with the Holy Spirit. We are simply the conduit of the Divine Plan. Success is not in our hands. The Researcher of Truth must, therefore, overcome the egotistical tendency of expecting cure whenever he lays his hands on a patient. All we can do is try to help and carry on with our duties and responsibilities. Occasionally you may witness healing phenomena that could shake you out of your wits. By simply laying your hand on a wound, for example, you may be able to speed up the healing process and cure a wound in a matter of moments. It is possible, however, that we may not be allowed to accomplish the most simple form of cure. To have a cure is more natural than not to have one. It is easier to succeed because it is the wish of the Absolute and of the Holy Spirit. When cure does not take place it implies that there is a karmic debt that cannot be overcome.'

'Is it not possible to know right from the beginning whether Karma will permit a cure and then act?' I probed further.

'No, this is not permissible. As I have already explained, the decision as to whether cure will take place is beyond our power. We as therapists should always be ready to offer our etheric energy to help someone in need. By our mere wish to be of help we automatically create a therapeutic elemental which remains on the aura of the patient. He may not perceive any immediate results but the elemental will stay on his aura. The karmic debt may be overcome at any moment in the future. When this happens the elemental will be activated and bring about the cure. For this reason no matter how many times a patient comes to you for help you must never refuse. We must be willing to repeat the same work without any concern as to whether therapy will take place or not. In our readiness to help the person we provide extra etheric energy that strengthens the therapeutic elemental resting on his aura. At no time did a therapist with a genuine wish to help another human being fail to do so physically or psychically.'

'Skeptics would say that healing is possible only because the patient himself believes in the healer and that cure results from powerful suggestions and autosuggestions. How do you confront this issue?' I asked again.

'They are right to a certain extent. Suggestion and autosuggestion are often the necessary conditions that can lead to therapy. The state of our health is after all the product of our thoughts and emotions. I am currently faced with great difficulties trying to help a policeman suffering from polio for the last twenty-five years. His indulgence in fantasies often become noxious autosuggestions which undermine his physical well being. We meet every week but whatever I create he destroys with his ill temper. I try to impress upon him that his attitude burns his etheric energy and prevents his cure. He doubts whether he can recover quickly. The doubt acts as a form of negative autosuggestion that retards his recovery.

'Let me now compare his case to that of an illiterate farmer. He claimed that one day as he was riding his tractor he was touched by something evil. As a result of this self-induced negative suggestion he became paralyzed. The doctors diagnosed his problem as multiple sclerosis. Nonsense. Whenever they fail to find the real cause of a problem they cook up a word and leave it at that. For three years this man remained in a wheelchair. He was a psychological ruin. He had five children to feed and his brother, who took over his tractor, gave him very little money. Eventually this farmer rebelled. One night while he was asleep his subconscious came in contact with mine. He saw my face and a voice in the dream urged him to go to the "Magus of Strovolos" who could cure him. I remember it was one o'clock in the morning when I heard knocks on my door. He came in his wheelchair along with his wife, brother and oldest son. He kept staring at me. "It is you!" he said with a stupefied look on his face. "What do you want from me?" I responded. "This son of a bitch brother of mine," he replied, "has been exploiting me for the last three years. He uses my tractor and gives me bread crumbs. I want to work for the sake of my children. I want to mount my tractor like before and go to work. I want to give him employment and not have to rely on his charity. I will get well. I know I will get well. That's why I came here." He was full of confidence and enthusiasm that he was in fact going to get cured. A healer must never allow such an opportunity to pass by. So I said, "Of course you will get well. Can you tell me how? I know, myself, but I also want you to tell me." "Come near me," he said. "Put your left hand on my shoulder and the other hand underneath and order me to stand up and I will stand up." Without losing a single moment I did exactly what he asked me to do. When I said, "Stand up

and walk," he got out of his wheelchair and began walking. He
took a few steps straight toward his brother and hit him on the
knee with his fist. "I am walking now, you son of a bitch," he
said to him. "Tomorrow I will be riding the tractor." He
looked at me and said, "What do you want me to do now?"
"Listen friend," I said, "tonight before you go to sleep I want
you to go to church and light a candle in front of the icon of
the Holy Virgin and that of Christ." "Why, is it necessary?" he
asked in surprise. "Yes. They made you well," I said. I
preferred that his faith rest upon something beyond the human,
beyond me, upon something transcendental. It would be
beneficial for his subconscious. In reality this is the Reality. The
next day he mounted his tractor. He has been working for three
years now without any problems. Where is the multiple
sclerosis?' Daskalos concluded with irony.

  'Is it possible to heal someone who does not believe or has
doubts?' I asked.

  'Yes, assuming that his subconscious does not interfere. I
prefer that such a person be unaware of my attempt to heal
him. When he is in a peaceful and receptive state of mind I can
have influence over him in the same way that the Holy Spirit
has an influence over his body in healing a wound. You will
learn that as a rule those who suffer do not help you at all
during the healing. In the great majority of cases they have
doubts. "How can this be possible?" is their first reaction. Do
not give them time to indulge in such doubts. You will often
have to carry on the healing without their being aware of what
you are doing.'

  Daskalos mentioned that when the individual is not in a
receptive mood he fortifies himself with elementals around him
that prevent the healing energy from penetrating his aura. He
advised his students that whenever they do healing, they should
make sure that non-believers are not present because with their
thoughts such people create negative elementals that may
interfere with the cure. Contrariwise, persons in attendance
with a supportive frame of mind can create vibrations that may
assist the healer with the therapy. When the psychotherapist
has sufficient power he may be in a position to neutralize
negative elementals created either by the patient or those in
attendance. It is always better, however, that the patient enter

into a receptive mood through appropriate suggestions by the healer and through autosuggestions on the patient's part. I had been earlier informed of an episode as to how Daskalos healed a cripple whom he accidentally met at a sea resort. Daskalos and Theophanis spent a day at the beach. As they were sun bathing they noticed a man in a wheelchair gazing at the horizon. They approached him and engaged him in a prolonged conversation. After they convinced him of their power to cure him, they proceeded right there and they were able to get him out of the wheelchair. His handicap was gone and he walked home.

Daskalos went on to argue that to become an effective healer you must become master of the different properties of the etheric-double. Unless one does that, he said, one can only have limited success. Many healers are not aware of what they do and often appear to behave hysterically in a healing session. They work in the dark. Daskalos did not discount the importance of 'blind faith' in healing. But we, he said, as Researchers of Truth must know what we are doing.

'Let me tell you of an experience I had with an English woman, a practicing healer in London, who visited me recently. She was present when someone suffering from acute arthritis came to see me. She asked whether I would let her take care of that case. I said, "Fine, go ahead. You can do it." The hand of the patient was swollen and his fingers were hurting a lot. She closed her eyes and began moving her hand up and down hysterically. Perhaps that was her way of gaining confidence and faith. "Move away, Daskale," she demanded, "because I will shake the evil off." She believed that she was "shaking" the evil off from his hand. She did succeed in curing the man. After he left I asked her to explain to me what she had done. "I removed the evil," she said. She was unaware that in reality, through the kinetic property of ether, she had transferred etheric energy. She placed herself in a semihypnotic state without being aware of it. Perhaps the patient, who was watching with his mouth open, was also semihypnotized. "Why did you shake your hand?" I asked. "Oh," she replied, "I had to throw the evil away." "Where? On the floor, on the marbles?" She was successful but she did not know why.

'As Researchers of Truth we must be fully conscious of what

we are doing. It is a much more powerful and effective way to healing than such hysterical methods that may cause healing phenomena to happen but may also create unnecessary disturbance within the subconscious. Most healers in Europe and elsewhere are not familiar with the nature and functions of the etheric-double. Their work is through blind faith. That is why their healing successes are often limited. For example, to be able to heal a broken spine one has to know not only how to master the various properties of ether but one must also learn human anatomy. Just today I took care of the spinal problems of a patient. Two sisters [students] were present and helped me out.'

Apparently Daskalos was alluding to another case similar to the one I had witnessed. The two sisters he referred to were present at the meeting and nodded affirmatively.

'This patient's vertebrae were out of position and she had terrible pains in her legs. In such a case the most a faith healer could do would probably be to remove the pain for a few days. It would be very difficult to handle such a problem through blind faith. It would be impossible to place the vertebrae in their right place unless one knows consciously how to employ etheric vitality and also have a knowledge of the structure of the spine.

'In this case, through the imprinting property of ether, we could create two etheric hands and place them inside the body of the patient. By mastering the sense property of ether, we could then feel on the edges of our etheric fingers the spinal problem and move the vertebrae into their proper place. Four hands are now at work, the material hands outside the body, and the etheric hands inside.'

Daskalos has repeatedly elaborated that etheric energy has four properties working simultaneously: the kinetic, sensate, imprinting and creative. The kinetic property is that which makes possible the ability of movement, such as blood flow, heart beat, pulsation of the lungs, movement of limbs, metabolism and so on. The sensate property is that part of the ether that makes possible the existence of sense experience, feelings and sentiments. The imprinting property enables us to construct noetic images, that is, it makes possible thought itself as well as phenomena such as telepathy, telekinesis and exomatosis. The creative property of ether is what makes possible the construction and maintenance of the body.

Without the creative property of ether, Daskalos went on to argue, no therapy could take place. He advised his students not to be preoccupied with this property of ether for the time being which, according to him, comes under the direct supervision and control of the Holy Spirit. Instead, he urged them to become masters, first, of the imprinting, kinetic and sense properties of etheric vitality.

'You should master these properties of ether by exercising with the construction of live and powerful visual images that can be applied in therapy. The moment you create such benign elementals they become automatically charged with the creative properties of ether which are the province of the Holy Spirit and of the Christ Logos. For the next fifteen days I would like you to do the following exercise. Close your eyes and see with your etheric eyes that you hold in your right hand a luminous ball of white light the size of a tennis ball. You are now exercising the imprinting property of ether. Feel it in your hand. It is alive and it vibrates with luminosity. This will train you in mastering the sense property of ether. What you have created is an elemental of thought-desire that can be used for therapy at a distance. Think of a person who is suffering from some illness and send this ball of light to cover his entire body. Now you are exercising the kinetic property of ether. The greater your ability to concentrate on the formation of this elemental, the greater its therapeutic value. The Holy Spirit will automatically fill this ball of light with creative energy.'

Daskalos then went on to argue that mastering the sense property of ether is crucial to determining a patient's problem from a distance. By holding his photograph one can come in contact with his magnetism and 'feel' the vibrations of that individual. A diagnosis of his problem can then follow.

Daskalos ended his talk. The tape recorders went off and everybody in the room began getting ready to leave. I had a last question and the tape recorders went on again. My query was in reference to the role of colors in therapy. Daskalos had repeatedly argued that therapy from a distance is possible by creating elementals of various colors that can be sent to patients. Presumably for each disease there is an appropriate color that a healer could project through thought.

'Do colors,' I inquired, 'have therapeutic qualities in themselves or do they bring about therapeutic effects because the healer himself imbues them with healing power?'

'First of all, colors do not exist,' Daskalos replied in no uncertain terms. 'There are only etheric vibrations that offer us the impression of colors. Color is also sound, light, movement, and a number of other things.

'When I say, for example, this color is red, it simply means that my eye absorbs the irritation of this frequency of vibrations which hits a part of my brain. The present self-conscious personality then interprets this irritation as red color. Whatever gives us the same vibration in our environment will create for us exactly this feeling of redness. Everything that exists is the result of frequencies of vibrations, including the composition of matter.

'We have observed that specific vibration frequencies and corresponding centers of the brain bring about certain results, say tranquility and calmness. We then conclude that this particular color has these qualities. We have noticed, for example, that there is a correspondence between the sentiment of altruistic love and that vibration which gives us the impression of the white-rose light. If you ask me why the vibrations that give me the feeling of white-rose light calm me down, I could not answer. I don't believe anyone can answer such a question. But I have this to add. A color that may calm one person could have the opposite effect on another. However, we can say that in general a color like the white-rose can have a soothing effect on most people. But if you cover a room with a white-rose color and place there a very nervous individual, that person may become more intense. I remember a case of a married couple that almost divorced because the wife painted the bedroom with such a color. Why did that color upset her husband? I was aware that earlier in his life he had fallen in love with a girl who habitually used to offer him a fragrant rose. Later they broke off the relationship. So the white-rose color subconsciously reminded him of a pain he had experienced in the past.

'In answer to your question, therefore, I have to add that in reality it is not only the vibrations that are responsible for a certain effect, but also the way we perceive things. In general terms, however, we have noticed that specific colors have a corresponding effect on the majority of individuals. In situations when you are not certain as to what color to project, simply send a ball of white light to the patient. That ball can envelop parts of his body or the entire body. When we deal with a specific disease and we know the appropriate color, then we employ that color. For example, in cases of anemia we could project with our minds white-rose or orange color. Never send red. Red will cause nervousness, confusion and despair. We should also never send red to someone suffering from high blood pressure. Deep red is permitted only on certain occasions and in small doses. In cases of cancer we will project a ball radiating violet color and place it inside the center of the tumor. We will keep it there until it destroys the tumor. Then we must remove this color elemental and destroy it. As a general rule of thumb, you should know that white is the safest color to use in any therapy. We never harm anybody when we project a vibrant white ball of light.'

Daskalos ended the lesson by urging his students to practice their meditation exercises and to systematically spend a few minutes every night in self-analysis. 'You must kill every trace of egotism from your personality.' It was an admonition that Daskalos repeated with monotonous frequency.

I made arrangements to meet with him the following day to continue the discussion on healing. I had many more questions to ask on the subject, particularly as it pertained to Mrs Katina's case. Daskalos was always willing to offer me 'private lessons.'

13
Materialization and Dematerialization

When I visited Daskalos it was nine in the morning. I found him watering his plants. He probably had the most varied and exotic collection of cacti on the island and he was very fond of them. 'This cactus,' he told me with pride, 'comes from the Amazon, a gift from an anthropologist friend of mine. This one is from Arizona, that one from Africa. . . .' I followed him about listening to his botanical lecture on the many varieties and attributes of cacti. 'This cactus,' he said, pointing at a large, round and menacing-looking creature, 'could harm you if you touch it unless you show it affection.' Daskalos then humorously described how one day he took it to a florist in order to find a special nutrient for it. The shopkeeper warned him never to touch that cactus because it is alive and the moment one lays a hand on it its prickles penetrate the flesh. Daskalos deliberately grabbed the cactus with his palm in front of the stupefied florist and kept it there for a couple of minutes. With a soft voice he then asked the plant, 'Let me go now, my love,' and the cactus opened up and let Daskalos remove his hand unharmed.

With the plants watered, we sat down and I began asking questions about the miraculous healing I had witnessed the other day.

'You must understand,' he said, 'that there was nothing miraculous about that case. If you call that a miracle, then all life should be considered a miracle. I simply mastered certain forces in Nature and applied them for healing purposes. I have become the cable through which that superintelligence, the Holy Spirit, works.' Daskalos then mentioned that the case I had witnessed the other day involved materialization and dematerialization. 'Materialization means harnessing and consolidating the substance by which matter is formed. What is this substance? The scientists call it energy, we call it vitality,

189

the Hindus call it Prana. Conversely, dematerialization means the transmutation of solid matter into energy or vitality. It is the release of harnessed and solidified vitality. Scientists can now transform matter into energy. We mystics have our own methods. We accomplish such feats by the sheer force of the will.

'Materialization and dematerialization have been experienced all through the ages in every corner of the Earth. Throughout the centuries mystics were able to materialize and dematerialize objects. We find such cases in the Bible, in the Old Testament, in the sacred books of Asia, of America, of the Aztecs ... It means that these phenomena are not the result of fraud or superstition. They are part of Reality. Most of the miracles of Jesus Christ were cases of materialization and dematerialization. One such case is when He harnessed energy from the universe and solidified it into fish and bread in order to feed the multitude.'

'When you say Jesus harnessed energy from the universe, do you imply the universe of the three dimensions?'

'No. I mean all the universes. We must not confine energy into invisible matter or substance of the three dimensional world. Because even invisible matter belongs to the three-dimensional world. We have also the fourth-dimensional, fifth-dimensional, the sixth- and seventh-dimensional universes. The mystic is working with his superconsciousness from these higher dimensions. Therefore to become master of materialization and dematerialization, one must develop and become master of his superconsciousness. To affect gross matter you must work from a higher dimension.'

'Are you saying that to harness this vitality and transform it into solid matter one has to work from within the fourth-dimensional, or psychic world?'

'Not exactly. Vitality exists in all the dimensions of Reality. You can get it from everywhere and then transmute it into hard solids.'

'How?'

'You must start working from the highest dimensions and descend through the lower levels until you reach the gross material plane. You must begin from the higher noetic world, the world of ideas, laws, causes, the world of noumena. From there on you proceed to lower the vibrations. You pass through the lower noetic world, the world of images and forms. Then you reach the psychic plane and further down you arrive at solid matter.'

Daskalos mentioned that he himself brought his abilities from previous incarnations. He did not acquire them in his present life. However, the first step in mastering such abilities presupposes learning how to concentrate and how to overcome one's egotism.

'One must set aside his present personality expressed as egotism and discover the real self within. He must also become master of his material body and its etheric counterpart. He has to learn how to work on the etheric-double, which is the invisible material part of oneself. The Researcher of Truth must become master of the various properties of ether or vitality, that is the kinetic property, the sense property, the imprinting property and the creative property, the latter being the most difficult. For example, you must learn how to create, through the imprinting property of the etheric-double, noetic images. It implies learning how to transform the formless vitality or substance of Mind which is everywhere within the universes into thought forms. Unless you master thought you can accomplish nothing. It means in reality mastering the power of concentration. If you are to materialize an object, you must first construct it in your mind and through undistracted intense concentration you charge it with etheric vitality. But with the slightest distraction the materialization vanishes. You must understand that the key to mastering matter is in concentration.'

'It is the most important quality of the mind,' I commented. 'Without concentration you cannot achieve anything in this life, period.'

'Good. This is particularly so in other dimensions of existence and is a precondition for becoming a psychotherapist.'

Daskalos then went on to elaborate on the differences between clairvoyance, exomatosis, and 'expansion' as various abilities of the mystic important in healing. I had had the opportunity to discuss with him on an earlier occasion the subject of clairvoyance and exomatosis but not that of 'expansion.' I asked for clarification.

'Clairvoyance means receiving vibrations from somewhere

which are then translated as "seeing." One may, for example, perceive clearly some event that takes place in London. That event is perceived in a similar manner as a television program from London. Clairvoyance means attuning oneself to vibrations of noetic or astral light, making possible perception of scenes from distant places.

'A more advanced mystic has other means of getting information. He can expand in space. Everything takes place within his consciousness. Whatever he receives and perceives is from himself. This is what we call expansion.'

'How is expansion different from exomatosis?' I probed.

'Expansion is a form of exomatosis but of a different quality. In ordinary exomatosis a master transports his consciousness to the place where he wants to work or get experiences. In expansion, however, a master spreads out his consciousness and brings everything within himself. Though he may cover a distance, still that distance is within him. We could call it exomatosis in the absence of a better term but I would rather call it expansion. In such a state of consciousness a mystic can receive vibrations simultaneously from several places, experience them all, feel them all, without confusion. It is a form of superconsciousness.

'Clairvoyance, exomatosis and expansion,' explained Daskalos, 'are different abilities and stages in the development of the mystic. Some mystics can use all three forms of psychic experience, others the first or second. The most difficult and most advanced of the three stages is expansion. To affect animate or inanimate matter presupposes the development of the third stage of psychic mastery.'

Many years back Daskalos had tried through expansion to experiment with the transmutation of metals. I assumed that it was a form of alchemy but Daskalos denied it.

'I wanted to transmute the twenty-karat gold wedding ring of my wife into silver. I placed the ring on the table and next to it a piece of silver, specifically a two-shilling coin. I then came out of my body and disconnected the link between my psychonoetic body and my material body.'

'Why was it necessary to do that?'

'Because the vibrations created through my will power were so intense that my body could have been burned. That is why I had to temporarily suspend the communication between the material body and the psychonoetic. In addition I had to abandon my psychic body and work only with the noetic. I had no need to go any higher, I was still in the world of forms and images. Through my noetic body I implanted my consciousness within the ring and observed the behavior of atoms. This is a form of expansion in consciousness; it is another ability of the mystic. He can come out of his body and rest on the petal of a flower and perceive it as a lawn, a long road or the runway of an airport. He may become smaller than an atom and observe its behavior yet it is always he, full and complete. Similarly he can expand within a city and be aware of whatever goes on within it. He can even expand within the entire solar system and beyond it, losing nothing of himself. He will not become bigger or smaller. There is no fear, therefore, of losing oneself, of becoming larger or smaller. By concentrating on a grain of sand it is no different than perceiving or expanding on a planet. Do you understand now what is implied when they chant in church "in His Universes"? The Pan-universal Logos is perfect and complete in His absolute superconsciousness within a grain of sand as well as within a galaxy.

'When I entered inside the ring I observed the behavior of the atoms. I saw the nucleus of the atom much more clearly than any scientific instrument could ever help me see. I noticed everything, the velocity of the electrons, their number within each atom of gold and their distance from one another. Then I came out of the gold ring and entered inside the silver coin. I made the same observations and noticed the difference between the atomic structure of gold and that of silver. Then I returned to the ring. Through my will power and concentration I was able to rearrange the atomic structure of a single gold atom so that it conformed with that of silver. By transforming a single atom a chain reaction was set into motion and eventually all the other atoms changed in the same direction. I then re-entered the silver coin and changed one silver atom into gold. Believe me it is not through fantasy that you achieve that. It is through observation and the power of creative thought.

'When I came out of the ring and returned to my body, the gold ring was still gold and the silver coin was still silver. Several of my students were present during the experiment.

They pointed out that nothing had happened. "No," I insisted, "the gold ring is now turning silver. Just wait awhile." They took it in their hands. It was still gold. A few seconds passed and I asked them to throw it down and concentrate on the sound of the ring. They followed my directions and after several repetitions they began to distinguish a marked change in the sound. The gold ring gradually became silver in their hands and the silver coin was transformed into gold. The following day I changed them back to their original state. You see, the transmutation of gold into silver or vice versa is a temporary state. Eventually the transmuted metals reverse to their natural condition.'

'Why is that so?'

'I do not know. Suppose I kept the ring in its silver state. In a year or two it would have become gold again. It would do so because it obeys the laws of the material universe.'

'But you said before that you were working within the laws of the universe?'

'Exactly. In this particular case the law means that if you transmute silver into gold or gold into silver, it will eventually return to its original state. Why? I have no idea.'

Daskalos then added humorously that someone he knew, after learning of the experiment, knocked at his door carrying along several bars of lead. He wanted Daskalos to transform them into gold. Daskalos got angry and sent him away.

'On a different occasion,' Daskalos went on, 'I wished to experiment with living substance and transmute it into inanimate substance. The moment that is achieved, living matter can no longer regain its original form. For example, if a plant is transformed into brass it can never return to life again. It will remain brass. I got a small branch of olive tree and a piece of rose bush. I placed next to them a piece of brass, a piastre coin. I followed the same method as before. When I woke up, the olive branch was still olive branch and the piece of rose bush was still a rose bush. But within minutes they were transformed into brass. I had turned living matter into inanimate matter. In reality, of course, there is no dead matter. Strictly speaking, all matter is alive. Anything that exists and vibrates is alive.

'A few days later a student of mine visited me. He taught

physics at the gymnasium. My wife, who had a habit of talking too much, mentioned to him what happened and showed him the leaves turned into brass. He lost no time. He booked a plane and went to Athens to see a professor of chemistry at the university. He brought the leaves along with him. He explained to this professor what he had seen and heard. The chemist responded: "Your master is a good hypnotist and a trickster and made you see what he wanted you to see." That professor thought that he had in his hands the evidence to expose a vagabond. He decided to test the leaves and reasoned that if his tests proved that it was chlorophyll transformed into brass, then it would have meant that the leaves were genuine. Otherwise they would be nothing more than good craftsmanship. He was shocked to find out that the leaves were indeed genuine. He rushed to Cyprus to visit me. "Sir," he said, "in the name of science I demand an explanation." "And I, sir," I replied, "show you the door and ask you to leave." '

'Why did you do that, Daskale?' I protested.

' "You are blind in your mind," I said to him. "In spite of your pride and fame, you cannot see the relevance of this phenomenon to the Divine." '

'You could have persuaded him with your arguments,' I persisted.

'He would have manufactured other explanations and idiocies. "What does God have to do with this?" he said. "If you cannot understand what life is," I replied, "I cannot explain to you what happened." I could have offered him an explanation which he would most probably have misunderstood and dismissed as nonsense. I just did not like his arrogance and pomposity.'

'Did you not say to me sometime ago that you would rather discuss such matters with rational and well-intentioned atheists than with religious fanatics?'

'With well-intentioned atheists I would. He was not one of them. He was a fanatical atheist like a religious zealot. He was not in a position to understand. I could not have convinced him of the existence of God even if I had presented God in front of him. "Don't talk to me about God," he said. "What does God mean? These are mysteries about the properties of matter that eventually will be explained by science. Everything else is coincidence. It is as if a glass breaks by itself and we cannot explain why it breaks." Since he was incapable of understanding, he could not perceive the nature of the laws at work. He was blind. He should, himself, have come to the understanding of the reality of God after studying the phenomenon. Had he been a person who came to me, not with humility towards me but towards the phenomenon he had witnessed, I would have helped him understand. I could not demand of him to accept a Christ who was born inside a stall with horses or to espouse a superstitious form of religious belief. Neither did I expect him to believe in an anthropomorphic God enthroned upon the clouds. But given what he saw, I expected him to be open to the possibility of an absolute intelligence behind the phenomenal world. That is why I had to send him away. You cannot convince people of the reality of the Absolute with phenomena. A mystic should avoid demonstrating his powers. Magicians can, through tricks, duplicate what a master can do. But no magician can heal a wound, remove a tumor or fix a broken spine. There is no sense in approaching a person unless he has reached a certain stage in his spiritual evolution, when he himself feels the need for knowing the Truth. When people reach that state of consciousness they will come to you. One does not chase people imploring them to have a glass of water. When they are thirsty they will ask for it themselves. There is no need, therefore, to explain to people who have no other motivation than simple curiosity about such phenomena. Those who are merely curious I send away. Those who have a genuine desire for knowledge I take by the hand and guide them into the mysteries in accordance with their abilities and level of understanding.'

After a half-hour break when Daskalos was giving advice to someone on the phone, we resumed our discussion. I asked Daskalos whether the case of Mrs Katina involved a form of materialization and dematerialization.

'It was that and more,' he replied.

Daskalos made use, in her case, of his etheric hands to dematerialize excessive tiny bones (*exosteosis*) that had accumulated around her spine causing extreme pain.

'By creating the etheric hands I was able to feel these little bones and then dematerialize them. I also had to create a new bone because as you may have seen on the X-ray plate, her spine was full of porosity at different spots. The bone was falling apart. Through materialization I created solid bone, a form of living matter.'

'Before you could accomplish this type of materialization, did you have to have an exact vision of what to create?' I asked.

'Definitely. I also had to first see, through her skin, what her problem was. In what way, you may ask, did I see, using my eyes? No. If I so wish I can see into your body with closed eyes. I can expand myself, enter inside the patient, and see everything in that person from all sides at the same time. I can close my eyes, for example, touch my hands to his side and examine the conditions of his kidneys. Are the molecules of my hands eyes to see? No. Yet I can see through, at any point I concentrate on, the patient's body or the body of any person.'

'Every molecule of your body becomes an eye,' I added.

'Exactly. But not only that. I can concentrate my eyes and enter inside you. I can expand and bring you within myself. I can expand in this room and whatever is here will be within me and I can observe it in me from every side. People come to me and tell me their problems. They sit on a chair in front of me, they talk, and I listen. While they do so I expand. I bring them within me so that I can feel and observe anything I want within their bodies and discover what their problems are. This is precisely how I cured your friend who had the accident.'

Stelios, a close friend of mine, had an auto accident that almost cost his life. When I visited him with Daskalos he was already out of the hospital and recuperating at home. He complained of persistent pains on the right-hand side below the navel. While Stelios was explaining his problem Daskalos appeared to focus his gaze on him. Then he explained that what caused the pain was a crushed gland that had to be removed lest it become carcinogenous. Then Daskalos abruptly stood up and asked me to follow him to the next room. 'Since you are eager to witness phenomena,' he said with mischief in his voice, 'let me show you one.' He unbuckled his belt, pulled up his shirt, pushed his pants low on his right side, and asked me to touch him on the spot where Stelios complained of pains. I saw and felt an inflated gland below the navel on Daskalos' right side. It was Stelios' gland, he explained, which he had dematerialized from my friend's body and transferred into himself. 'He is freed of his problem now,' he said. 'His cancerous gland is in me now. I will get rid of it gradually at my own pace.'

I was in no way able to determine whether my friend's gland was actually transferred into Daskalos' body! Unlike Mrs Katina's case, for which I had held the empirical evidence in my hands, there was no way to test and ascertain whether Daskalos' diagnosis of Stelios' problem was valid and whether cure had actually taken place. Daskalos was not the least concerned as to whether I was convinced or not. I must admit the thought crossed my mind that perhaps the inflated gland was already in Daskalos' body before we arrived at my friend's home, that it was pure coincidence. But one thing was clear. My friend was relieved of his pain after our visit. Furthermore, I had no doubt that Daskalos was not trying to fool or deceive me with 'phenomena' so that I might be impressed. I had observed him in many instances of healing not to be unduly suspicious as I had been at the beginning of our acquaintance. By this time I had developed great respect for and admiration of Daskalos' healing powers.

Daskalos went on as he referred to my friend's case, 'I noticed the cancerous gland during our conversation. While talking to you, part of my consciousness was focused on you. But at the same time another part of my consciousness was within his body observing and examining everything. How many people know what is taking place inside their own bodies? Once I expand I can be not only in my own body but also in your body, in everybody's body. When I noticed the gland, I had to dematerialize it in his body and then transfer it into myself so that I can gradually dissolve it.'

'Why was it necessary to take in into yourself?' I wondered.

'Had I dematerialized it that very moment when I noticed it, I would not have been able to dissolve it completely. It would most probably have reappeared later on. I had to transfer it into myself and quietly dematerialize it completely. Many healers do not know the appropriate method of dematerializing cancerous tumors. They may bring about a cure but in the course of time the problem could reappear. One has to learn the right way of healing. This is what we try to teach the would-be psychotherapist. As I mentioned, the most difficult but most successful method of healing is through expansion, namely bringing the entire body of the patient within my consciousness and working from within myself. The other method is to project an etheric hand, implant it within the body of the patient, and then proceed with dematerialization. This is not the safest and most effective method. I prefer to expand my consciousness and work from all sides at once.' Daskalos leaned back in his chair and paused for a few moments.

I was told by an eye witness that on one occasion Daskalos removed a cancerous tumor from the body of a woman and transferred it to the thumb of his left hand. His relatives wanted to rush him to the hospital and have the thumb amputated. He reassured them that in a few days the cancer would disappear. Indeed, in two days the tumor on his thumb was gone.

Daskalos claimed that one of the preconditions for mastering healing through expansion is the ability to truly love your fellow man. 'You must reach that state of consciousness,' he said, 'whereby you may "love thy neighbor as thyself." When you reach that state, healing is easy. Unless you genuinely love you cannot heal and you cannot accomplish much in the area of what people call the paranormal.'

'I suppose,' I pointed out, 'this is a safety valve on how much evil a black sorcerer can inflict.'

'The word "evil" means little to me,' Daskalos answered sharply. 'Who is really a black sorcerer but an ignorant fellow who has mastered certain forces in nature and misused them? What is considered as evil is, in reality, the wrong utilization of divine forces. That is why I consider the word "evil" inappropriate. When we speak of evil I prefer to imply the expression of oneself in an ignorant manner. In the course of time one learns through the law of cause and effect.'

'I suppose,' I ventured to add, 'this is what Socrates had in mind when he argued that nobody does evil knowingly.'

'Precisely. Evil is ignorance.'

'Daskale,' I asked, shifting the conversation back to the topic of materialization, 'is it possible for an advanced mystic to dematerialize himself or rematerialize at another place?' I raised this question because the notion of teleportation, no matter how bizarre it may sound, is considered a fact in the literature on occultism. For example, Castaneda reported that he experienced such a phenomenon while he was an apprentice to Don Juan. I also met an Indian professor of music, the husband of the Indian ambassadress to a European state, who confided in me in all seriousness that he had witnessed teleportation performed by an Indian yogi.

'Yes it is possible to dematerialize and rematerialize your body somewhere else,' Daskalos went on, 'but why do it that way? Why not construct and materialize another body by drawing energy from the universal ether?'

'You mean you can suddenly appear in front of me "just like that"?' I replied smiling.

'Exactly,' Daskalos replied seriously, as if this were a most common phenomenon. 'You can see me and shake hands with me, talk to me as if I were physically present. But I can only materialize myself when the masters from above permit it. There has to be a serious reason. I would not even have to interrupt what I might be preoccupied with at the moment. When you reach a certain stage of superconsciousness you can express yourself in several places simultaneously.'

'Have you had such experiences?'

'Yes, many times.'

'How were you able to verify to yourself that they were real experiences?'

'People saw me and then came to ask me questions. I have had repeated experiences of this type.' Upon my probing, Daskalos proceeded to narrate such an experience.

'One day I was writing a letter when I felt that someone in Karpasia, seventy miles away, was in distress and was planning to commit suicide. I received his vibrations subconsciously. I saw him leave the coffeeshop and walk slowly towards the pier. His intention was to throw himself into the sea. It was a stormy day. High winds were blowing and waves were crashing over the pier. In the few minutes it took him to reach his destination, I learned everything about him and the reasons that drove him to the brink of suicide. By coordinating myself with his mind I discovered that he was married to a Greek woman from another island and had three children by her. Her younger sister, who was on a visit to Cyprus, began having an affair with him. She was prettier and more seductive than his wife. The younger sister had no scruples that the man she was having the affair with was her sister's husband. In fact she wanted him to divorce his wife and then marry her. She persuaded him to abandon his wife and children and follow her to Greece. His wife knew of the affair and of their plans to elope. She was desperate. The man, not knowing what to do, since he still loved his family, decided, like a fool, to put an end to his life. This is what came to me in those few moments. You see, one must first develop the ability to feel and get information in a single moment that would normally require hours of conversation. As an invisible helper you know instantly what is happening to a person and you act with speed.'

'Had you never seen nor met these people before this episode?' I asked.

'Never.'

'Why should these impressions come to you?'

'I am not sure. Most likely other forces implanted them so that I would intervene and save his life. I had to act quickly. There was no time to waste. I materialized myself at the edge of the pier and suddenly appeared in front of him. I stood there dressed in my white robe. I raised my hands and cried out, "What are you doing?" He looked at me in a state of shock and turned pale. He could not believe his eyes. How could a man appear from the middle of nowhere on the edge of the pier splashed by waves in that most tempestuous night? "I don't know what to do," he muttered. "Go back to your wife and children," I commanded, "and send the other woman away." He covered his eyes with his hands, turned around and walked away. I then dematerialized instantly. He soon sent his sister-in-law back to Greece and lived peacefully with his family.

'Several months later some friends asked the man to drive them to Nicosia to visit the "Magus of Strovolos." His friends were afraid their child had epilepsy. They were wrong. The child had worms in the bowels. We healed the child. When they came to the house my wife opened the door. I was sitting in my study when they brought the child there. I happened to be wearing my white robe that day. When he saw my face he started to choke and began to tremble. "What is it?" I said. "Was it you?" he asked. I told him to keep silent and that we would talk later privately. When I finished with the child I took him by the arm and we went into another room. "Now," I said, "you are with your wife and children. Everything is fine, is it not? You sent the other woman away." He embraced me and began to cry. "I thought you were an angel sent by God to save my life for the love of my children," he said in tears. I explained the nature of our work and talked about the invisible helpers. "If God," I added, "sends angels to assist human beings, why can he not also send human beings to assist their own brethren?" That fellow became one of our most dedicated students in the circles for the Research of Truth. He is now living with his family in South Africa. Their children are grown up.

'Based on my own experience,' Daskalos began after a half-hour's break, 'I could identify three types of materialization. First, the invisible and tangible materialization. Second, the visible but intangible materialization. Third, the visible and tangible, or solid, materialization. The first type involves the construction of solid but invisible substance. It is the form of materialization that has the greatest force when working within the three dimensions. You can move objects, for example, that would normally require the combined strength of several men, such as a very heavy piece of furniture. Yet the hand or the force which causes the movement remains invisible to the material eye. It is this type of materialization that I used in the case that you know about, of the scissors.'

'In that episode, Daskale, could someone have seen your hand pushing the scissors from the top of the chest?'

'Probably not. It was invisible but tangible materialization, the type which is at work in the séance rooms in Europe. The second type of materialization, that is, visible but intangible, has no power to affect solid objects. You may see a hand floating or a person appearing in ghostly form. It might look like a mist in the image of solid matter. Yet you can pass your hand through it and not even notice it. The third kind of materialization is visible and solid. It is not always the most appropriate or desirable because it can harm the material body. For example, if you construct a visible and tangible materialization of your body from a distance and someone hits it, the wound will appear on your material body no matter how far away you may be. Whatever you inflict on the materialization will be transferred to the body. Actually such a risk exists to some extent in the case of invisible but tangible materialization. That is why one should make sure that one disconnects the communication between the materialization and one's body. For example, if you materialize on a battlefield and you are invisible you must disconnect that materialization from the etheric of your body so that bullets that may pierce it will not inflict wounds on the material body.

'There are also ways that one can employ to disconnect the communication between one's body and a materialization which is visible and tangible. Once that is achieved nothing can happen to one's body, otherwise it is very dangerous. On several occasions I failed to disconnect my body from my materialization and consequently I suffered from wounds inflicted on the materialization. One night, for example, I was sitting with my wife in our living room. It was midnight and I began to feel uneasy. I saw that one hundred miles away there was a ship in trouble. It was a small boat carrying cargo to nearby countries. One of the two masts was broken and the propeller was not working properly. The crewmen were trying desperately to maneuver their ship in the right direction. I found myself there on time to be of help. The captain was unable to keep his hands steady at the helm so I materialized two hands in order to help. The man saw them and wondered whether he was asleep or awake. I had much more power in my hands than the captain did. In that particular case I applied both the visible and invisible but tangible materializations. He saw my hands appear and reappear over and over again. In reality, however, my hands were always there, steadily holding the helm.'

'How did you manage that?' I asked, and my question provoked laughter from Daskalos.

'I managed to do it, but don't ask me how. The water you drink is transmuted within your body into blood and flesh. Can you tell me how that is done? Yet it is done. I partly know how materialization is accomplished, not through knowledge but through action. I instinctively know, just as you know how to drink water which later becomes blood. In the case of materialization tremendous will power and concentration are required.

'When the danger was over,' Daskalos continued, 'I thought of returning to my body. The crew was now in a position to steer the ship into the harbor. Suddenly the other mast crashed and fell on the deck with a tremendous roar. I was fully materialized but my body was still invisible. The mast hit me in the face. There was no disconnection between my physical body, which was in a trance, and my materialization. When I woke up I realized that my mouth was bleeding and I had a terrible headache.

'When we leave our bodies and we materialize somewhere else, we must close the door behind. We must disconnect the body from the materialization.'

'But if you do that, is it not as if you die in a way? Must you not, of necessity, have the connection?' I inquired.

'No. You have the connection but not the conscious connection. When you leave your body you carry with you, as I believe, part of the etheric matter, but not the etheric-double. The etheric-double cannot leave the body, otherwise it will die. When you are outside of the body you always carry some of the etheric substance with you.'

'Why?'

'So that your mind will be connected with your body. So that you will be able to remember and return. As we have said many times, it is through the etheric that we are able to project elementals of thought and desire. However, if you carry more etheric than you need for the return trip, the connection between your body and the materialization remains wide open.'

'When you say that you were fully materialized on the boat, you were invisible to the others. But you were there and what hit you was the etheric part of the mast,' I commented.

'No. The mast itself hit me.'

'But if you were invisible, why could it not go through you without hitting you?'

'It is of no consequence. I am still affected. I said that when you are in a state of invisible but tangible materialization, you will have the effects of the physical body unless you take special precautions. It is the same with the visible and tangible materialization. Only with visible but intangible materialization will there be no effect.'

'What kind of measures can you take to protect your body?'

'While away you disconnect it by only thinking and impressing in your subconscious that nothing will happen to your material body. You say to yourself, "No matter what kind of experiences I will undergo, nothing will happen to my material body." Everything is worked out on the subconscious level. The subconscious is the ruler of the material body. Whether you are inside or outside your material body, you can exercise your subconscious to accomplish acts that appear superhuman. For example, a heavy object may require the power of several people before it can be moved. Yet if I put you into a certain trance or hypnotic state (there are many levels of trance states) you may be able to lift it with only one hand. How so, you may ask. I believe the work is actually done not by your hand but by a materialized force inside it. The bones and muscles of the individual hardly play a role. I need to study this phenomenon further. I tell you, there is a great fascination for me in exploring further. Yet the cry of pain is so intense around us that I cannot afford the time to satisfy my curiosity.'

'Is it possible for a great master to dematerialize someone else and rematerialize him somewhere else?' I asked, having in mind an incident that Carlos Castaneda allegedly experienced during his apprenticeship with Don Juan.

'Yes. But only a great master can do that. Not just a master. Anyhow, I cannot do such a thing myself.'

'And you cannot do it on yourself,' I stated.

'I can do it on myself if I want to. But what for? Only in an extreme emergency would I do such a thing. If, for example, I need to materialize somewhere and it would be unsafe to leave my body behind because others might destroy it, then I could dematerialize it.'

'Have you ever done so?'

'No. I never faced such an emergency. Suppose I must travel a long distance instantly for a particular purpose. There is no reason to dematerialize my body here. I can materialize a body at the spot where I want to be by drawing etheric energy from the source itself which is everywhere in the universe. You do not need to deplete the reservoir of existing vitality within your body.'

I briefly talked to Daskalos about the work of Castaneda. I specifically mentioned the incident described in one of his books when Don Juan supposedly gave a sudden push to Castaneda and the latter instantly found himself walking two miles away. 'Is that possible?' I asked.

'Yes. But what makes you think that Don Juan actually dematerialized Castaneda's body and then rematerialized it two miles away? What may have happened could be that Don Juan transplaced Castaneda's consciousness and made his body invisible to the passersby. It is not necessary to dematerialize a body in order to make it invisible. Perhaps the master placed the body of his student on a chair and created for him a new etheric body two miles away within which he transplanted his self-consciousness. There are ways that you can make a material object, even a human body, invisible to others.'

'How is it done?' I asked somewhat incredulously. In Daskalos' customary manner, he began answering my query by narrating a story.

'An English scientist visited me once. "I have been to India and was greatly disappointed and disillusioned," he complained. "Why?" I asked. "I met in the streets a half-naked fakir and a small boy who had in front of him a piece of rope and a plate for throwing money into. About twenty people gathered. The fakir began to play a tune on his flute. Suddenly the rope got loosened and stood vertically on itself like a pole. The boy then climbed up the rope. He stood there a few minutes, smiled, moved his hands, and then stepped down. The rope began to come down and bundled itself up again. The next day I visited this fakir with a friend of mine. We brought along a camera. When the same episode unfolded we took photographs. But when we developed the pictures they showed that the boy was sitting on the ground and the rope remained where it was. This fakir deceived us but could not deceive the camera."

'I laughed when I heard his story. "Is that the reason why you were disappointed?" I asked him. "Why did you not study the phenomenon which you had witnessed twice with your own eyes? Why did you not raise the question 'how come'? What did actually happen?" "I'll think about it," he said.

'I told him that had that fakir been a much more powerful yogi he could have literally made the rope move up and climb on it. And there have been such phenomena that have been photographed. I explained to him what must have happened.

"The fakir spread his aura around and put the audience inside. Then he began to think intensely and he created with his mind all those images you were 'seeing'." '

'I suppose, Daskale,' I said, 'he was creating the elemental of the child climbing the rope.'

'Exactly. "Seeing" means that light hits something, bounces back at our eyes and, via the optical nerve, provides an irritation at a particular center of the brain. Therefore, that fakir was able to create this irritation on that center of the brain of those in attendance through his method of intense concentration. "Why not study this phenomenon carefully," I further suggested to the Englishman, "instead of dismissing it as a trick? Why not study the nature of thought, of concrete thought? That fakir did something substantial which deserves serious attention." '

'Why can't we say, Daskale, that the fakir hypnotized his audience and made them "see" things that never happened?' I suggested.

'Hypnotism is a different phenomenon altogether. In hypnotism the hypnotist uses powerful suggestions through words or the help of some instrument, to an audience which is receptive and cooperative. This fakir used the power of his thought to influence his unaware audience telepathically and made them "see" things that did not exist on the gross material plane. I am not aware of any conventional hypnotist who can do that. If we want to call that hypnotism, fine. But it is not hypnotism as it is commonly understood, or misunderstood.'

Daskalos then concluded that just as it is possible to make people 'see' things that in reality do not exist, it is also possible through a similar procedure to make people not see objects or human bodies that do exist.

'I wonder what happened to the English scientist,' I mused.

'He went back to India for further study,' Daskalos said with a loud laugh.

'I tell you,' Daskalos continued, 'thousands of such phenomena take place all the time, in Asia, in India, in Tibet, everywhere, even in Greece. I met a Lama in Athens who can make a body invisible. He can also train people to levitate after they pay a certain amount of money. I am personally against this. A student of mine paid three hundred pounds in order to learn how to levitate. This Lama isolated a group, including my student, for fifteen days with no contact with the outside. They ate and drank whatever he gave them. They meditated continuously, using a specific mantra, and on the fifteenth day most of them levitated. He semi-hypnotized them during this period of isolation, cultivating in their subconscious the belief that they could succeed in levitating. It is the subconscious that makes levitation possible. This Lama succeeded, but in what? Levitating a few moments on the air and then down again. What for? I told my student that she just wasted three hundred pounds. She could have helped so many people in need instead of satisfying her curiosity.'

I commented that with levitation the laws of the material universe are reversed. I asked Daskalos, wondering about it, whether what is involved in levitation is similar to the manner with which a rocket is being propelled, that is, through the consumption of energy. 'No,' he said. 'In levitation the body becomes lighter than air.

'When you implant within your subconscious that kind of faith, you literally can accomplish so-called miracles,' Daskalos continued. 'That was what Jesus Christ meant when he said that if you have faith equivalent to a seed of mustard, you can move mountains. Believe me it is true. "But how is it done?" someone will ask. I know how but it is not easy to teach it to others, particularly when their interest is nothing more than curiosity.'

'You mean, Daskale, you can move mountains?' I said jokingly.

'Why should I? Why not go over the mountains? It is a more practical way,' Daskalos replied, laughing. 'All I am really doing is harnessing and employing certain forces in Nature unknown to ordinary people.'

I realized that I had been talking to Daskalos for several hours. His eleven-year-old granddaughter came into the room and announced that her mother was getting impatient. She expected Daskalos to go over to their house for certain errands. The girl sat on her grandfather's lap as I fired my last question. Daskalos had jokingly said to some of the other students one day that I was an incurable interrogator. I never stop asking questions even in the psychic plane where, he said, 'We frequently meet and have lessons.'

'I often wonder,' I said, 'how enjoyable and fascinating it must be to do all the wondrous things you say you are doing; leaving your body, materializing, dematerializing. . . . Had I been able to have such experiences myself, the world would have been a really magical place to be, a true "enchanted garden."' Daskalos was silent for a few moments as he pondered my question while caressing the hair of his granddaughter.

'When I was a young man, these experiences were giving me great fascination, great pleasure. I remember I used to travel to Africa and, from the other side, observe and study beautiful exotic flowers and trees. One day I spread myself over the north of Canada, near the Pole and I saw the Eskimos digging holes into the ice and fishing. I had never known that something like that was possible. I learned about it in exomatosis. When I was younger I used to experiment a lot. I wanted to learn more and my curiosity would often get me into trouble. These experiences were fascinating to me. But something which used to give me great pleasure as a young man might not give me as great a pleasure now. With the course of time one realizes new values in life. Instead of finding satisfaction in seeing, perceiving and enjoying new phenomena, I now find great joy in being of service to my fellow human beings. I now set aside what is purely pleasurable and preoccupy myself primarily with what is necessary to help alleviate the pain about me.'

14

Afterthoughts

Two years had passed since the summer of 1981 when I last saw Daskalos. By January, 1983, he had fallen seriously ill. He had several operations on his right foot and was bedridden. One of his close disciples, a fifty-year-old housewife, informed me on the phone that Daskalos' days were sadly numbered. The wound on his foot would not heal.

In June of 1983, as soon as the academic year was over, I flew to Cyprus. The day after my arrival, still struggling to adjust from the dizziness of an eight-hour time lag, I visited Daskalos at Strovolos. Under my arm I had the manuscript of this book which was almost completed.

I softly knocked at the half-open door trying not to create noise in case he was asleep. There seemed to be nobody home.

'Come on in,' I heard his voice. I entered, closed the door behind me and walked towards the bedroom.

'Welcome,' Daskalos said, smiling as he extended his hand towards me. He was lying in bed wearing only his undershirt and the lower part of his pajamas. It was mid-June and the temperature was beginning to soar. His right foot was bundled up in gauze. I shook hands, bent down and kissed him on both of his unshaven cheeks.

'I was told you were in serious trouble,' I said, 'and I have come to see you.'

'Oh . . . they don't know what they are talking about,' Daskalos replied and waved his hand with impatience. 'I am fine. The Karma has been paid. I promise you that in one week I will be on my feet.'

I was not sure whether Daskalos was trying to give me encouragement or whether he meant what he said. Kostas, with whom I talked on the phone a while ago, complained with exasperation that Daskalos was reckless and did not take his illness seriously. But Daskalos seemed far from being at the threshold of death as I had been led to believe. His spirits were high, ever ready for endless conversations and hilarious anecdotes.

'How did you manage to stay in bed for so many months?' I asked, trying to match his lighthearted frame of mind.

'Who told you I was in bed for all these months?' Daskalos replied with raised eyebrows. 'Believe me had I remained in bed for six months I would have gone mad. My body was in bed. I have been out of it most of the time.'

'I see . . . ,' I said, and smiled. 'Daskale,' I went on, 'I am just about done with the book. Here it is.'

He took the manuscript, read the title and flipped the pages for a few seconds. 'You said you were going to do it and you did,' he murmured and handed it back to me. I did not think he cared to read it but he asked for a copy as soon as it was published. I asked him why he had not bothered to put his teachings on paper himself and waited for an academic 'idler' like myself to do so. Daskalos responded that he had more important tasks to attend to in this life than writing books. 'Besides,' he went on, 'that is your job.' He then talked of his illness and the operations that he had to go through. The surgeon had already amputated one of his toes and it was a toss-up whether his leg would be spared. He was under strict orders not to put any pressure on his leg and to remain in bed for an indefinite period, until the wound healed.

Before I had a chance to ask more questions about his condition and the issue of healing in general, two nurses came to the house. I assumed they had arrived to attend to Daskalos' medical needs. Instead they had come for a lesson, not on the world beyond, but for a more mundane task, to get instruction in the English language! In exchange for the good care the two nurses took of Daskalos during his hospitalization he volunteered to give them language lessons so that they could continue their training in England.

When I went to Strovolos the following morning, he was sitting in bed freshly shaven. Next to him there was Marios wearing his roller skates and attentively listening to his grandfather's fairy tales. Now in his seventh year, Marios had gone through a cyst operation himself, unusual for his age, and had just recovered. I sat on a chair waiting and listening to

Daskalos' yarn. Then the boy noisily rolled out of the house and rushed into the neighborhood to play with friends.

'It is puzzling,' I commented, 'how a healer has to go through these pains. You cure others but not yourself. And Marios had to go through the excruciating pains of an operation. Why could you not heal both yourself and Marios? Why the need for surgery? One of my colleagues in America,' I went on, 'wishes to know what the limitations of a healer are and what can a conventional physician do that a healer cannot?'

'Do you remember what I said to you sometime ago? That I was planning to assume the Karma of my son-in-law? There it is,' Daskalos responded smiling and triumphantly pointing at his foot. 'Had I not done so my son-in-law would have been dead by now, believe me! Why do you suppose Marios had such an unusual operation? He also took upon himself part of the Karma of his father. I diagnosed my grandchild's illness at a time when the doctor insisted that the probability of the child's having such a complication was infinitesimal. Then the tests showed that my diagnosis was correct. But I could do nothing to cure the child. He had to go through the suffering of the operation because karmic laws were at work. As for myself I could employ healing powers, even in the condition I am now, to help others but I would not do it on myself. If I heal myself now before the karmic debt is completely exhausted, the illness will automatically be transferred onto my son-in-law. To answer your friend's question, therefore, I will say this. There is nothing a medical doctor can do that a healer, who is master of materialization and dematerialization, cannot do. But the limitations of the healer are always the nature of the patient's Karma. No matter how powerful a healer may be, if it is not permitted by Holy Providence, healing will not take place. Similarly, a medical doctor can do what his science makes possible for him to do, and no more. But, again, he can heal only if Holy Providence allows it.'

'Why was it necessary to take up the Karma of your son-in-law?' I asked.

'Because his Karma was too heavy. It would have been impossible to bear it alone. It would have killed him,' Daskalos replied and repeated some of the ideas he mentioned to me in earlier conversations on how and under what circumstances one assumes the Karma of another. Then he proceeded to state that in the case of his son-in-law he employed 'spiritual healing' as distinct from 'psycho-therapy' or what people commonly call 'psychic healing.' I mentioned that it was the first time I had heard of such a distinction and urged him to elaborate.

'In psychic healing the psychotherapist transfers energy from his own etheric-double to that of the patient with the wish that he be cured. In such a case most of the Karma of the patient is already exhausted and therefore healing is easy. Anybody can become a psychic healer. In spiritual healing, on the other hand, the healer shares the Karma of the patient and suffers as a result. My grandson went under the surgeon's lancet to save his father. I have stayed in bed for over six months for the same reason. One never pays for someone else unless one volunteers to do so. And the force that prompts one to shoulder the burden of another is always love.'

'Is it possible,' I asked, 'for one to take up the Karma of another without being aware of it?'

'No! You share the Karma of another only superconsciously.'

'But I thought you said to me sometime ago that one can in fact take up the Karma of a beloved one subconsciously.'

'Yes, one could do that, but not in therapy. In spiritual healing the therapist is fully conscious of what he is doing through his superconsciousness.'

After further questioning on my part Daskalos explained that in the case of Mrs Katina, the patient suffering from her spine, he employed 'simple' methods of psychic healing. In her case Daskalos did not take up any of her Karma. It was the same with the case of my friend Stelios. Daskalos claimed that when he 'transferred' the potentially cancerous gland on himself it was nothing more than a better technique of dematerializing it. He did not shoulder Stelios' karmic debts.

'Let me demonstrate what I mean with a phenomenon,' Daskalos said abruptly. 'Remember now that normally I am not allowed to do phenomena but I'll make an exception.'

I saw a look of mischief in Daskalos' face, as if he were about to do something to shake me out of my wits. I stared at him for a few seconds not knowing what to expect.

'The doctor said,' Daskalos went on, and there was obvious

disrespect in his voice for what the doctor said, 'that I should remain in bed and never step on my right foot under any circumstances because the wound would open up again. I have not been out of this wretched bed for six months. Now I shall remove this Karma from myself for a while.'

Daskalos closed his eyes in a state of deep meditation and slowly passed his hand over his right leg. After about a minute he opened his eyes and without the slightest of reluctance got out of bed.

'What are you going to do?' I mumbled and my face dropped. I felt that Daskalos was about to do something foolish. My intuition did not fail me. He stood on his feet and without giving me time to breathe he began hopping around the room on his injured leg.

'Sit down for God's sake!' I shouted and felt like grabbing him around the waist and forcing him back to bed. Kostas' words about Daskalos' recklessness flashed through my mind. I thought for a moment that perhaps the old man had lost his wits. He continued hopping around the room for about half a minute with a smile on his face and totally oblivious to my agony and pleas for sanity. Then he went back to bed and lay down as if nothing had happened.

'Now I must get the Karma back,' Daskalos said and closed his eyes. He breathed deeply for several seconds and slowly passed his hand over the operated-on leg. After a minute he opened his eyes.

'Don't worry,' he reassured me as he noticed the anxiety in my face. 'Nothing happened to my leg. Now that the Karma is back I could not possibly do what I did awhile ago. Do you understand now?'

'I have a hard time,' I murmured wryly and with some relief that Daskalos' histrionics were over. There seemed to be no damage to his foot.

'You should have seen how scared Harry Edwards was when he was initiated into our circles and was introduced into spiritual healing.' Daskalos went on and giggled as he reminisced about the Englishman.

I first learned of Harry Edwards one day when I was casually looking at a pile of old pictures lying on top of Daskalos' dresser. My eyes focused on a fair, British-looking, stocky man ın his fifties. He stood in the Stoa next to Daskalos in a meditative position among others of Daskalos' disciples. When I asked him who the fellow was he explained that he was the well known (among occultists) British psychic. Edwards visited the island for his initiation into Daskalos' inner circle. The picture was taken during the ritual. It was dated April 1st, 1954. When I returned to the United States I accidentally came across a book with Harry Edwards' photo portrait. It was identical to the man I saw in Daskalos' old picture.

'Daskale,' I went on, 'my colleague in America has several more questions that he would like answered.'

'I am listening.'

'He was puzzled by what you said you did with the demon that protects your flowers. "How is it possible," he asked, "that an evil spirit could be transformed into a benign entity?" '

'Remember what I told you before, evil in reality does not exist. Let me give you an example. Suppose you mix water with soil and you end up with a bad-smelling mud. It is a temporary phenomenon. Fire, which is an element on a higher level than water, by generating heat, will transform this bad-smelling mud into pure water and soil again. The bad-smelling mud does not exist any more. Yet the water and the soil still exist in a different form. Likewise evil is a temporary phenomenon. An evil thought or an evil emotion are both Mind in different rates of vibrations. Higher agents, love and reason, can transform evil thoughts and evil emotions again into pure Mind essence. You see, there are no evil men in reality. They are human beings whose material brains combine thoughts and emotions in a manner that resembles something like the bad-smelling mud. Reason and love can change all that.

'The same principle applies to the realm of the so-called evil spirits or demons. According to the Scriptures evil spirits are fallen angels. If that is possible why then can we not accept that these evil spirits can ascend back to the realm of the angels? If we allow to humanity the idea of salvation and restoration, why can we not do the same for other emanations from God?'

'I believe your explanation will satisfy my friend,' I added. 'But he has another question. "Why is evil necessary?" '

Daskalos sat carefully on his bed in order not to put any strain on his right foot and prepared to answer my question.

He paused for a few seconds and then continued.

'A painter uses various colors in order to present on a two-dimensional surface a landscape of the three-dimensional world. To give life to his picture and the sense of depth a painter would use the black color. What he paints does not exist on the three-dimensional locality. Yet the black color provides the impression of a three-dimensional reality on the painting. Likewise the idea of evil is necessary to give to the three-dimensional world of matter and life an impression of reality. As I pointed out to you in our earlier encounters, within the gross material, psychic and noetic worlds one experiences only relative reality. These dimensions of reality which offer us the sense of understanding also give us the sense of evil, something non-existent in ultimate reality. The impression of evil exists only in the worlds of emotions and thoughts.'

When I left Daskalos' house that day he assured me once more that the Karma had been paid off and that he would begin to walk within a week. He kept his promise. When I visited him six days later he was in his studio completing a painting he had begun before his illness. He walked carefully so as not to put extra weight on his right foot. Days later his recovery was complete. He moved about at a normal pace and made plans for his annual trip to Greece to give lessons at his circles in Athens and Salonica. The Karma of his son-in-law had been exhausted.

I spent the following week camping out and spear fishing at Lara, a remote beach at the southwest coast of the island, away from tourists, concrete and traffic. I was with Neophytos, an American-trained Cypriot sociologist and former colleague at the Cyprus Social Research Centre. In between breaks from our amateurish and fruitless fishing adventures I told him for the first time about my research activities during the past four years. He listened with fascination to my story. He too was aware of the tales told of the 'Magus of Strovolos,' but he had never met him. Like myself Neophytos was beginning to feel disillusioned with scientific materialism and was by now more willing to entertain alternative conceptions of reality.

'Tell me,' my friend asked, 'do you believe in what Daskalos is teaching? Has your life changed since you met him?'

'It is not the first time I have been asked this question,' I said, 'and it is one that I often raise in my own mind. I have no easy answers.'

I mentioned how, ever since meeting Daskalos, I have puzzled over repeated coincidences that, after a while, forced me to wonder whether they were in fact coincidences. I then described to Neophytos a few of the many episodes that puzzled me.

I once saw Daskalos in a dream talking to me. Suddenly he disappeared. I turned around and saw him walking towards me from behind. When I met him the following morning I casually mentioned that I had seen him in my dream the night before. I gave no further details. 'Oh yes,' he nodded, 'I was giving you a lesson on the nature of space in the fourth dimension.'

On another occasion Daskalos described to me in stunning detail the inside of our house in Maine. To the best of my knowledge there was no way that he could have known the details of our home. He 'visited' us, he claimed, many times, particularly when I thought of him with intensity.

One day, Iacovos and I were searching for Daskalos all over Larnaca. He was nowhere to be found. We assumed he was already at Theano's place where a meeting was scheduled. As we walked towards her house I humorously remarked to Iacovos that perhaps he visited some mistress of his and that was why we could not find him. When we reached Theano's place Daskalos was there surrounded by several of his adepts. 'Daskale,' I exclaimed, 'we looked all over town for you. Where have you been?' 'At my mistress',' he snapped with sarcasm and laughter. 'I heard your silly chat,' he went on and continued laughing.

When we returned to America Emily began having severe pains in her right knee. One day we received a letter from Iacovos. He suggested that Emily visit a doctor to have her right leg examined because he and Daskalos 'saw' that there was something wrong with her right knee! He reassured us that he and Daskalos were working on her but that she should consult a physician in any case. We had never mentioned anything to anybody in Cyprus about this problem. Emily's pains were gone in a few days after receiving Iacovos' letter. She never went to a doctor.

I went on to mention to Neophytos an incident that occurred

the day before I boarded the plane for Cyprus. A colleague at the University of Maine, a hellenist, brought to my attention the ancient meaning of my name. I had assumed it was a derivative of 'kyrie,' meaning 'lord' as in 'Kyrie Eleison' chanted in church services. 'Not so,' my friend, an expert on classical Greek, assured me. He sent me to the Liddell and Scott Greek–English Lexicon. Based on a Greek magical papyrus discovered in Egypt it said that 'Kyriacos' was 'a spirit invoked in magic.'

'One thing that I am certain of about Daskalos,' I said to my friend, 'is that he has extraordinary powers at diagnosing and healing illnesses. Through Daskalos', I went on, 'I have come to recognize in a more concrete manner what philosophers, mystics, some contemporary physicists and brain researchers have been saying, that mind has power over matter. It is not the other way around as materialists of all political and scientific colorations have been insisting over the last two hundred years with so much ferocity and religious zeal.

'As for the details of the teachings,' I said, 'I cannot make any statement. I remain a Doubting Thomas, but one who is at least ready to place his fingers on the scars of the Master to examine and experience their authenticity.

'If you are honest with yourself,' I continued, 'it is impossible to be exposed to Daskalos for a long time and not wonder about the possibility that the observable empirical world may be indeed a hierophany, an expression of a higher reality hidden from ordinary consciousness.'

I then cited a quotation from Philip Slater, a sociologist turned mystic, that 'all the errors and follies of magic, religion, and mystical traditions are outweighted by the one great wisdom they contained – the awareness of humanity's organic embeddedness in a complex natural system.' 'It is imperative,' I said to my friend, 'that this awareness becomes the motif of everyday consciousness. The very survival of humankind depends on it.'

Neophytos puffed his pipe a few times and gazed at the sea, pondering what we had been discussing over the last few days.

'I would like to meet Daskalos,' he said with determination, as if suddenly overcoming a childhood taboo.

When I introduced them to one another Daskalos burst into

laughter. Neophytos stood with wide open eyes for a few seconds as he discovered that his deceased father, a venerated judge, was a close friend, secret disciple and a first cousin of Daskalos. The 'Magus of Strovolos' was my friend's uncle!

Before leaving Cyprus I went to bid farewell to Daskalos. He kissed me on the forehead and murmured a prayer as he made the sign of the cross over my head.

'Whenever you need me,' he said reassuringly, 'think of me intensely and I will be with you.'

'I'll do that,' I said, and got into the taxi for the one-hour drive to Larnaca airport.

Glossary

Chakras Psychonoetic centers on the etheric-double of the individual. It is through the chakras that the human personality absorbs etheric vitality for its maintenance. Through appropriate discipline and meditation exercises the mystic tries to open his chakras for the acquisition of psychonoetic powers. To a clairvoyant the chakras appear like revolving discs.

Elementals Thought forms. Any feeling or any thought that an individual projects is an elemental. They have shape and a life of their own independent of the one who projected them.

Etheric-double The energy field that keeps the three bodies of man (the gross material, psychic and noetic) alive and linked to one another. Each particle of man's body has its corresponding etheric-double. It is etheric vitality that makes healing possible. The universe is filled with etheric energy. It can be transferred from one individual to another, and it is absorbed through the chakras.

Exomatosis The ability to willfully abandon one's body, live fully conscious within the psychonoetic dimensions and then return back to the body. It implies remembering whatever one experiences in the out-of-the-body state.

Gross material body One of the three bodies that make up the present self-conscious personality. The material body of man. That part of one's personality that lives within the gross material world, the three-dimensional world. The lowest expression of self. The center of the gross material body is the chakra of the solar plexus.

Higher noetic world The world of ideas, of the archetypes. The world of causes and laws that provide the foundations of all phenomenal reality.

Holy Monad The component parts of the Absolute. Each Holy Monad emanates myriads of rays that pass through different

220

archetypes and acquire shape and phenomenal existence. When one such irradiation passes through the Idea of Man a human personality is constructed. Humans who belong to the same Holy Monad have a particular affinity for one another.

Holy Spirit The impersonal superconsciousness which expresses the power of the Absolute, making the creation of the universe possible. The dynamic part of the Absolute.

Holyspiritual That which pertains only to the Holy Spirit. Animals live within a holyspiritual state. They lack the logoic expression of the Absolute, that is, they lack self-consciousness. Man is both logoic and holyspiritual.

Idea of Man An eternal archetype within the Absolute. Once an emanation of a Holy Monad passes through the Idea of Man, human existence begins.

Invisible helpers Masters who live on the psychic and noetic dimensions and are invisible to material eyes. Also masters who live within the gross material dimension but who carry out exomatosis and assist humans living within the gross as well as the other dimensions.

Karma The law of cause and effect. The sum total of a person's actions, thoughts and feelings that determine his successive states of existence. A person is fully responsible for the creation of his Karma, his destiny. The attainment of Theosis implies transcending one's Karma.

Law of cause and effect See Karma.

Logos The part of the Absolute that makes possible the existence of self-consciousness and free will. As eternal entities men are both logoic and holyspiritual. Animals are only holyspiritual. Jesus as the Christ Logos represents the most complete expression of the logoic nature of the Absolute. The more spiritually advanced a human entity is, the more the logoic part in him is dominant.

Mind The means by which the unmanifest Absolute expresses Itself. Mind is the supersubstance by which all the universes, all the dimensions of existence, are constructed. Everything is Mind.

Noetic body One of the three bodies that makes up the present self-conscious personality. The body of thoughts. The noetic body exists within the noetic world, the fifth dimension. Its image is identical with the other two bodies. The center of the noetic body is the chakra of the head.

Noetic world The fifth dimension. Within the noetic world, space as well as time are transcended. A human entity living within the noetic world can travel instantly, not only over vast distances but also across time.

Permanent personality That part of ourselves upon which the incarnational experiences are recorded and are transferred from one life to the next. Our inner self.

Present personality What is commonly known as the personality of the individual. It is made up of the noetic, psychic and gross material bodies. The present personality is the lowest expression of ourselves which is constantly evolving and tends to become one with the permanent personality.

Psychic body One of the three bodies that constitutes the present self-conscious personality. The body of feelings and sentiments having as its center the chakra of the heart. The psychic body lives within the psychic world, the fourth dimension. Its image is identical with the other two bodies, the gross material and the noetic.

Psychic world The fourth dimension. Within the psychic world space is transcended. An individual living within the psychic world can travel instantly over vast distances.

Sacred discs See Chakras.

Soul That part of ourselves which is pure and uncolored by earthly experience. The soul is beyond the Idea of Man, beyond all manifestation. It has never been born and it will never die. It is that part of ourselves which is qualitatively identical with the Absolute. The soul is our divine essence, unchangeable and eternal.

Theosis The final stage in the evolution of the self after it has undergone the experience of gross matter through successive incarnations. Re-unification with the Godhead.

World of ideas See Higher noetic world.

ARKANA – NEW-AGE BOOKS FOR MIND, BODY AND SPIRIT

A selection of titles

With over 200 titles currently in print, Arkana is the leading name in quality new-age books for mind, body and spirit. Arkana encompasses the spirituality of both East and West, ancient and new, in fiction and non-fiction. A vast range of interests is covered, including Psychology and Transformation, Health, Science and Mysticism, Women's Spirituality and Astrology.

If you would like a catalogue of Arkana books, please write to:

Arkana Marketing Department
Penguin Books Ltd
27 Wright's Lane
London W8 5TZ

ARKANA – NEW-AGE BOOKS FOR MIND, BODY AND SPIRIT

A selection of titles

Neal's Yard Natural Remedies Susan Curtis, Romy Fraser and Irene Kohler

Natural remedies for common ailments from the pioneering Neal's Yard Apothecary Shop. An invaluable resource for everyone wishing to take responsibility for their own health, enabling you to make your own choice from homeopathy, aromatherapy and herbalism.

Zen in the Art of Archery Eugen Herrigel

Few in the West have strived as hard as Eugen Herrigel to learn Zen from a Master. His classic text gives an unsparing account of his initiation into the 'Great Doctrine' of archery. Baffled by its teachings he gradually began to glimpse the depth of wisdom behind the paradoxes.

The Absent Father: Crisis and Creativity Alix Pirani

Freud used Oedipus to explain human nature; but Alix Pirani believes that the myth of Danae and Perseus has most to teach an age which offers 'new responsibilities for women and challenging questions for men' – a myth which can help us face the darker side of our personalities and break the patterns inherited from our parents.

Woman Awake: A Celebration of Women's Wisdom Christina Feldman

In this inspiring book, Christina Feldman suggests that it *is* possible to break out of those negative patterns instilled into us by our social conditioning as women: conformity, passivity and surrender of self. Through a growing awareness of the dignity of all life and its connection with us, we can regain our sense of power and worth.

Water and Sexuality Michel Odent

Taking as his starting point his world-famous work on underwater childbirth at Pithiviers, Michel Odent considers the meaning and importance of water as a symbol: in the past – expressed through myths and legends – and today, from an advertisers' tool to a metaphor for aspects of the psyche.

ARKANA – NEW-AGE BOOKS FOR MIND, BODY AND SPIRIT

A selection of titles

The Revised Waite's Compendium of Natal Astrology
Alan Candlish

This completely revised edition retains the basic structure of Waite's classic work while making major improvements to accuracy and readability.

Aromatherapy for Everyone Robert Tisserand

The therapeutic value of essential oils was recognized as far back as Ancient Egyptian times. Today there is an upsurge in the use of these fragrant and medicinal oils to soothe and heal both mind and body. Here is a comprehensive guide to every aspect of aromatherapy by the man whose name is synonymous with its practice and teaching.

Tao Te Ching The Richard Wilhelm Edition

Encompassing philosophical speculation and mystical reflection, the *Tao Te Ching* has been translated more often than any other book except the Bible, and more analysed than any other Chinese classic. Richard Wilhelm's acclaimed 1910 translation is here made available in English.

The Book of the Dead E. A. Wallis Budge

Intended to give the deceased immortality, the Ancient Egyptian *Book of the Dead* was a vital piece of 'luggage' on the soul's journey to the other world, providing for every need: victory over enemies, the procurement of friendship and – ultimately – entry into the kingdom of Osiris.

Yoga: Immortality and Freedom Mircea Eliade

Eliade's excellent volume explores the tradition of yoga with exceptional directness and detail.

'One of the most important and exhaustive single-volume studies of the major ascetic techniques of India and their history yet to appear in English' – *San Francisco Chronicle*

ARKANA – NEW-AGE BOOKS FOR MIND, BODY AND SPIRIT

A selection of titles

Weavers of Wisdom: Women Mystics of the Twentieth Century Anne Bancroft

Throughout history women have sought answers to eternal questions about existence and beyond – yet most gurus, philosophers and religious leaders have been men. Through exploring the teachings of fifteen women mystics – each with her own approach to what she calls 'the truth that goes beyond the ordinary' – Anne Bancroft gives a rare, cohesive and fascinating insight into the diversity of female approaches to mysticism.

Dynamics of the Unconscious: Seminars in Psychological Astrology Volume II Liz Greene and Howard Sasportas

The authors of *The Development of the Personality* team up again to show how the dynamics of depth psychology interact with your birth chart. They shed new light on the psychology and astrology of aggression and depression – the darker elements of the adult personality that we must confront if we are to grow to find the wisdom within.

The Myth of Eternal Return: Cosmos and History Mircea Eliade

'A luminous, profound, and extremely stimulating work . . . Eliade's thesis is that ancient man envisaged events not as constituting a linear, progressive history, but simply as so many creative repetitions of primordial archetypes . . . This is an essay which everyone interested in the history of religion and in the mentality of ancient man will have to read. It is difficult to speak too highly of it' – Theodore H. Gaster in *Review of Religion*

The Second Krishnamurti Reader Edited by Mary Lutyens

In this reader bringing together two of Krishnamurti's most popular works, *The Only Revolution* and *The Urgency of Change*, the spiritual teacher who rebelled against religion points to a new order arising when we have ceased to be envious and vicious. Krishnamurti says, simply: 'When you are not, love is.' 'Seeing,' he declares, 'is the greatest of all skills.' In these pages, gently, he helps us to open our hearts and eyes.

ARKANA – NEW-AGE BOOKS FOR MIND, BODY AND SPIRIT

A selection of titles

A Course in Miracles: The Course, Workbook for Students and Manual for Teachers

Hailed as 'one of the most remarkable systems of spiritual truth available today', *A Course in Miracles* is a self-study course designed to shift our perceptions, heal our minds and change our behaviour, teaching us to experience miracles – 'natural expressions of love' – rather than problems generated by fear in our lives.

Sorcerers Jacob Needleman

'An extraordinarily absorbing tale' – John Cleese.

'A fascinating story that merges the pains of growing up with the intrigue of magic . . . constantly engrossing' – *San Francisco Chronicle*

Arthur and the Sovereignty of Britain: Goddess and Tradition in the Mabinogion Caitlín Matthews

Rich in legend and the primitive magic of the Celtic Otherworld, the stories of the *Mabinogion* heralded the first flowering of European literature and became the source of Arthurian legend. Caitlín Matthews illuminates these stories, shedding light on Sovereignty, the Goddess of the Land and the spiritual principle of the Feminine.

Shamanism: Archaic Techniques of Ecstasy Mircea Eliade

Throughout Siberia and Central Asia, religious life traditionally centres around the figure of the shaman: magician and medicine man, healer and miracle-doer, priest and poet.

'Has become the standard work on the subject and justifies its claim to be the first book to study the phenomenon over a wide field and in a properly religious context' – *The Times Literary Supplement*